Volumes in this series:

Wings Like Eagles

Reflections on Life in the Lord

Volume Four: Matthew – John

David King

Forward by Chris Huntley

Published by
Spiritbuilding Publishers
9700 Ferry Road, Waynesville, OH 45068
(800) 282-4901

WINGS LIKE EAGLES: Reflections on Life in the Lord (Volume 4)
by David King
ISBN 978-1-955285-65-0

Printed in the United States

Cover design by Adam Moore
Cover photo by Bruno van der Kraan on Unsplash
Author portrait by Joanna Roseborough

Spiritbuilding
PUBLISHERS

spiritbuilding.com

He gives power to the weak,
And to those who have no might
He increases strength.
Even the youths shall faint and be weary,
And the young men shall utterly fall,
But those who wait on the LORD
Shall renew their strength;
They shall mount up with wings like eagles,
They shall run and not be weary,
They shall walk and not faint.

— Isaiah 40:29-31

Other Bible translations referenced in this volume:

CSB	Christian Standard Bible (Holman Bible Publishers)
ESV	English Standard Version (Crossway)
LXX	The Septuagint Version of the Old Testament (Zondervan Publishing House)
Message	*The Message* (Eugene Peterson)
NASB	New American Standard Bible (Lockman Foundation)
NIV	New International Version (New York International Bible Society)
NLT	New Living Translation (Tyndale House Publishers)
RSV	Revised Standard Version (National Council of Churches of Christ in the USA)

*To the Savior who
found me when I was lost,
loved me when I was unlovable,
and is patiently waiting to
welcome me home.
Come, Lord Jesus!*

Contents

Forward

by Chris Huntley

David King has been one of the most influential men in my life. As a freshman in college, I met his daughter, Julia, and quickly became enamored. Within a few short years, Julia and I were wed and I became a part of the family. What I didn't realize at the time was how great a blessing Julia's family would become, particularly my relationship with David.

From the very beginning, David became a mentor in every respect of the word, providing wisdom in various areas of my life, not the least of which concerns my approach to God's word. Knowing that I desired to devote my life to preaching, David began to pass his accumulated wisdom to me. He has helped me navigate through tough waters in my own understanding and practice, especially in the early years. I can still vividly remember sitting in his office as he would patiently listen to me, a young upstart know-it-all, wax eloquently concerning my vast wisdom and understanding of complicated matters, after which he would gently guide me to the Bible and help me see the truth in the text, which often was at odds with my ideas. Though certainly warranted, there was never any judgment or censure, but always a calm and encouraging correction by answering straight from the text.

David's greatest strengths come not only from his knowledge of the Bible, but also his ability to see how those texts practically apply to the various situations in which Christians find themselves. His wisdom is earned not only from his life experience, but also by placing that life experience within the framework of the word of God. And in this series, *Wings Like Eagles: Reflections on Life in the Lord*, this wisdom is on full display.

In David's typical manner, he steps out of the way and allows the text of God's word to speak to a twenty-first century audience. Even when he deals with various controversial topics (and David is not afraid to confront topics that need to be confronted), he does so by allowing the text to make the argument. Just as he did with a brash, young preacher so many years ago, he derives the answers for these topics by focusing on the proper cultural and textual contexts, avoiding the pitfalls of many similar treatments which simply engage in proof-texted passages that serve as token verses to talk about their subjects. Though each installment is short, it is packed with exegesis, explanation, and application presented in an accessible and succinct style. Unlike the preacher caricature of verbosity, David speaks volumes with few words.

In this current volume, *Volume 4: Matthew–John*, David focuses on the writings concerning the wisest man who has ever lived: Jesus, God in the flesh. I thoroughly appreciate that David divides his writings according to the gospels instead of following a chronological harmonization of the gospels. In this way, each author is given his own voice. David goes through these gospels bringing Jesus' wisdom to an audience that faces many of the same challenges that the gospel authors' original audiences faced. The conclusions are just as pertinent today as they were roughly two thousand years ago.

I invite you to join with me as we have a seat in David's office with him and allow him to expound on the text to help us see the truth concerning the questions of life that are answered by the word of God, particularly the words of the Son of God himself.

Preface

In his book, *Reading the Gospels Wisely* (2012), New Testament scholar Jonathan Pennington confessed to treating the four gospels with indifference early in his career:

> *My lack of interest in the Gospels was manifested by how little time I really spent teaching or preaching from them. It was a case of benign neglect that revealed my lack of true affection. . . . We know doctrine is important, and we know the Bible makes claims about theology and how we ought to live, so we love Paul. He's a straight shooter; he nails it on the head; he lays out the truth in powerful and straightforward ways. He provides a clear map of the theological landscape and the moral path for our lives. But the Gospels? Well, certainly it is nice to see Jesus in action, taking down the Pharisees, doing cool water-walking miracles and all, but sometimes his teaching is confusing* (p. 36-37).

Pennington's admission strikes close to home, because my early preaching career followed a similar path. Some of the Bibles I used in those early years show evidence of unbalanced study habits: The epistles are dog-eared and grimy from use, while the gospels are comparatively clean. I did not ignore the gospels, but neither did I give them the intense study they deserve. Of course, Jesus is the greatest character in the Bible; but He is largely a figurehead for the deeper theological platform fleshed out in the epistles—or so I thought.

However, the fact that the story of Jesus consumes almost one-half of the New Testament offers a clue about the foundational role these books and their chief character should play in our theology. Like Pennington, as I began to spend more time in the gospels, I began to gain a deeper appreciation for them. Their value can be seen in three areas:

First, *they serve as the foundation of the entire Biblical narrative.* Pennington likens the gospels to the keystone in a great Roman arch, tying together the books of the Old Testament on the left and the remaining New Testament books on the right. Without the gospels, the entire edifice collapses. Indeed, we cannot make sense of the rest of the Bible without a firm grasp of the story of Jesus.

Second, *they highlight the spiritual nature of God's kingdom.* Both in His teaching and His behavior, Jesus turned the entire human enterprise of power-seeking on its head. His version of how we achieve greatness in our lives—and how we respond to the forces of evil that would subvert it—contradict everything this world tells us about getting ahead.

Finally, *they display as no other biography can what God intends humanity to be.* Jesus is more than just a wise teacher and miracle worker. He is the penultimate Hero, the exemplar whose exploits are free of the flaws and failings that tarnish the legacy of other heroes. Our destiny is not defined by the cold logic of law, but by the spirit of unselfish service displayed in the life of the only Man who got it perfectly right—then sacrificed it all for a race of creatures so undeserving of it.

Unless otherwise noted, all Scripture citations are from the New King James Version. The interpretations, as well as any mistakes, are my own.

Chris Huntley deserves special thanks for providing the Forward. As always, I am so grateful to Matthew Allen and Adam Moore for their roles in bringing this volume to press.

Valley Center KS
April 2023

Introduction

We call the first four books of the New Testament the "gospels," but that label is a misnomer. There is only one gospel, presented in four parallel accounts (notice the title of each book: "The Gospel According to" so-and-so).

But why *four* books? Would it not have been easier and less messy for all the Jesus pericopes to be compiled into one grand volume that tells the whole story from beginning to end? In that single source, there would be no discrepancies to resolve, no confusion over chronology, no puzzling questions regarding names, places, or events. Instead, we're stuck with four versions of the life of Christ that, while harmonizing on the general facts of His life, require a good deal of sifting and sorting to tease out the complete picture.

There are two reasons for the Spirit's diversified approach to documenting the Jesus story.

The first involves *the nature of investigational testimony in establishing truth*. In the Law of Moses, civil judgments had to be based on the testimony of two or three witnesses (Deut. 19:15). In capital cases especially, the testimony of a single witness was inadmissable (Deut. 17:6). So in establishing the veracity of the Jesus story, we have not two or three witnesses, but *four*. Two of the witnesses (Matthew and John) were His apostles, and the other two were companions of two other apostles (Mark for Peter, Luke for Paul). Like all witnesses, each of these four authors had his own perspective on the events he was documenting, so it is unreasonable to expect exact duplication in their records. The differences among these accounts may be puzzling, but they are not insurmountable. Rather than weakening the case for Jesus, the testimony of these four sources serves to reinforce our confidence in the basic integrity of the history they tell.

The second reason for having four accounts involves *the different audiences for whom they were written.*

Matthew wrote for a *Jewish* audience, highlighting Jesus as the Messiah of the Old Testament. He quotes extensively from the Jewish Scriptures, linking details in Jesus' life to Old Testament prophecies. He traces the genealogy of Jesus only back to Abraham, emphasizing Jesus as the fulfillment of the Abrahamic promise, a distinctly Jewish hope.

Mark's gospel targeted a *Roman* audience, people who were impressed more by what a man accomplishes than what he says. Mark's account, therefore, is short on talk and long on action. (Notice how often Mark uses the word "immediately" to describe people getting things done.)

Luke's gospel is the first part of a two-volume history that explains the origins of the Christian faith to a predominately *Gentile* audience. Luke focuses on Jesus' work among the marginalized, the powerless, the weak of society, those who comprise the vast bulk of humanity, people who long for some scrap of dignity in a world of hardship.

John's account, written long after the others, assumes a prior knowledge of the earlier accounts. His biography is deeper and more theologically dense, suggesting that it was written to strengthen *Christians* in their faith.

Despite the differences that make each book unique, there is an underlying unity that binds them together. They tell a single narrative about a God-man who came to earth, lived life as an ordinary but perfect human, challenged all of us with a body of teaching that overturns our view of what's important, paid an awful price for His integrity—then shocked the world by conquering death itself.

History has never seen such a Man. His story should consume our hearts and minds like nothing else.

The Pedigree of a King

Bible genealogies tend to put us to sleep, but the New Testament opens with a genealogy that screams a key message about our Messiah.

The book of the genealogy of Jesus Christ, the Son of David, the Son of Abraham (Matt. 1:1).

෴

In one respect, it is unfortunate that the first chapter of the New Testament begins with a genealogy, one of those long lists of hard-to-pronounce names that puts us to sleep when we try to read it. Surely, a book of such importance should have a more engaging introduction.

But this genealogy is here for a reason, and the careful reader can glean some useful information from studying it. For example, the first verse identifies Jesus as the descendant of Abraham and David. That makes Him the fulfillment of two of the greatest promises of the Old Testament (Gen. 12: 1-3; 2 Sam. 7:12-16). That detail alone would catch the attention of every Jewish patriot who was longing for the arrival of his Messiah.

But another curious detail stands out: Why are several *women* included in this list? All Bible genealogies are concerned only with male lineage; the mothers were not deemed noteworthy. But Matthew goes out of his way to mention four women. Even more puzzling is the fact that all four of these women were of questionable background. Tamar (v. 3) played the harlot with her father-in-law, Judah. Rahab (v. 5) was a Canaanite prostitute. Ruth (v. 5) was a Moabite, of whom God had said they "shall not enter the assembly of the

Lord; even to the tenth generation" (Deut. 23:3). Bathsheba (identified as "her who had been the wife of Uriah," v. 6) committed adultery with David. Matthew seems to be going out of his way to mention four women who would have been shunned by all polite Jewish society of his day.

That's no accident. Matthew is making a bold statement here in the very first lines of his biography of Jesus: The Messiah came from a line of broken, imperfect people, in order to save broken, imperfect people. He could be a friend of sinners, because He had sinners in His pedigree. Whatever their flaws, God could use them to accomplish something great.

God can use you, too. Whatever your shortcomings, failures, and disadvantages, you have value in God's eyes. Don't get discouraged. Don't give up. You have no idea what God may have in store for you or your descendants in some far distant scenario. Trust Him and do your best, and He will take care of the rest.

"The Bible Teaches..."

We like to quote Scripture to defend our beliefs. But so what? Even Satan can do that. We must be careful how we interpret what we read.

Then the devil took Him up into the holy city, set Him on the pinnacle of the temple, and said to Him, "If You are the Son of God, throw Yourself down. For it is written: 'He shall give His angels charge over you,' and, 'In their hands they shall bear you up, lest you dash your foot against a stone.'" Jesus said to him, "It is written again, 'You shall not tempt the Lord your God'" (Matt. 4:5-7).

. . . In which are some things hard to understand, which untaught and unstable people twist to their own destruction, as they do also the rest of the Scriptures (2 Pet. 3:16).

৩৵৶

We pride ourselves on being a people of the Book. Whatever the issue before us, "the Bible teaches. . . " is the final word. If the Bible teaches it, we believe it; if not, we don't. It's safer that way, right?

But while this may sound good in theory, in practice it carries a considerable degree of risk. For all its value, the Bible can become a stumbling block if we are careless in how we use it.

Consider, for example, how Satan sought to derail Jesus' mission. He took Jesus to the pinnacle of the temple and urged Him to jump off, apparently to get Jesus to show off His special connection with God. After all, did not the Bible teach that legions of angels would swoop down to rescue Him (Psa. 91:11-12)? What better way to prove His

Messiahship than to put on a grand display of power before thousands of witnesses in the very shadow of the temple!

The problem with this challenge, of course, was that instead of trusting God to care for Him, such a foolish stunt would have been forcing God's hand. That's pride, not faith—which is why Jesus declined to take the bait (by quoting a clarifying Scripture).

This exchange, pitting one Scripture against another, illustrates the danger that hangs over our use of the Bible. Whether by carelessness or by stubbornness, we can easily follow Satan's lead and use a bit or two of Scripture to promote a concept that God never sanctioned. We can, in Peter's words, "twist the Scriptures" to our own destruction.

How can we avoid abusing the Scriptures in this fashion?

The first rule is to always, *always*, study the context. Who is speaking? To whom are they speaking? What is the purpose? What is the setting? For example, Job 4:8 ("Those who plow iniquity and sow trouble reap the same") sounds like a great text for a sermon—until we realize that it was spoken by Eliphaz, who was unfairly seeking to blame Job for bringing his tragedy upon himself. That context forces us to temper the message we draw from his words.

A second rule—one used by Jesus in His duel with Satan—is to harmonize passages with other texts dealing with the same theme. The Bible is often its own best interpreter, but it requires a good deal of careful study to connect all the dots that will reveal the full portrait of truth.

There are other safeguards that should govern our use of the Scriptures, but these are adequate to illustrate the problem. Simply declaring "the Bible teaches . . . !" doesn't necessarily prove what we think it proves.

Shortcuts

Much of the damage we inflict upon ourselves is the result of trying to find an easy path to life's purpose. Satan couldn't be happier.

And [Satan] said to Him, "All these things I will give You if You will fall down and worship me." Then Jesus said to him, "Away with you, Satan! For it is written, 'You shall worship the Lord your God, and Him only you shall serve'" (Matt. 4:9-10).

"Be faithful until death, and I will give you the crown of life" (Rev. 2:10).

ക്കൈ

God's plan was for Jesus to become ruler over all creation. But the path to that glory would require that He first sacrifice Himself for the sins of humanity. There would be no crown without the cross.

At the very beginning of His ministry, however, at a vulnerable moment when He was tired and hungry, Jesus was offered a shortcut. Satan promised to deliver all the kingdoms of the world into His hands. Even better, the price was right; all He had to do was fall down and worship him. All the gain without the pain.

Jesus refused the offer. First, could Satan really deliver on that promise? Jesus was familiar with Satan's track record as the father of bait-and-switch lies (Jn. 8:44). This had all the earmarks of another lie.

Of course, from Jesus' perspective, whatever Satan could or couldn't deliver was irrelevant. There was really nothing to consider here. Jesus was not about to renounce his allegiance to his Father. His heart was steadfast in its intention: "Him only you shall serve." Jesus resisted this temptation—and many others that followed—completing His mission and securing our salvation. Thank God.

The story of Jesus' encounter with Satan holds a more personal message for each one us. Like Jesus, the path before us is not easy. Like Him, we must face many hardships and sacrifices before we receive our own crown of life. "Be faithful until death" is not easy.

Just as he did with Jesus, Satan tempts us with shortcuts. Every day we encounter opportunities great and small to cut corners, fudge the truth, slack off, give ourselves a little break from the pressure. Of course, once we start taking these shortcuts, we soon end up worshiping the wrong Master. We've sold our soul to the devil for an easy out, and forfeited our claim to glory in the hereafter.

Friend, when the going gets tough and you see an opportunity to bypass the pain by cheating just a little, don't take the bait. Satan is offering you a crown without the cross. Fix your eyes on Jesus, "the author and finisher of our faith, who for the joy that was set before Him endured the cross, despising the shame, and has sat down at the right hand of the throne of God" (Heb. 12:2).

Go and do likewise.

Why Teaching?

A major objective in Jesus' earthly sojourn
involved teaching people how to live a better life.
His words still have transformative power today.

From that time Jesus began to preach and to say, "Repent, for the kingdom of heaven is at hand." . . . And Jesus went about all Galilee, teaching in their synagogues, preaching the gospel of the kingdom (Matt. 4:17, 23).

Now early in the morning He came again into the temple, and all the people came to Him; and He sat down and taught them (Jn. 8:2).

৩৫৫৫

The signs and wonders that Jesus performed drew large crowds, but it was His teaching that had the biggest impact on His contemporaries. Whether in a synagogue, from a boat, on a mountainside, in the temple, or in a private home, Jesus never passed up an opportunity to impart a message that challenged His listeners. His teaching spanned a wide range of subject matter: rebuking sin, encouraging the weak, enlightening the foolish, foretelling the future. Even now, two thousand years later, people are still astonished at the wisdom of what He taught.

Jesus devoted so much of His career to teaching because we humans are so ignorant of life. We live out our days beset by a cascade of problems. Some of these issues are not our fault, but many can be linked directly to our own poor decision-making; then we exacerbate the troubles by our bungling attempts to deal with them. As the problems pile up, so do our anxieties. We end up lost in a world of pain and heartache, having no hope of finding our way out of the mess we're in.

This is the world Jesus came to confront. He knew that humanity's problems cannot be fixed by doling out free goodies and empty platitudes. What we need more than anything are changed attitudes and behaviors. "Repent!" is the plea of a God who knows what we are capable of becoming, and weeps at our failure to realize that potential.

The only way to change hearts and lives is through a steady diet of didactic instruction. People must be trained to think more clearly, to behave with dignity and honor, to talk more optimistically, to react to adversity with greater maturity. Somebody has to *teach* them how to do all that.

That's why we have the Bible. That's why we have parents and elders and preachers and teachers and mentors. We all need to spend more time reading the Bible and listening to those who instruct us from it. If we're serious about self-improvement, it will begin by submitting ourselves to the teaching of God's word, especially the words of Jesus.

Pay attention, class . . . .

The Moment of Decision

If our quality of life is a function of the decisions we make, it is important that we learn how to make them prudently—and decisively.

And Jesus, walking by the Sea of Galilee, saw two brothers, Simon called Peter, and Andrew his brother, casting a net into the sea; for they were fishermen. Then He said to them, "Follow Me, and I will make you fishers of men." They immediately left their nets and followed Him. Going on from there, He saw two other brothers, James the son of Zebedee, and John his brother, in the boat with Zebedee their father, mending their nets. He called them, and immediately they left the boat and their father, and followed Him (Matt. 4:18-22).

৵৽৹

When Jesus called these four men to be His disciples, they wasted no time making a decision. "They immediately left their nets and followed Him . . . Immediately they left the boat and their father, and followed Him." Their quick reaction was not as impulsive as it sounds. According to John, they were already familiar with Jesus (see Jn. 1:35-42), and likely had been weighing the pros and cons of such a move for some time. This calling was merely a formality.

So when the moment of decision came, these men did not stall for time or offer half-measures. They made up their minds to accept the challenge, said goodbye to the past, and stepped boldly into their new careers. They remained committed disciples of the Master for the rest of their lives and radically altered the course of human history. But it all began when they "immediately left . . . and followed."

Most people struggle with the difficult life decisions that come their way. They will procrastinate, or let someone else make their decisions for them, or dither over the available options until the opportunity is lost. When Elijah challenged the Israelites of his day to decide which god they were going to follow, Yahweh or Baal, the people "answered him not a word" (1 Kgs. 18:21)—they couldn't make up their minds. Only after God gave a dramatic display of His power—when it became obvious which way the wind was blowing—did they come down on the Lord's side (v. 38-39). Of course, their enthusiasm was short-lived, and they were soon back to their old fickle ways.

When an individual is confronted with the need for a change in his life, the decision to make that change does not grow easier with time. After seeing the resurrected Lord, Saul of Tarsus spent three days in Damascus agonizing over his condition. It took a firm nudge from Ananias to stir him to action: "Why are you waiting? Arise and be baptized and wash away your sins" (Ac. 22:16). Further delay would have only made the decision harder.

The same principle applies to a local church. Its future depends on the presence of people who can make decisions and carry through on them. A congregation that is comprised of members who stand around looking at each other, waiting for somebody to "do something," or who make commitments that are never carried out because everyone is "too busy," will accomplish very little for the Lord, and eventually expire.

Peter, Andrew, James, and John were effective servants of the Lord because they were men of action who did not shrink back in the face of hard commitments. Even when their decisions turned out to be flawed, they learned from their mistakes and became better men.

Similar decisions face us in life. How will we respond?

The Gospel of the Kingdom

The Sermon on the Mount is an iconic summary of what Jesus taught, providing a deeper insight into what it means to be a citizen of God's kingdom.

Jesus went about all Galilee, teaching in their synagogues, preaching the gospel of the kingdom, and healing all kinds of sickness and all kinds of disease among the people (Matt. 4:23).

৸৹৵

What was this "gospel of the kingdom" that Jesus was preaching? The answer is found in the three chapters that immediately follow (5-7), a lengthy discourse that we now call the Sermon on the Mount. If we want to preach the gospel today, this sermon is a good place to start.

Before digging into the details, it's helpful to notice two broad subtexts that run throughout this sermon: (a) life is hard, and (b) the secret to success in life is a pure heart. Keep these two ideas in mind as you read these chapters, and the Sermon will reveal a world of meaning.

Jesus begins with the Beatitudes (5:3-16), inner qualities that allow us to find genuine contentment in life. Our purpose in life is not defined by possessions or status, but by building the right character, a character that is constructed from the inside out.

This emphasis on the heart sets up the next section (5:17-48). Unlike the scribes and Pharisees—moralists who were so careful to maintain an *outward* display of righteousness—disciples of Jesus concentrate on harnessing the *inner thoughts* that drive behaviors. This raises the bar, producing an ethos that more closely resembles that of God—especially in how we view our enemies.

Even when we perform acts of goodness, they mean nothing if done for selfish ends (6:1-18). Our objective in doing good must never be to receive glory from men, but for the sake of the good itself. Even if my good deeds are never noticed by others, I'm fine with that, because my desire is to do the right thing for its own sake, not to promote myself.

The vicissitudes of life plunge many people into worry about their physical affairs. But because they seek a higher destiny in life, disciples of Jesus are not eaten up with anxiety (6:19-34). They face life with a calmness of spirit.

In a world of people with wildly different backgrounds and outlooks, friction with others is inevitable. But there is a right and wrong way to handle those conflicts, and discerning the difference requires a great deal of wisdom. That should drive us to our knees seeking guidance from God (7:1-12).

Finally, Jesus warns that the path of wisdom He lays out in this sermon is not easy, and many charlatans will offer attractive alternatives to His teaching. We mustn't take the bait, choosing instead to stay on the straight and narrow (7:13-27).

This sermon does not exhaust the gospel message. Paul later identified the death and resurrection of Christ as the foundation of the gospel (1 Cor. 15), an event that lay in the future as Jesus spoke. Neither does this sermon address topics such as church organization, worship, or discipline, all of which are addressed elsewhere in the epistles. This sermon was not intended to be the complete package, but *an introduction to a radical new way of looking at life.* It forces the reader to wrestle with the fact that the path to God is primarily a function of the heart. Outward forms of righteousness, while important, flow out of that deeper well. In the absence of that foundation, religion becomes an exercise in empty—even destructive—theater.

Jesus' audience was "astonished" at this message (7:28). We would be too, if we really understood the significance of this "gospel of the kingdom."

A Sermon Like No Other

The fact that the Sermon on the Mount is found at the very beginning of the New Testament should tell us something about its value and purpose.

Seeing the multitudes, He went up on a mountain, and when He was seated His disciples came to Him. Then He opened His mouth and taught them (Matt. 5:1-2).

And so it was, when Jesus had ended these sayings, that the people were astonished at His teaching, for He taught them as one having authority, and not as the scribes (Matt. 7:28-29).

လ**ာ**

Between these verses lies the greatest body of instruction the world has ever known: Jesus' Sermon on the Mount. Fragments of this Sermon can be found throughout the other Gospels, but nowhere else do we find such a comprehensive and powerful summary of Jesus' message to humanity.

Some of Jesus' best known sayings are found in this Sermon: the Beatitudes, the Golden Rule, the Lord's Prayer, the warning of the wide and narrow gates, the parable of the Wise and Foolish Builders, and others. Jesus touches all the hot buttons of our daily lives, concentrating especially on attitudes of the heart. He speaks plainly about the dangers of materialism, hypocrisy, worry, empty formalism, sexual sin, and false teachers. His instructions on how to manage our relationships with others, especially our enemies, are unparalleled in their practical simplicity, even if they are hard to implement. If we want a master course on developing character, the Sermon on the Mount is a good place to start.

However, to the first-time reader, this Sermon can be a jolting experience. In the 1980s, a composition professor at Texas A&M University, Virginia Stem Owens, had her freshman students read the Sermon on the Mount and write their impressions in an essay. Even this professor was shocked at the dismissive responses she received. One student complained that the Sermon "was hard to read and made me feel like I had to be perfect, and no one is." Another student labeled the ethical demands of this Sermon as "absurd," and pointed to Jesus' statement about lusting after a woman (5:28) as "the most extreme, stupid, un-human statement that I have ever heard." (Read the professor's full description of this episode at https://andynaselli.com/why-people-hate-the-sermon-on-the-mount.)

Maybe that's why the Lord has placed this Sermon at the very beginning of the New Testament. Before we learn anything else about Jesus, we are confronted with the core message He came to deliver. It's as though God is telling those who are curious about this Jewish Messiah to consider what following Him entails. Jesus does not call us to a country club of nice people, or to a philosophy study group, but to a radical new way of looking at ourselves and life. Those who take seriously what Jesus teaches here will undergo a personal transformation unlike anything else they will experience in their life.

Reading the three chapters of this Sermon takes only a few minutes. Learning and internalizing its lessons takes a lifetime. Make the Sermon on the Mount a frequent part of your Bible study, and your life will be enriched.

General Omar Bradley once said, "We have men of science, too few men of God. We have grasped the mystery of the atom and rejected the Sermon on the Mount. The world has achieved brilliance without conscience. Ours is a world of nuclear giants and ethical infants" (Armistice Day speech, Boston, MA, Nov. 11, 1948).

It's time we all get busy and rectify that deficiency.

The Peacemakers

In a world racked by conflict, it is a rare breed of individual who can calm troubled waters and restore harmony among warring factions.

"Blessed are the peacemakers, for they shall be called sons of God" (Matt. 5:9).

Let us pursue the things which make for peace and the things by which one may edify another (Rom. 14:19).

Now the fruit of righteousness is sown in peace by those who make peace (Jas. 3:18).

He who would love life and see good days, let him refrain his tongue from evil, and his lips from speaking deceit, let him turn away from evil and do good; let him seek peace and pursue it (1 Pet. 3:10-11).

☙

When *four* New Testament speakers call for God's people to be peacemakers, it's a sure bet we're dealing with a serious topic. The sad history of discord and conflict among humans, even in the church, bears witness to a glaring deficiency in this area. We should study the contexts of all four passages to learn more about how to be peacemakers.

Jesus' blessing upon peacemakers introduces His Sermon on the Mount (ch. 5–7), a discourse on personal character that deals extensively with interpersonal relationships. In this sermon, Jesus addresses themes like anger (5:21-26), retaliation (5:38-42), unconditional love (5:43-48), forgiveness (6:14-15), and harsh judging (7:1-5), all of which play major roles in how we get along with others, especially our adversaries. Those who successfully implement

His teaching on these topics come closest to being "sons of God."

In Romans 14, Paul offers counsel on how to handle "disputes over doubtful things" (v. 1). Before we start drawing lines over the minutiae of God's law, we need to weigh the impact of the battle we're about to engage. Is this issue worth the damage we will inflict on others and on the cause of Christ if we push it? Or would we all be better off by simply respecting the scruples of others (v. 3)?

James contrasts the behavior of peacemakers with those who are driven by "bitter envy and self-seeking" (v. 14, 16). Most fights are sparked by somebody who is miffed because they are not getting their way. Peacemakers, on the other hand, are people who are "willing to yield" (v. 17). They recognize a higher principle in play beyond their own selfish interests, and figure out a way to adapt to the needs of the larger community.

Finally, Peter borrows directly from a psalm of David (Psa. 34:12-16) that emphasizes the primacy of the Lord in all our affairs. If we fear Him (v. 7, 9), seek Him (v. 4, 10), and trust Him (v. 8, 22), we will have no need to defend our interests at any cost, for we know that the Lord will deliver us in His own good time (v. 6-7, 17, 19, 22).

As a bonus, those who have mastered the art of bridging differences with others in their own relationships are also qualified to intervene in disputes among others. Their wise and calming presence can help bring down the temperature and get people talking rationally again.

Peacemakers are a rare breed, but the world would be an even darker place without their steady influence. We all need to learn how to do it better.

The Greatest Evangelistic Tool

Evangelism should be a major focus of God's people. But the most effective evangelism tool is often overlooked in our outreach programs.

"Let your light so shine before men, that they may see your good works and glorify your Father in heaven" (Matt. 5:16).

ॐ

Every church that takes its mission seriously is concerned with evangelism. Churches are constantly on the lookout for more effective ways to take the message of salvation to a lost world. This usually involves gospel meetings, programs, campaigns, training sessions, or special outreach events. Churches that are really aggressive about evangelism tap the energy of their members, sending them out to knock on doors, hand out tracts, or put bumper stickers on their cars. Sometimes these tools work; but most of the time they generate a brief burst of enthusiasm that soon fades away.

Actually, the New Testament says very little about evangelism as an obligation of the average Christian. Evangelism was certainly a major activity in the early church—we read of numerous people who devoted their lives to spreading the Word—but it is never described as a universal requirement of all Christians. The reason is not hard to figure out. Teaching is an art that requires good people skills and communication skills. Not everyone can do it—or should even try (Jas. 3:1).

But there is one thing that every Christian *can* do to help spread the Word, and God fully expects each one of us to be active in this work. *We can live our faith in our daily lives.*

The good works that define our personal character will do more to attract people to our religion than all the sermons we could ever preach. As Jesus put it, our good works serve as a light to help others see God more clearly.

Unbelieving husbands, for example, can be converted "without a word . . . by the conduct of their wives" (1 Pet. 3:1). Later in that same chapter, Peter urges us to "be ready to give a defense to everyone who asks you a reason for the hope that is in you" (3:15), implying that unbelievers can be attracted to our faith simply by witnessing how we live, not by all the gospel pamphlets we hand out. Jesus said that God is glorified when His disciples "bear much fruit" (Jn. 15:8)— defined elsewhere as love, joy, peace, longsuffering, kindness, goodness, faithfulness, gentleness, self-control (Gal. 5:22-23). A few people displaying these qualities in their community are the best possible advertising for Christianity.

That's why so much of New Testament instruction is devoted, not to overt evangelism, but to training believers to live right. Most of the teaching of Jesus and His apostles is designed to improve attitudes and behaviors, to prepare people to deal patiently with hardship, to promote service to others. It is this kind of lifestyle that will attract people to the gospel. (Incidentally, these attitudes and behaviors begin among ourselves. Christians who cannot get along with each other discredit their faith and drive people away.)

None of this should be construed as discouraging churches from promoting evangelism by their members. But churches would do well to remember that the greatest evangelistic tool available to them is the active good will of their members in their community. Concentrate on that, and evangelism will take care of itself.

You Have Heard...

Much of what people "know" about the Bible is a garbled version of the original source. We can't believe everything we hear in popular discourse.

"You have heard that it was said to those of old . . ." (Matt. 5:21).

"Furthermore it has been said, . . ." (Matt. 5:31).

৩৽৵

No less than six times in this chapter, Jesus addressed a popular piece of theology by introducing something His audience was familiar with, a bit of wisdom they "had heard" was true. But in all six cases, Jesus argued, these rabbinic axioms pointed the people in the wrong direction. What they had heard—and what everybody assumed to be true—was in fact dangerously flawed.

One of the greatest stumbling blocks in our journey toward God is the mountain of misinformation that obscures the way, much of it coming from people who mean well. God has provided a reliable source of truth in the Bible, but countless "you have heard" truisms, many based on some fragment of Biblical truth, send us off on tangents that obscure what God would have us to know.

Sometimes what we have heard is taken directly from the Bible, but it's an isolated sliver of truth that ignores a wider context of information. The result of such a cherry-picked exegesis is an unwarranted conclusion that sets us up for trouble.

Sometimes what we have heard is an unnecessary inference based on a jumble of unrelated passages. Numerous verses can be stitched together in such a manner as to create the illusion of a Biblical mandate where none exists. The outcome is a man-made "rule" that God never intended.

Sometimes what we have heard has been fabricated by men. It's simply made up. It may be packaged in such a way as to sound spiritual, but God had nothing to do with it.

In a culture like ours, with a long history of exposure to Biblical theology, we should not be surprised to find that the popular version of "Christianity" in which we are immersed is contaminated by many of these distortions. Consequently, depending on "what we have heard" as a foundation for establishing truth can send us down a dangerous path.

Jesus corrected all six of those popular maxims in His Sermon, and spent the rest of His career correcting others. In our search for God's truth, we must take care to measure "what we have heard" against our own careful, methodical reading of the Bible. Let the Bible interpret itself, and we can spare ourselves the frustration of being misled by "what we have heard."

The Perils of Porn

Adultery in the flesh starts with adultery in the heart. Jesus' solution to all sexual sin is to train the heart not to desire it.

"I say to you that whoever looks at a woman to lust for her has already committed adultery with her in his heart. If your right eye causes you to sin, pluck it out and cast it from you; for it is more profitable for you that one of your members perish, than for your whole body to be cast into hell" (Matt. 5:28-29).

৩৵৽

There was a time when a man who wished to see pornography had to go out of his way to find it. Today, thanks to the internet, that's no longer the case. Vast quantities of pornography are readily available to anyone with a few clicks of a mouse. Consider the following statistics from 2006 (via *Internet Filter Review*):

- Number of pornographic websites: 42 million.
- Percentage of internet users who view online pornography: 42.7%
- Number of U.S. adults who regularly visit pornographic websites: 40 million
- Average age of first internet exposure to pornography: 11 years old
- Number of "Christians" who say that pornography is a major problem in the home: 47%

Clearly, pornography is a growing problem that poses a real threat to the moral foundation of our society.

As with every other moral issue, dealing with this problem places us in a position contrary to the prevailing culture. Pornography is now so widespread that many accept it as just a normal part of life, something that we shouldn't get all upset over. After all, "everybody does it," so what's the big deal, right?

Actually, there is much about pornography that is harmful.

First, *pornography victimizes those who create it.* Women who have left the porn industry relate horrible stories of what that career did to their lives. Whatever "act" they put on in front of the camera, the women who star in these productions hate what they are doing. They're in it strictly for the money, and those who watch their performances contribute to their degradation.

Second, *pornography teaches men a perverted image of what sexual intimacy is about.* Young men who enter marriage educated only by what they have viewed on porn sites are in for a rude shock when they have to build a relationship with a "real" woman.

Third, *pornography is addictive.* Like alcohol, gambling, and other behaviors driven by our baser instincts, viewing porn can become a consuming activity that takes over one's life. In extreme cases, pornography can become the springboard to criminal activity involving sexual assault, or worse.

Finally, *pornography destroys homes.* It throws marriages into conflict, and tears families apart. And all in exchange for . . . what?

How can we avoid the harmful effects of pornography? Obviously, we must choose not to view it. But if you're already struggling with it, take Jesus' advice: "Pluck out your eye"—that is, take whatever drastic steps are necessary to get it out of your life. Yank the internet connection, get involved in a support group, seek counseling—whatever it takes.

The greatest peril of porn is the threat to your soul. Hell is not worth it.

Jesus On Divorce

In a society that treats divorce casually, Jesus challenges the assumptions that legitimize it. Our divorce epidemic must face a similar reckoning.

"It has been said, 'Whoever divorces his wife, let him give her a certificate of divorce.' But I say to you that whoever divorces his wife for any reason except sexual immorality causes her to commit adultery; and whoever marries a woman who is divorced commits adultery (Matt. 5:31-32).

❧

Like everything else in His Sermon on the Mount, Jesus' treatment of divorce landed like a hammer blow on the people who heard it. We can't appreciate the impact of what He said without considering the popular view of divorce that prevailed in His day, and the historical background behind it.

Moses addressed the topic of divorce only to regulate it (Deut. 24:1-4). Once divorced and remarried, a woman could never return to her first husband. This prohibition served as a deterrent to men impulsively dumping their wives in a fit of passion. The Pharisees ignored the intent behind this law, focusing instead on the "certificate of divorce" that formalized the separation. In their legalistic view, divorce is no big deal, so long as the paperwork is in order. The practical effect of this flawed interpretation, of course, was a nightmare for the poor women whose lives were turned upside down by husbands who didn't take their marriage vows seriously.

As with everything else in this sermon, Jesus attacked the root of the problem. Notice that Jesus addressed the impact on the *woman* who is divorced, not on the *husband* doing the divorcing. That distinction is significant. In the popular view, a man was doing his wife a favor by giving her a certificate of divorce; she was a free woman, available to the next man who wanted her. This legal jujitsu sounded noble, but the practical effects of casting out one's wife—emotional, familial, societal, financial—were devastating, especially to the woman.

We know what the Pharisees thought of adultery. They once brought to Jesus a woman caught "in the very act," and pressed Him on whether she should be stoned (Jn. 8:4-5). So when Jesus labeled as "adultery" the wife's second marriage (which was essential to her survival), He was charging these men as being accomplices to the very sin they themselves condemned. Their fallacious exegesis of Deut. 24 mocked the divine purpose for marriage.

And that is Jesus' point here: *Every divorce involves sin.* Whether the grounds for divorce are infidelity or incompatibility, every divorce involves a corruption of God's original intention for marriage. In His eyes, marriage is not a relationship of convenience, but a permanent bond. When people jump in and out of serial marriages, they are no different from the cad who sleeps around behind his spouse's back.

Our society's casual treatment of marriage and divorce doubles down on the depravity of the Pharisees. Even among those who seek to uphold God's original intention for marriage, the words of Jesus are parsed to such excruciating detail that we lose sight of His core message: *Marriage is a lifetime bond that must be preserved at all costs.* When we divorce, we spit on God's design for human happiness.

How can we counter the rising rate of divorce in our society? Condemning divorce is a good start, but the more effective strategy is to educate people on the sacred value of marriage, and the life skills essential to making it successful.

Loving Is Not Liking

The command to "love your enemies" seems
hopelessly unrealistic—but not if we grasp the
distinction between "liking" and "loving" others.

---

*"You have heard that it was said, 'You shall love your
neighbor and hate your enemy.' But I say to you, love your
enemies, bless those who curse you, do good to those who
hate you, and pray for those who spitefully use you and per-
secute you, that you may be sons of your Father in heaven"
(Matt. 5:43-45).*

სოლ

No ethical system challenges humanity more than Jesus'
Sermon on the Mount. The demands that Jesus makes in this
Sermon seem to contradict everything we think we know
about human relations. Skeptics dismiss it as unrealistic.
Even believers struggle to understand and apply it.

The counterintuitive nature of the Sermon is nowhere
more glaring than in the command to "love your enemies."
When others treat us with hate and contempt, it is only natural that we respond in kind. Yet Jesus insists that we not only
not hate our enemy, but *love* him. How is this even possible?

To implement this principle in our lives, we first have to
understand the terminology. By treating "love" and "like" as
synonymous, we create a roadblock that prevents us from
grasping what Jesus is saying. But the two concepts are quite
different.

We "like" those things that bring us some kind of emotional pleasure or enjoyment. We like little puppies because
they're cute and playful; we like ice cream because it's cold

and sweet; and we like our friends because they are so much like us, with common interests, beliefs, experiences, and backgrounds. They probably even look like us. We like them because their presence in our lives validates our comfortable identity. None of that applies to our enemies, nor can it.

But to love someone in the Biblical sense involves none of those qualities. Biblical love is defined as "active good-will" toward others. It is a genuine desire for whatever is in the best interest of another, whether we like them or not, and is demonstrated in sincere acts of kindness and compassion. We don't have to *like* someone to *love* them.

The greatest example of this kind of unselfish love is God Himself. "God demonstrates His own love toward us, in that while we were still sinners, Christ died for us. . . . When we were enemies we were reconciled to God through the death of His Son" (Rom. 5:8, 10). God doesn't just demand that we love our enemies; He models that behavior Himself, in a very practical manner.

The implications of this principle have a far-reaching effect on human relations. Consider its application in marriage. Two people fall madly in love, get married, and take on the world together. But after a few years the fun wears off and the two people who once couldn't bear to be apart now can't stand each other. They don't even like each other any more. They have become enemies, inflicting enormous pain on each other. Can their marriage be saved? Yes, but only if both parties are willing to do what Jesus said: bless instead of curse, do good instead of evil, and pray fervently for one another. They have to learn how to truly *love* each other, despite their differences.

Loving our enemies is not only possible, it is essential to human flourishing. We mustn't allow our dislike of others to keep us from doing them good.

Seeking Perfection in an Imperfect World

God wants us to be perfect, but He knows we will never become so. Knowing how to balance those two realities is essential to our mental health.

"Therefore you shall be perfect, just as your Father in heaven is perfect" (Matt. 5:48).

"For there is not a just man on earth who does good and does not sin" (Eccl. 7:20).

❧

These two verses illustrate the conundrum with which every conscientious child of God struggles throughout life. On the one hand, we are told to "be perfect" and "do not sin" (1 Cor. 15:34). That means no mistakes. Yet on the other hand, we are told that we'll never achieve that lofty goal (Eccl. 7:20; 1 Jn. 1:8). No one will ever be sinlessly perfect, at least not on their own merit. Our challenge is to find a happy balance between these two principles, both in our dealings with others, and with ourselves.

Some people fixate on the first principle ("be perfect") to the neglect of the second. These folks either beat themselves up over their own shortcomings and dwell on their failures; or they minimize their own shortcomings by loudly criticizing everyone else's flaws. Either way, those who are obsessed with perfection are insufferable to be around.

Other people avoid that extreme by embracing the other principle ("no one is perfect"). These people just shrug their shoulders at the whole idea of improvement or excellence, and tolerate all manner of behaviors, both in themselves and in others. We can't be judgmental, you know.

Put all these people together, and you end up with a toxic mix: Some people are determined to straighten out everyone else's lives; others are equally determined to remove any rules or restrictions on any behavior; and others are a psychotic mess, unable to live with themselves or with others. The result is chaos—which pretty much explains why the world is in the shape it's in today.

The solution to all this confusion, of course, is to appreciate how these two principles really do harmonize with each other.

First, we must realize that although no one will ever achieve sinless perfection in this life, it is the *striving* for that goal that is the source of every advancement in human endeavor. When people push themselves—or are pushed—to reach higher levels of performance, they will achieve victories they never thought they could accomplish, even if they don't reach their original goals. So it is good to set our sights high, and to gently prod others to do the same.

Second, we must respect the role of *forgiveness* in this equation. God forgives our mistakes; we should forgive the mistakes of others; and we should forgive ourselves. Forgiveness is not the same as indifferent toleration. By definition, forgiveness implies a failure to meet a standard. But the beauty of forgiveness is that our failures are not fatal. We are given another chance to get it right, and another, and another. It is this environment of mercy that allows people to grow and improve, without becoming despondent over their imperfections.

The biblical injunction to "be perfect" is not inconsistent with the declaration that no one will ever be so. In fact, they are perfect complements to each other, providing just the right combination of discipline and reassurance that can inspire us to reach our full potential.

Why Pray?

If God already knows our heart before we pray, what's the point in telling Him? Actually, there are several good reasons why we should talk to God.

"And when you pray, do not use vain repetitions as the heathen do. For they think that they will be heard for their many words. Therefore do not be like them. For your Father knows the things you have need of before you ask Him" (Matt. 6:7-8).

৩৵৶

Elsewhere in the Bible we are encouraged to "let your requests be made known to God" (Phil. 4:6). Yet in this passage, Jesus tells us that God already knows our needs even before we ask for them. So why bother praying?

This is a puzzle only if we view prayer as informing God of our feelings and our needs—that is, a means of bringing Him up to speed with what's going on in our life.

But prayer is not for God's benefit. Rather, *we* are the ones who stand to gain from this activity. Consider how prayer benefits us.

First, *prayer strengthens our faith in God.* If a person does not really believe that God is "out there" somewhere listening, he's obviously not going to waste time mumbling some private thoughts to Him. That's why atheists generally do not pray. However, if we start with just a seed of faith in God, and develop the habit of talking to Him regularly, that seed will grow into a firm conviction that He really is there, and that He listens, understands, and cares about our life.

Second, *prayer prepares our hearts to listen and understand God's word.* As our faith in God deepens, we develop a hunger and thirst to know more about Him. That longing, of course, leads us to the Bible, the story of God's long involvement in human affairs. As our prayer life grows, we begin to read the Bible with a fresh perspective, with hearts more keen to pick up lessons that we can apply in our lives. In that sense, we can say that our prayers open our hearts to gain wisdom.

Third, *prayer enhances our sense of dependence on God.* In the act of expressing our needs and desires to God, we remind ourselves that we are not autonomous. We owe our lives and everything in them to God. We cannot thump our chest and boast of our achievements and skills. We depend on Him for everything, even the air we breathe. Our prayers remind of us of that basic reality.

Finally, *prayer fosters a spirit of gratitude in our hearts.* Thankfulness is a major component of prayer. And as we repeatedly thank God for His goodness in our lives, we slowly train ourselves not to take our blessings for granted. We develop a deeper appreciation for the good things in our lives— and even some of the not-so-good things. Furthermore, grateful people are generous people. The more we appreciate what we have, the more we sympathize with those who do not share our good fortune, and are motivated to share with them.

So does this mean that prayer is merely a tool of personal psychological healing, and nothing more? Of course not. God does answer prayers, often involving active providential intervention in our lives. But He intervenes only in behalf of those whose prayer life demonstrates that they are truly seeking Him.

When we pray, we cannot tell God anything He does not already know. The real question at stake in our prayer life is: What do *we* know?

Where Is Your Heart?

What we treasure—value, cherish, hold dear—
reveals the true state of our heart. It is not hard,
therefore, to identify where our heart really lies.

"Do not lay up for yourselves treasures on earth, where moth and rust destroy and where thieves break in and steal; but lay up for yourselves treasures in heaven, where neither moth nor rust destroys and where thieves do no break in and steal. For where your treasure is there your heart will be also" (Matt. 6:19-21).

৵৽

In a world where everybody is madly chasing after riches, Jesus admonished His disciples to adopt a wholly different value system. Our treasure should be in heaven, not here on earth. The basis of that different perspective is a simple principle of human nature: "Where your treasure is there your heart will be also." A study of this little proverb provides a good exercise in self-examination.

"Treasure" is what I value, what I consider to be most important in my life, that for which I will make the greatest sacrifices. Whatever occupies that role in my life is what my heart will be focused on. Expressed another way, my heart belongs to whatever I consider to be of greatest importance. If the vast majority of my life is spent on making money or accumulating worldly possessions, then *that* is what I love more than anything else; *that* is where my heart lies.

So in order to determine where my heart lies, all I need to do is look at what I consider to be of greatest value. Where do I choose to spend the bulk of my energy and resources?

What do I prefer to do with my free time? What is so important to me that I will spend my hard-earned money on it? These questions can be used to construct a series of simple tests to determine if my heart is in the right place on a number of issues. For example:

Christian: Do you love God and your brethren? If so, how much time in your daily routine is spent on the things of God? Do you really enjoy spending time reading God's Word and being with God's people? Or do you see those activities as a burden to be borne? What does your checkbook say about how much you value this aspect of your life?

Husbands and wives: Do you love your spouse? Given a choice, do you prefer to spend more time with your spouse than with any other activity? Do you delight in making your spouse happy, whatever the cost? Do you treat your spouse as the most important person in your life, next to God? Answer these questions honestly, and you have a good indication of whether or not you really do love him/her.

Parents: Do you love your children? If so, how much of your uninterrupted time do you give them? What do you sacrifice to ensure that their moral, spiritual, intellectual, and physical needs are met? Do you treat them as precious gifts from God, or as nuisances that get in the way of other activities? You may fool yourself, but your children know whether or not you value them by how you treat them.

Obviously, not all of these relationships can be Number One. We have to set priorities and apportion our time and resources accordingly. But it is important that each of these relationships—rather than money or possessions—receive dedicated attention in our lives. That's the only way we can demonstrate where our heart truly lies.

Parenting: How Birds Do It

We make child-raising more complicated than it needs to be. Watching the simplest of God's creatures raise their young can teach us much.

"Look at the birds of the air, for they neither sow nor reap nor gather into barns; yet your heavenly Father feeds them. Are you not of more value than they?" (Matt. 6:26).

ഇം

Jesus often used birds to illustrate lessons about life. There's something about the simple life that birds lead that helps clear away the clutter and see life for what it really is. In recent years, this has become more obvious to me while watching swallows raise their young in the sturdy little nests they have built under the eaves of our house. We humans can learn a lot about parenting from these little creatures, if we will take the time to learn.

Parenting is a collaborative effort between a male and a female. Invariably, a mating pair remains committed to the work of raising their young. They do not experiment with single parenthood, step families, same-sex parenting, communal families, or other variations on the traditional model. They instinctively know what we humans have forgotten, that the best, most efficient form of parenting is a father and mother working together in a committed relationship to raise their young.

Parenting is hard work. Both parents stay busy cleaning the nest, catching bugs for their little ones, and warding off dangers to the nest. Mom and dad might fly off for a few minutes of aerial fun, but they are soon back at the nest tending to their primary task. They never seem surprised at the amount of work involved in raising their young, or get too involved in other activities and neglect them. And I have never seen a pair abandon their nest altogether. With these birds there is no question what comes first.

Parenting requires protecting the offspring. Swallows are fiercely protective of their families. If someone walks near their nest, they will buzz the intruder repeatedly, with loud chirps to scare away the threat. There is a risk involved in this behavior, but it usually works. How many of us humans will spring into action to protect our children from the threats to their welfare that come from television, the internet, even their schools? If their own parents won't protect them, who will?

Parenting, if successful, results in an empty nest. After the eggs hatch and the little chicks get big enough to spread their wings, mom and dad will spend hours swooping and fluttering in front of the nest teaching their brood how to fly. Eventually, the little ones get the courage to jump, and off they go. For several days thereafter, little swallows are flying around all over the place, but soon they are gone, never to return. Mom and dad do not sit around the nest, pining for the kids. Life goes on, and so do they. No "empty nest" syndrome here.

One final lesson: *Parenting does not require a library of self-help books written by experts.* Birds come by it quite naturally—and so do we humans, if we will listen to our instincts and do what we know is right.

What Is the Kingdom?

The "kingdom" metaphor in the New Testament
has a range of meanings. We err trying to make
one definition fit every occurrence of the word.

*"Seek first the kingdom of God and His righteousness,
and all these things shall be added to you" (Matt. 6:33).*

സ⌘യ

We are conditioned to give a quick answer to that question: it's the *church*—the body of the saved, all the redeemed—ruled by its king, Jesus Christ. That's at least partially true, but trying to fit that definition into every New Testament passage that mentions the "kingdom" creates some problems.

There are at least three different ways in which the concept of "the kingdom" is used in the New Testament.

First, of course, are those passages where the word "kingdom" clearly refers to the church. Jesus told Peter, "On this rock I will build My *church*, . . . and I will give you the keys of the *kingdom* of heaven" (Matt. 16:18-19). "He has made us to be a *kingdom*, priests to His God and Father" (Rev. 1:6, NASB). "He has delivered us from the power of darkness and translated us into the *kingdom* of the Son of His love" (Col. 1:13). These passages represent the fulfillment of the Old Testament promises of a coming kingdom, ruled by the Son of David (2 Sam. 7:12-16).

But in other passages the word is used to describe a future reward that we have not yet seen. For example, Peter urged his readers to "make your calling and election sure . . . for so an entrance will be supplied to you abundantly into the everlasting *kingdom* of our Lord and Savior Jesus Christ" (2 Pet. 1:10-11). At the final judgment, the faithful will be told, "Come, you blessed of My Father, inherit the *kingdom* prepared for you from the foundation of the world" (Matt. 25:34). Paul looked forward to that day when Lord would "deliver me from every evil work and preserve me for His heavenly *kingdom*" (2 Tim. 4:18). The "kingdom" in all these passages is obviously heaven itself, the dwelling place of the King.

Other passages imply a third variation. Jesus told the Pharisees, "the *kingdom* of God does not come with observation; . . . For indeed, the *kingdom* of God is within you" (Lk. 17:20-21). Neither of the previous definitions fits very well here. It is best to think of this "kingdom within" as *the rule of God in the lives of individuals.* As people enthrone God in their hearts, He "rules" there.

Likewise, when a scribe gave an accurate summary of the two greatest commandments, Jesus assured him, "You are not far from the kingdom of God" (Mk. 12:28-34). Jesus was not referring to a map or a calendar, but to the scribe's own relationship with God. This definition also seems to fit best in Jesus' plea to "seek first the *kingdom* of God and His righteousness" (Matt. 6:33). We seek God's kingdom when we seek to incorporate His righteousness in our personal lives. Study the parables of Jesus with this concept in mind, and they become much more personal and useful.

Actually, all three definitions are related: Those who submit to God's rule in their lives are added to the church, and are rewarded with a home in heaven. Truly, the kingdom of God is the greatest of all kingdoms!

Are Christians Judgmental?

"You're so judgmental!" The best way to avoid that label is not to avoid expressing opinions, but to use exercise good sense in making judgments.

"Judge not, that you be not judged" (Matt. 7:1).

"Solid food belongs to those who are of full age, that is, those who by reason of use have their senses exercised to discern both good and evil" (Heb. 5:14).

৩∞৩

One of the most common epithets that gets thrown at Christians is the label, "judgmental." Any attempt to express a Biblical opinion on a subject (especially those involving morality) is met with a sneering "Oh, you Christians are so judgmental!" We get slammed with that criticism so much that many of us now shy away from expressing our faith. Better to be quiet than to be tarred as an extremist.

What does this word mean? Why do people use it to describe us? And what can we do to avoid it?

The dictionary defines *judgmental* as "displaying an excessively critical point of view." Sadly, many Christians indeed fit that definition. They are quick to condemn and slow to listen. They are harsh in their treatment of those they disagree with. And the opinions they push with such arrogance are often poorly informed and delivered with disdain for the hearer. Worse, this even describes how they often treat their fellow Christians!

But guess what? Many atheists and free thinkers are also judgmental, guilty of all the above. They can be just as hateful, just as harsh, just as close-minded, as any Christian. (If you don't believe that, spend time reading the comments section on some apologetics blogs.) You see, being judgmental is not a Christian problem; it's a *human* problem. All of us—including those who claim an enlightened understanding of tolerance—have a tendency to pounce on others who do not agree with us.

But consider a variation on this theme: Have you noticed that people who exercise good judgment are generally not considered judgmental? You know the type: They seem to know exactly when to insert themselves into a situation to resolve a problem—and when to quietly back away to avoid creating a problem. They are skilled at dealing with people, with a knack for saying the right thing at the right time, and nothing more. Even when they rebuke, they do so with a gentle firmness that evokes concern, not animosity.

In other words, these people have a highly developed sense of moral discernment; they "have their senses exercised to discern good and evil." They make judgments all the time regarding people, situations, and behaviors. But their judgments are thoughtful, accurate, measured, careful, calm. Everybody—atheist and believer alike—appreciates the beauty in that kind of character.

The problem is not that we make judgments; it's *how* we make them. True, the "judgmental" label is sometimes just a knee-jerk reaction to a contrary opinion. But all too often it's a legitimate complaint. The best way to avoid that insult is to be a person of good judgment. Educate yourself on the topic at hand; carefully consider all the factors involved before blurting out an opinion; think through the implications of what you say before you say it; and speak with gentleness and respect for your opponent. People still may not agree with you, but they will respect you as a person of good judgment.

Living the Golden Rule

No other Biblical command has been given its own name. It's so simple and practical, yet we struggle to practice it. There is a reason why.

"Therefore, whatever you want men to do to you, do also to them, for this is the Law and the Prophets" (Matt. 7:12).

༺༻

We call this precept "The Golden Rule," because no other law is so valuable a guide for making moral decisions in life. If all of us treated others with the same courtesy and consideration that we expect them to show us, the world would be a much happier place.

Of course, that's not happening. Everyone admires the Golden Rule as a reliable standard of conduct, and admits that it's the answer to most of humanity's social problems. Yet most people struggle to live it consistently. Even among those who claim to follow Jesus, the compliance level is often quite low. Like so many other Biblical injunctions, profession and practice don't always match up. Why?

We can suggest a couple of reasons. First, there are some people who have been so damaged in their upbringing that they struggle to understand the concept of treating others "as you want others to do to you." They despise themselves, and expect others to despise them too. They have no sense of self-worth by which they can appreciate the needs of others, so they are incapable of that kind of empathy. There is no personal frame of reference that would allow them to recognize the need for treating others with respect. Before these people can practice the Golden Rule effectively, they first need to do a major reconstruction of their own self-image. Only then can they appreciate the value of treating others with dignity.

For the rest of us, the Golden Rule is great in theory, but impractical in real life because of the sacrifices that such a way of life would entail. For example:

- We expect others to go out of their way to defer to our needs or wishes . . . but I don't have the time or resources to do the same to them!
- We expect others to swallow their pride and apologize for their offenses . . . but what I did to them was no big deal, they should just get over it!
- We expect others to overlook our mistakes and short-comings (they should try to walk in my shoes for a day) . . . but their mistakes are inexcusable!

We have no problem recognizing how people ought to treat us, but extending those same favors to others is just too much to ask. We can offer all kinds of reasons for treating others in a manner that benefits us, rather than the way we would like to be treated if the roles were reversed.

The root problem here, of course, is *selfishness*. The desire for personal aggrandizement blinds us to a fair comparison of what we want and what others want. We hold one standard for others and a different standard for ourselves—and cannot see a problem in that imbalance. In order for the Golden Rule to work, we have to redirect our attention away from ourselves and toward others. We have to genuinely desire what is best for them above what we want.

That's not easy—but there are no shortcuts. We must make whatever sacrifices are necessary to make the Golden Rule central to our character—including reconstructing our self-image, if necessary. That process begins by reflecting on the work of the One who loved us and sacrificed so much for us.

Fruit Inspectors

The threat of false teachers requires diligence on our part. Jesus provides a simple test to help us identify these threats before we take the bait.

"Beware of false prophets, who come to you in sheep's clothing, but inwardly they are ravenous wolves. You will know them by their fruits. Do men gather grapes from thorn-bushes or figs from thistles? Even so, every good tree bears good fruit, but a bad tree bears bad fruit. A good tree cannot bear bad fruit, nor can a bad tree bear good fruit. Every tree that does not bear good fruit is cut down and thrown into the fire. Therefore by their fruits you will know them" (Matt. 7:15-20).

৩০৵৶

Jesus' Sermon on the Mount (Matt. 5–7) is a positive affirmation of the character of those who would be His disciples. The attitudes and behaviors that He promotes as creating happiness in life have been validated in the lives of countless people through the ages.

But as Jesus began to draw His sermon to a close, He issued a warning regarding those who would lead us down a different path. There are false prophets, He says, who will offer us the same benefits—but via dangerous short cuts.

How can we identify these false teachers? The usual answer is that we must compare what men teach with what Jesus and His apostles taught; if it does not match up, it's false teaching and should be rejected.

While that is certainly valid, that's not the answer Jesus gave here. Instead, He invites us to look beyond the teaching to the *fruits* of the teaching; that is, examine what the teaching produces. What impact does a teaching have on the lives of those who follow it or are influenced by it? You don't have to be a Bible scholar to recognize rotten fruit when you see it.

For example, in contrast to the high standard of sexual ethics that Jesus taught, modern culture offers a much more casual standard. Sexuality is considered just another adventure to be explored with others, without boundaries or restrictions. Millions of young people have bought into this liberating philosophy—but at a terrible price. Broken hearts, jealous rages, psychological and emotional baggage, STDs, and a host of other issues are the fruit of this no-rules lifestyle. The fruit is bad because the root (teaching) from which it springs is bad, and it's a wise young person who spots that connection before taking the bait.

At the opposite extreme are those who zealously push a religion of artificial rules designed to ensure that no mistakes are ever made. Every extension of every detail is carefully thought out and made an article of faith and a test of fellowship. The problem with this approach, of course, is that no two people agree on every detail, so the result is endless wrangling over excruciatingly complex interpretations. In other words, the fruit of endless strife and conflict exposes the core teaching as bogus. That's not the religion Jesus promoted.

If we want to inoculate ourselves against the influence of false teachers, we would do well to study the fruits of truth and error, such as described in Gal. 5:19-26, 2 Cor. 12:20-21, and Jas. 3:13-18. Learn to recognize the symptoms of false teaching, and it will be easier to identify the teaching as true or false. That does not relieve us of the responsibility to study the content of the teaching, of course, but it's a good place to start.

Who's Going to Heaven?

Knowing how to respond to a popular prejudicial retort can move the discussion toward a more profitable outcome.

"Not everyone who says to Me, 'Lord, Lord,' shall enter the kingdom of heaven, but he who does the will of My Father in heaven" (Matt. 7:21).

❧

When trying to teach others what the New Testament says about salvation and the church, people will often respond with a question that puts us on the defensive: "So you think you're the only ones going to heaven?" The implication is that we are narrow-minded, intolerant, judgmental, and arrogant. How is the best way to respond?

First, we should recognize that this question is meaningful only among those who believe there is a final judgment and a reward/punishment beyond. If the questioner is a committed secularist who denies God, an afterlife, judgment, heaven, hell, or anything beyond the molecules we are made of, then there is no point in carrying the discussion further. If none of those things exist, then there is no objective morality to which we owe our allegiance, and we're all going to rot in the grave, without any distinctions whatsoever. The greater question we should be discussing with these people is, why should we even bother trying to live a moral life at all? But that's a question for another article.

So let's assume we both believe in God, an afterlife and a final judgment. Given that shared belief, let's turn this question around: Do you think *everyone* is going to heaven, regardless of what they do or don't do? Child molesters? Rapists? Serial killers? Hitler? White male Republicans? Very few people are so open-minded that they recognize absolutely no limits on human behavior. But once you acknowledge *any* restrictions on who is going to heaven, you're in the same position I am. We may have different perspectives on what the boundaries are and how to determine them, but we both agree that only a subset of the human race is going to heaven.

So the question, "Do you think you're the only ones going to heaven" is misleading, and even a little dishonest. If we agree that some people are going to heaven and others are not, then the more appropriate question should be, "Who is going to heaven?"

Fortunately, we do not have to speculate on the answer to that question. Let's listen to what Jesus said: "Not everyone who says to Me, 'Lord, Lord,' shall enter the kingdom of heaven, but he who does the will of My Father in heaven." This is a simple, unambiguous declaration. It is those who do God's will who are going to heaven. It is not narrow-minded, intolerant, or hateful to bring this fact to people's attention.

Of course, in the end God has the last word, and nothing we believe or say will influence His judgment of others. They have to answer for their lives, and we have to answer for ours. Our purpose in pointing out Biblical truth concerning salvation and the church is not to pass judgment on people, but to prompt an honest consideration of what God has revealed, and to encourage compliance. This is fair and reasonable.

A final word of caution: If we present this truth in a disdainful manner that reeks of arrogance, we deserve the scorn we receive. Humility must govern our conduct in discussing these topics, knowing that we are still in the process of learning truth ourselves, and will be judged like everyone else.

Doing the Will of the Father

The condition for entering heaven seems simple enough, until we take a closer look at what it requires of us—and what it does *not* require.

"Not everyone who says to Me, 'Lord, Lord,' shall enter the kingdom of heaven, but he who does the will of My Father in heaven" (Matt. 7:21).

৵৽৻

These words of Jesus should settle once and for all the question of what is required to go to heaven. Mere expressions of loyalty are not enough. Faith without action is not enough. Warm, fuzzy feelings about God and Jesus are not enough. No, it is only the one who "does the will of My Father" who shall enter the kingdom of heaven.

So let's take this principle for a test drive. Consider the Pharisee in Jesus' parable, for example, a man who could boast to God, "I thank You that I am not like other men—extortioners, unjust, adulterers, or even as this tax collector. I fast twice a week, I give tithes of all that I possess" (Lk. 18:11-12). It's an abbreviated list, no doubt, but he appears to qualify as heavenly material, right? Especially compared to the tax collector, who could only beg, "Be merciful to me a sinner" (v. 13). Clearly, the tax collector fell short, while the Pharisee passed with flying colors. But Jesus turns our expectation upside down with His conclusion: The tax collector "went down to his house justified rather than the other" (v. 14). The one who "did the will of the Father" was rejected, while the "sinner" got in. How does that work?

The same conundrum appears in the parable of the Prodigal Son (Lk. 15:11-32). The younger son went wild with sin, yet was eagerly embraced by his father when he returned home. The older brother, who "never transgressed your commandment at any time" (v. 29), was the one left out of the banquet. Here, too, the rule seems to break down.

So Jesus declares that going to heaven is predicated on obedience; yet His stories seem to suggest that those who obey actually have *less* of a chance of making it than those whose lives are an unholy mess. What's going on here?

Jesus is not contradicting Himself. The solution is to revisit our definition of "doing the will of the Father." Look at the context of both parables and you'll notice that Jesus was not emphasizing the details of outward conduct, but *the manner in which we approach God*. The external behavior is important, certainly; but the *inward attitude* with which we come into God's presence is more important. The tax collector and the younger brother in the two parables made a lot of mistakes, but they humbled themselves and came clean before their fathers. The Pharisee and the older brother, on the other hand, were proud of their performances, confident that their own goodness had earned their way in. God was just their cheering section.

Here's the bottom line: "Doing the will of the Father" first requires that we cleanse our hearts of all the stubbornness, pride, and smug self-righteousness that prevents us from coming into His presence. This humbling of the heart is the one act of obedience without which all the others are meaningless.

Then, having fixed what's broken on the inside, a remarkable thing will happen: What's on the outside will begin to undergo a natural and gradual transformation into a life of genuine purity, as an outgrowth of the new heart. We are prepared for heaven, not by our superior achievement, but by the power of God's grace working in the inner man.

Profession vs. Performance

Calling Jesus "Lord" is easy. The challenge comes when His commands are hard. That's when the genuineness of our faith is put to the test.

"Not everyone who says to me, 'Lord, Lord,' shall enter the kingdom of heaven, but he who does the will of My Father in heaven" (Matt. 7:21).

"But why do you call Me 'Lord, Lord,' and not do the things which I say?" (Lk. 6:46).

❧

In an age when followers of Jesus are considered religious kooks, it takes courage to declare allegiance to Him. "No one can say that Jesus is Lord except by the Holy Spirit" (1 Cor. 12:3), so we have to give credit to anyone who is willing make that confession.

But confessing Jesus as Lord only gets us started on the life of faith. The confession must be followed by allegience to the guidance of the one we call our Lord. Otherwise, the confession is just empty talk.

Unfortunately, many believers never get beyond the confession stage. They talk about God and Jesus and the Bible, but their lives are a glaring contradiction to everything the religion of Jesus stands for. Their performance does not match their profession.

The first letter to the Corinthians was addressed to "all who in every place call on the name of Jesus Christ our Lord" (1 Cor. 1:2); but the next sixteen chapters were spent trying to get these people who called Jesus their Lord to understand how that confession should be demonstrated in their daily lives. They still struggled with the old carnal attitudes and behaviors from their previous way of life; in some cases, the failures were spectacularly bad. Paul insisted that this had to change. If the Corinthians were going to represent Christ in their community, their lives had to show qualities that made them stand out from their unbelieving neighbors. Otherwise, what's the point of following Jesus?

The problem that plagued the church at Corinth continues to plague Christianity today. Millions of people claim allegiance to Jesus, but their lives are a sorry reflection of the high standard set by their Savior. The world notices the contradiction, and does not hesitate to rub it in our faces. We can and must do better.

But a word of caution: In highlighting the importance of obedience, we must be careful not to stretch Jesus' words beyond their intended meaning. Jesus is not demanding sinless perfection as a condition for salvation. Nor is He granting us a license to criticize every flaw and wart in a brother. His words must be reconciled with Paul's warning that "as many as are of the works of the law are under the curse; for it is written, 'Cursed is everyone who does not continue in all things which are written in the book of the law, to do them'" (Gal. 3:10). If we begin to think that our obedience is so good that it will earn us our salvation, we're already doomed. Try as hard as we may, our obedience will always be incomplete. That's why Jesus died for us.

But the fact that our obedience will never be perfect does not release us from the obligation to *try*. That is what Jesus is looking for: People who love Him so much that they will do everything within their power to honor Him with their lives. They will make mistakes, of course; but they will never give up, always striving to honor the one they call "Lord."

Proximity Is Not Faith

Those who claim to follow Jesus often confuse their close relationship with the Master with "faith." The two are not necessarily the same.

When Jesus heard it, He marveled, and said to those who followed, "Assuredly, I say to you, I have not found such great faith, not even in Israel!" (Matt. 8:10).

But He said to them, "Why are you fearful, O you of little faith?" Then He arose and rebuked the winds and the sea, and there was a great calm (Matt. 8:26).

❧

The fact that these two stories—found next to each other in Matthew's gospel—feature one party with "great faith" and another with "little faith" suggests a deliberate lesson in contrasts. The lesson becomes even more remarkable when we look at the two parties whose faith is being contrasted.

The first story involves a centurion (v. 5), a Roman soldier whose sworn duty was to subjugate the people of God under the heel of their pagan overlords. But this centurion was not here to throw his weight around. On the contrary, Luke records that this Roman was kindly disposed to the Jews, having financed the building of a synagogue for them. Even the Jewish elders spoke highly of him (Lk. 7:4-5).

The centurion sought Jesus in behalf of his servant, sick and near death. He had heard of Jesus' miracles, and hoped to secure one for his servant. But when Jesus agreed to come to his house, the centurion protested that he was not worthy of such an honor; Jesus could perform the miracle from His current location. The centurion was familiar with the concept of authority; if Jesus could do it at all, He could do it from anywhere, with only a word (v. 8-9). It was an expression of faith that left Jesus amazed.

The second story involves not a Roman, nor critics from among the Jewish leadership, nor even the multitudes who followed Him. Rather, it features His own disciples, the apostles. While crossing the Sea of Galilee with Jesus, they encountered a storm that threatened to swamp their small boat. Overcome with panic, they pleaded to Jesus for deliverance: "Lord, save us! We are perishing!" (v. 25). It never occurred to them that they already had Jesus with them in the boat; were they really in any serious danger? In their minds, having Jesus in their midst offered no protection from the danger around them. Jesus' rebuke was well-deserved: "Why are you fearful, O you of little faith?" If they feared for their lives with Jesus right there in the boat with them, did they have any faith at all?

The contrast in these two stories could not be more stark. On the one hand, a pagan Roman (decent, but still a pagan) displayed absolute confidence in Jesus' ability to work a miracle remotely. On the other hand, Jesus' closest companions, when faced with a minor threat, fell to pieces in terror.

Faith is not a function of our proximity to the Lord. That's why regular church-goers are routinely put to shame by drug addicts and prostitutes. One group is proud of their connection with the Creator, but struggles to leverage that relationship for strength in their daily lives. The other group knows their lives are in shambles and flee to Jesus for refuge. They cling tightly to Him with all their might, because they need Him. That is the faith that saves.

Do you have faith? Or are you just along for the ride?

A Compassionate Shepherd

People need leaders who can guide them well.
But too many leaders lose sight of what the
people need, leaving them lost and discouraged.

---

*But when He saw the multitudes, He was moved with
compassion for them, because they were weary and scattered,
like sheep having no shepherd. Then He said to His disciples,
"The harvest truly is plentiful, but the laborers are few.
Therefore pray the Lord of the harvest to send out laborers
into His harvest" (Matt. 9:36-38).*

*And Jesus, when He came out, saw a great multitude and
was moved with compassion for them, because they were like
sheep not having a shepherd. So He began to teach them
many things (Mk. 6:34).*

৩৯৫

These two passages, although similar, document separate episodes in the life of Christ. Together, they teach us
some important lessons about the role of *compassion* in the
ministry of Jesus, and how that example should guide our
own dealings with others.

First, consider the metaphor the authors use to describe
the multitudes: "like sheep having no shepherd." This figure
of speech sums up how most people go through life: wandering about with no well-defined sense of purpose or direction.
That journey of aimlessness exposes them to temptation, sin,
and all its evil consequences. They are not just scattered—
they are "*weary* and scattered," tired of life and its hassles.

Second, notice how Jesus expressed His compassion to
these lost souls: He taught them. Of course, Jesus did more

than just teach people. Other passages describe how Jesus' compassion led Him to heal the sick (Matt. 14:14) or feed the hungry (Matt. 15:32). But these were temporary fixes for a deeper, more serious problem, namely, the people's lack of purpose in life. Modern notions of social justice that tie human happiness to material possessions are based on a false sense of compassion, and leave people just as starved as before. Jesus' solution was not food or medicine, but instructions on how to live. Notice in the teachings of Jesus the themes that come up again and again: attitudes, relationships, covetousness, preparing for life after death. These are the issues that need to be addressed if people are to find meaning in their lives. In His teachings, Jesus helped them deal with those issues.

Finally, we can learn a lesson from what Jesus did *not* do in response to the people's plight: He did not ignore them. He did not look down on them with contempt or disdain. He did not brush them aside as ignorant rubes who got what they deserved. These were weak, misguided people who could give Jesus nothing in return; yet He genuinely cared for their well-being, and took the time to help them. The fact that He took any interest in them at all is a remarkable testament to the depth of His love for humanity.

Jesus was a realist. He knew that not everyone was a "lost sheep" who needed compassion. Some were scoundrels who needed a good scolding, and He could dish it out when necessary (Matt. 23). Others were lazy opportunists who were just looking for a free lunch; He refused to play that game (Jn. 6:26-27). But to the rest, Jesus was a friend who was genuinely interested in their welfare, and expressed it in the guidance He provided them. If we are serious about following His example, we should go and do likewise.

Why Do We Criticize?

The human tendency to criticize is destructive, even to the critic. So why do we do it? And how can we train ourselves not to be so negative?

"But to what shall I liken this generation? It is like children sitting in the marketplaces and calling to their companions and saying: 'We played the flute for you, and you did not dance; We mourned to you, and you did not lament.' For John came neither eating nor drinking, and they say, 'He has a demon.' The Son of Man came eating and drinking, and they say, 'Look, a glutton and a winebibber, a friend of tax collectors and sinners!' But wisdom is justified by her children" (Matt. 11:16-19).

৵৽

The generation to whom John the Baptist and Jesus preached could never be satisfied. John was too ascetic, and Jesus was too loose in the company He kept. No matter what approach God took with these people, they would find something to criticize. As a result, they could never see the truth God was trying to bring into their lives.

Before we mock these critics for their foolishness, we would do well to reflect on our own habit of criticizing. How often do we castigate our spouse, our kids, our co-workers, our politicians, or our brethren? Impersonal circumstances and events also draw our wrath: the weather, health issues, economic downturns, mechanical breakdowns, or a thousand other little dramas that routinely intrude upon our lives. Of course, our grumbling doesn't fix the problems—but at least we feel better about it.

Why do we do this? Several reasons come to mind:

When it comes to denouncing others, *envy* often plays a role. If we can spot a defect in someone who is smarter, stronger, more popular, or better off than us, a well-aimed strike can even the score and elevate our status (or so we think).

Sometimes the bashing is driven by a desire to *shift attention away from our own faults*. By highlighting everything that is broken around us, our own imperfections may be less noticeable. In some cases, the defects we grouse about in others may even play a role in our own failures, which comes in handy: "See?! It's not my fault!"

But one issue almost always lies at the root of a hyper-critical personality: *pride*. Drawing attention to the problems in the world around us makes us feel superior to the world. If everything were run the way *we* think it should be run, life would be so much better. Of course, we're not in charge, so our role is reduced to one job: criticize.

Chronic criticism is destructive. Nobody likes to be in the presence of someone who makes a living belittling everything and everyone around him. Unbeknownst to the critic, the greater damage is inflicted on himself. His incessant harping on what's wrong "out there" blinds him to the good that is in the world (which is considerable). It also gradually eats away at his ability to enjoy life. Every facet of his life becomes poisoned by his complaining about the negative.

How can we get this bad habit under control? First, *we must address our pride problem.* We must admit that we don't know everything, and that often *we* are the ones who need fixing—or maybe educating. A stiff dose of humility will go a long way toward tempering our desire to criticize.

Second, *we must train ourselves to recognize and appreciate what is good in this world.* Certainly, some things in life need to be criticized. But those critiques will be more effective if they come from someone who has earned a reputation as an encourager, a beacon of light who promotes good cheer in a dark world of negativity.

Jesus Was a Scoundrel

Our opinion of others can be tainted by biased testimony from critics. That's why we should withhold judgment until we've heard both sides.

"Look, a glutton and a winebibber, a friend of tax collectors and sinners!" (Matt. 11:19).

"We found this fellow perverting the nation, and forbidding to pay taxes to Caesar" (Lk. 23:2).

"This man blasphemes!" (Matt. 9:3).

"He is out of His mind" (Mk. 3:21).

৵৵

These verses are just a sampling of what the Bible says about Jesus. In fact, the Bible portrays Jesus as an evil snake who "is deserving of death" (Matt. 26:66). The evidence of the Bible is incontrovertible: Jesus was a reprobate who deserved what He got.

Of course, you don't have to be a Bible scholar to recognize the error I have committed here. These quotations are taken from the mouths of Jesus' *enemies*, men who were out to destroy Him. (The sole exception is the "out of His mind" statement, which was the opinion of His own family, spoken from ignorance, not hate.) All of these charges were highly prejudicial and one-sided. It is a gross misrepresentation of history to try to pass this testimony off as the truth about who Jesus was.

Yes, Jesus was a scoundrel—if we listen only to His critics. But if we take the time to listen to the Man Himself and the testimony of others who knew Him well, we come away with an entirely different opinion.

But therein lies the problem, doesn't it? Before we can form a well-rounded opinion of someone, we must be careful to hear all the evidence relating to their character. We cannot afford simply to pick up whatever snippets of hearsay are being tossed about to form our conclusion. We need to listen not only to a man's critics, but also to his friends. If possible, our own interactions with an individual can inform our understanding of his character. It is this kind of balanced evaluation has led millions of people to conclude that Jesus was most certainly *not* a scoundrel, but the Savior of humanity.

This simple exercise in biblical hermeneutics teaches us two important lessons in dealing with people.

First, before we charge someone with gross error, we need to carefully *examine our own motives in doing so*. Are we genuinely interested in promoting the truth, or are we merely out to "get" an enemy? Are we presenting a balanced picture, or are we withholding key information that would significantly alter the story, if it was known? In short, are we being honest with the facts ourselves?

Second, when we hear serious charges being spoken against someone, we should resist accepting it as truth until we have had an opportunity to *examine the matter ourselves*. Salacious accusations are almost always exaggerated and inaccurate. "The first one to plead his cause seems right, until his neighbor comes and examines him" (Prov. 18:17). If we take pains to hear both sides, we will come much closer to learning the truth of a matter.

One more lesson can be learned from this little study. Just because someone quotes a lot of Scripture doesn't necessarily prove he is teaching the truth. The conclusion being promoted may not be what God intends. We must search the scriptures ourselves, to find out if these things are so (Ac. 17:11).

A Light Burden

Life in a broken world involves hardship; there's no avoiding that reality. But we do have a choice as to which burdens we carry along the way.

"Take My yoke upon you and learn from Me, for I am gentle and lowly in heart, and you will find rest for your souls. For My yoke is easy and My burden is light" (Matt. 11:29-30).

For this is the love of God, that we keep His commandments. And His commandments are not burdensome (1 Jn. 5:3).

"For they bind heavy burdens, hard to bear, and lay them on men's shoulders; but they themselves will not move them with one of their fingers" (Matt. 23:4).

❧

By any definition, life is a struggle. We live in a world that almost seems designed to disappoint, and the toil and trouble that is required just to survive can be a crushing load.

Religion is humanity's attempt to mitigate this experience. Whatever the teachings and rules and rituals, the goal of every faith system is always the same: to provide a meaningful framework by which we can cope with the struggles of human existence. Even if we deny any external deity and worship only ourselves, the goal is still the same: How can we find purpose and strength in life?

Unfortunately, most religious systems make the problem worse, not better. The rhetoric may be lofty, but the philosophical underpinnings are often flawed and the practical effects misguided, even dangerous. There is a reason that religion today has a reputation as being the source of most of the world's problems.

Even the religion of the Bible is not immune to this risk. In the hands of leaders like the scribes and Pharisees, God's instructions can be twisted into a millstone that further grinds people into the ground, rather than helping them.

Authentic Christianity—not the cheap dime-store variety—is not a hardship, but a blessing. Studying the Bible, especially the words of Jesus and His apostles unadulterated by human traditions, is not only a simple exercise, it resonates beautifully with the human heart. It calms the troubled spirit and nourishes the soul. It instills a hope that enables us to take on life with optimism and confidence. Such a life is not always easy, but it's a "light" load compared to the exhausting alternative.

Every one of us must bear some burden in life. The question is, which burden will we choose to carry? Jesus offers a yoke that is "easy" and "light." But finding that bearable burden requires the courage to shove aside all the baggage that men try to pile on top of it. Study the teachings of Jesus. Allow the meaning of His life, death, and resurrection to penetrate your heart. Open your life to His influence—and you will find rest for your soul.

The Sabbath Controversies

The numerous clashes between Jesus and His
critics over His Sabbath activities hold important
lessons in how to apply God's instructions today.

---

*At that time Jesus went through the grainfields on the
Sabbath. And His disciples were hungry, and began to pluck
heads of grain and to eat. And when the Pharisees saw it,
they said to Him, "Look, Your disciples are doing what is not
lawful to do on the Sabbath!" (Matt. 12:1-2).*

*"But if you had known what this means, 'I desire mercy
and not sacrifice,' you would not have condemned the guilt-
less" (Matt. 12:7).*

ഔ

The Jewish leaders had many complaints against Jesus,
but one complaint gets more coverage than any other in the
gospels: their accusation that Jesus violated the Sabbath.
There are at least five separate occasions where this was an
issue. Four of the incidents involved acts of healing: the man
with a withered hand (Mk. 3:1-6; Lk. 14:1-5); the woman
with a stooped back (Lk. 13:10-17); the paralytic at the spring
of Bethesda (Jn. 5:1-18; 7:21-24); and the blind man healed
at the pool of Siloam (Jn. 9:1-16). The fifth incident involved
the disciples of Jesus plucking grain for a meal on a Sabbath
day (Matt. 12:1-14; Mk. 2:23-28; Lk. 6:1-11).

There was a Sabbath law; neither side disputed that (Ex.
20:8-10; 31:12-17). The basis of this conflict was how these
two parties interpreted and applied that law. A study of these
Sabbath controversies provides an insight into how the enemies of Jesus viewed the Law, and explains why they saw

Jesus as such a threat. Likewise, it reveals Jesus' own view of what constitutes true religion. All of which can help us in our own efforts to properly understand and apply God's word.

To the Jewish mind, the Sabbath—like all of God's commands—was an arbitrary test to see how well man can obey God. In order to pass this test, every conceivable angle of this law's application had to be teased out and correctly applied. Thus, a whole body of regulations arose around the Sabbath law, many of which appear silly to modern ears. (For example, a woman could not look into a mirror on the Sabbath day, lest she see a gray hair and be tempted to pluck it out.) One false move and you failed the test. It was this kind of theology that viewed Jesus' behavior as unlawful, even shocking. To these people, Jesus was a dangerous liberal who treated God's law with a careless disdain for details.

Jesus, on the other hand, saw the Sabbath law as a practical instruction given for man's good. "The Sabbath was made for man, and not man for the Sabbath" (Mk. 2:27). By its very nature there was a certain level of ambiguity in that law, and God expected people to use common sense in applying it. The intent of the law was not violated, for example, by pulling out an ox that fell into a ditch (Lk. 14:5), or leading a donkey to water (Lk. 13:15)—and certainly not by healing a sick person or grabbing a quick snack of grain while passing through a field. Properly understood, the Sabbath law was a guideline to make man's life more enjoyable, not to make it more tedious.

God's law must be respected. But that respect requires that we not turn His law into a regulatory minefield. Keep it simple and practical, as God intended.

Blaspheming the Holy Spirit

Jesus identifies one sin as unforgivable. But a
closer look at the context reveals a reasonable—
and sobering—explanation.

---

*"Therefore I say to you, every sin and blasphemy will be
forgiven men, but the blasphemy against the Spirit will not be
forgiven men. Anyone who speaks a word against the Son of
Man, it will be forgiven him; but whoever speaks against the
Holy Spirit, it will not be forgiven him, either in this age or in
the age to come" (Matt. 12:31-32).*

తిజ

Amidst all the New Testament language about God's
amazing mercy and His willingness to forgive even the most
vile sins, this passage delivers an unexpected jolt. It sounds
as though Jesus is designating one sin as beyond God's grace.
Commit this one, and you're toast, no matter how many
apologies you offer or tears you shed.

Why is an insult against the Holy Spirit so much more
deadly than an insult against Jesus Himself? Is there really no
hope for someone who has committed this sin—even inadvertently? As with most such questions, the context provides
useful clues to help us unravel this mystery.

Jesus had just healed a man who was demon-possessed,
blind, and mute (v. 22). To counter the impact of this miracle
on the crowd, the Pharisees discounted the miracle as an act
of Satan (v. 24). This explanation, of course, was logically
inconsistent—why would Satan cast out his own demons
(v. 25-26)?

But Jesus was concerned with a much more serious error in their thinking. He claimed to cast out demons "by the Spirit of God" (v. 28). If they refused to believe that God's Spirit was behind this miracle, what avenue was left by which Jesus could convince them of His credentials? What further proof could God provide to change their minds?

The answer, of course, was there was nothing else that God could do. By denying the power of the Holy Spirit, displayed in such a dramatic and unmistakable fashion, they effectively destroyed their last remaining opportunity of ever coming to accept Jesus as the Servant of God.

That's why their blasphemy against the Spirit was such an egregious sin. It was not because the Holy Spirit is more important than Jesus, but because the Spirit's work, particularly through the miracles, provided the best evidence of Jesus' legitimacy. By rejecting that, there was nothing else God could do to bridge the gap between Himself and their stubborn pride. They were doomed.

The same principle is in play today. We do not have modern-day apostles and miracles, but we do have a validated record of the miracles of long ago. That documentation—inspired and revealed by the Holy Spirit—still serves as God's message to the human race (2 Tim. 3:16-17; Eph. 3:4-5). Today, as then, "no one can say that Jesus is Lord except by the Holy Spirit" (1 Cor. 12:3); that is, the Spirit's testimony recorded in the word draws men to the Savior. But if people, for whatever reason, choose to reject the testimony of the Spirit—by dismissing the Bible as a fabrication, or rejecting its message as an ancient myth—then there is nothing else God can do to reach them. By denying the Spirit's work, they have eliminated any possibility of ever accepting Jesus as Lord.

And by blaspheming the Spirit in that fashion, they have placed themselves beyond God's mercy. They cannot be forgiven, because they do not *want* to be forgiven.

Tribute to a Good Man

In our decadent society, a good man is a rarity. But to those who are privileged to know such a man—especially his children—he is a godsend.

"A good man out of the good treasure of his heart brings forth good things . . ." (Matt. 12:35).

ଐ

He grew up in the piney woods of East Texas with three brothers, his mother, and no father. He was seven years old when the Great Depression hit, but his family didn't notice it much because they were already dirt poor. He spent many a day tromping through the woods of the Neches River bottom, learning how to shoot, fish, swim, and live off the land. Life may have been tough, but that was no excuse for not learning how to survive.

By the time he left high school, he was ready to see the world. So like many young men of his day, he joined the military, little knowing that his generation would soon be called upon to fight the most terrible war the world had ever seen. He served in the army air corps, doing his small part to win the war, and learning the value of freedom in the process. For the rest of his life, he would be an ardent patriot, with little patience for flag-burners and draft dodgers.

After the war, he returned to Texas to build a new life. He married and settled down in a field job with an oil company. It was not a glamorous job, and he didn't make a lot of money, but it was honorable work, and he was proud to do it. The idea of complaining about his "mistreatment" as a worker never crossed his mind.

His childhood poverty had taught him the value of money, and he learned that lesson well. He never spent a nickel that didn't need to be spent. He was not miserly, just thrifty. He didn't have a lot of money to invest, but he did the best he could, and by his later years, his frugality had earned him a comfortable standard of living.

Because he had grown up without a dad, he was determined to be the best father he could be. His wife and kids were the center of his life. Most of his vacation time was spent taking them on camping trips throughout the western U. S. He once had an opportunity to work on an assignment overseas that would have dramatically increased his income, but he turned it down because of the impact he knew it would have on his family. Here was a man who had his priorities straight.

He was a man of uncompromising integrity. His creed in life was simple, but rooted in rock-solid common sense: Work hard, be honest, respect authority, accept responsibility for your actions, help your fellow man. The world would be a happier place if everyone lived by these rules.

Underlying all of this was a quiet faith in God. He believed in the value of true religion in making people better, and insisted that church be an important part of his family's life. But church was not mere window-dressing. He lived what he taught.

Thanks, Dad, for showing me and many others what it means to be a good man.

In memory of a good man, Elmo Joe King, 1922-2002

A Lesson in Repentance

Many people think they have repented, but have no idea what real repentance is. Jesus points to an example of repentance that clarifies the topic.

"The men of Nineveh will rise up in the judgment with this generation and condemn it, because they repented at the preaching of Jonah; and indeed a greater than Jonah is here" (Matt. 12:41).

৵৽

Jesus says that the men of Nineveh "repented at the preaching of Jonah." But if we go back and read the book of Jonah, we find that the word "repent" is found nowhere in the text. What happened that led Jesus to see repentance in these people?

Recall that Jonah was sent by God to Nineveh to preach a message of judgment ("Cry out against it; for their wickedness has come up before Me," 1:2). After a slight detour involving a big fish, Jonah delivered God's message in the great city: "Yet forty days, and Nineveh shall be overthrown!" (3:4).

Jonah's preaching got results: "The people of Nineveh believed God" and "cried mightily to God" (3:5, 8). Even Nineveh's king humbled himself in sackcloth and fasting, and ordered his subjects to "every one turn from his evil way and from the violence that is in his hands" (3:8). The people took this message to heart, for "God saw their works, that they turned from their evil way; and God relented from the disaster that He had said He would bring upon them, and He did not do it" (3:10).

Note the sequence of events: the people believed God, they expressed remorse for their sins, and they turned from their evil ways. All three of these elements combined to make up what Jesus called "repentance."

What many people call "repentance" does not fit this Biblical model. For example, some people—after getting burned yet again by the destructive effects of their foolish conduct—change their lives only out of a desire for self-preservation. God had nothing to do with their reformation. That's not repentance.

Or consider the rowdy young man who cleans up his act and "gets religion" in order to win his girlfriend. Has he repented? Not necessarily. He may have turned from his evil ways, but if the change was motivated by something other than faith in God and grief for his sins, the changed life won't last long. (And his girlfriend will find out soon enough after she marries him.)

On the other hand, there are those people who sincerely believe in God and are so, so sorry for their sins—but not enough to give them up. They remain mired in a web of fleshly appetites and lazy indifference to what God wants them to be. Their weak efforts to turn their lives around are ineffective and short-lived. Repentance has not yet taken hold in these people.

If we truly desire to repent, the same three elements that turned the people of Nineveh around must operate in our lives: First, we must cast ourselves completely on God's mercy, recognizing Him as our Creator and Judge; second, we must agonize over the imperfections that tarnish our lives; and third, we must harness every fiber of our being to actually change our behavior.

One final thought: Repentance is not a one-time event. It should be an ongoing process throughout our lives, always driving us closer to what God wants us to be.

How to Build a Better Society

The building of a good and just society depends
on the development of good and just people.
There is no shortcut to achieving that goal.

---

*"The kingdom of heaven is like a mustard seed, which a
man took and sowed in his field, which indeed is the least of
all the seeds; but when it is grown it is greater than the herbs
and becomes a tree, so that the birds of the air come and nest
in its branches." Another parable He spoke to them: "The
kingdom of heaven is like leaven, which a woman took and
hid in three measures of meal till it was all leavened" (Matt.
13:31-33).*

৯৽৽

These two parables of Jesus illustrate an important feature of His kingdom. Its growth in the world is slow and
imperceptible, not spectacular and quick. Its influence is profound, but not after the manner of most human enterprises.
This truth holds an important lesson for a society struggling
to find its way through perilous times.

Humans are not perfect, so we should not expect any
human society to be perfect. To witness a nation of over three
hundred million people struggling to function smoothly,
therefore, should not come as a surprise to us.

What faces our country now, however, is an existential
threat that involves more than mere human imperfection.
Two starkly different visions of how to deal with our social
failings are competing for dominance. One view insists that
societal dysfunctions can only be fixed by dismantling and
rebuilding the institutions that form the foundation of society,

by revolution, if necessary. Destroy it all and start over. In its current manifestation, this Utopian project emphasizes tribal identity; some groups must be demoted and punished based entirely on their innate characteristics, while other groups are to be promoted based solely on their group markers. The result, predictably, is open warfare—with no winners.

Jesus advocated a different view. He taught that society is a reflection of the character of the individuals who comprise it. For society to change for the better, the people in it must change for the better. The standard of measurement that defines character is moral integrity, a value that transcends group identity. Using the illustrations of a growing mustard seed and leaven in a loaf of bread, Jesus taught that a society is slowly transformed as individual hearts and lives are transformed. The changes may be small, slow, and inconspicuous, but they are real—and involve a minimum of destructive disruption.

The men who built our nation understood that principle, and designed a system of government around it. John Adams, the second President, wrote, "Our Constitution was made only for a moral and religious people. It is wholly inadequate to the government of any other" (letter to Massachusetts militia, Oct. 11, 1798). Under this system of governance, personal character and responsibility are given more weight than government edict. This is as it should be.

Cultural critic Dennis Prager summed up the challenge facing us thusly: "You can't make society better unless you first make its people better" (YouTube video, "How Do We Make Society Better?" Pt. 5). But in the current crisis, that is the very thing that is being ignored, even denigrated. As a nation we first abandoned God; now we are struggling to replace Him with something else. It will never work.

If I want to make society better, that's a laudable goal. But it starts with making *me* a better person. That's the message our neighbors need to hear, and it begins with us modeling it in our own lives.

The Feeding of the 5,000

Only one miracle of Jesus is recorded in all four gospel accounts. It stands out from the rest for the sobering lessons it provides.

Then He commanded the multitudes to sit down on the grass. And He took the five loaves and the two fish, and looking up to heaven, He blessed and broke and gave the loaves to the disciples; and the disciples gave to the multitudes. So they all ate and were filled, and they took up twelve baskets full of the fragments that remained. Now those who had eaten were about five thousand men, besides women and children (Matt. 14:19-21).

ও৵৹

We call this miracle "the feeding of the five thousand," but that is a misnomer, since that figure does not include the women and children who were present. Jesus performed a similar miracle several months later with a smaller, predominantly Gentile crowd (Mk. 7:31; 8:1-10). The sheer scale of these two miracles puts them in a category all by themselves, but our attention is drawn to the earlier event, since it is the only miracle recorded in all four gospel accounts. There was something unique about this one that deserves a closer look.

Consider the circumstances surrounding this miracle. John's account mentions that the feast of the Passover was drawing near (Jn. 6:4). That time stamp places this miracle one year before the final Passover, when Jesus was crucified. The preceding chapters indicate that the enthusiasm that had accompanied His early ministry was starting to wane. Although He still attracted crowds, many were beginning to tire of His enigmatic teaching (Matt. 13:53-58), and His enemies were becoming more bold and confrontational (Matt. 12:2, 14, 24). The final blow came when Jesus received word that His cousin, John the Baptist, had been executed (Matt. 14:1-13). It was in response to that news that Jesus took His apostles into a remote area to "rest a while" (Mk. 6:31).

With that background in mind, take a closer look at the miracle itself. Despite His own grief and His desire to escape the crowds, Jesus could not turn His back on them. He "was moved with compassion," and taught them and healed their sick (Matt. 14:14; Mk. 6:34). He also challenged His apostles to feed them: "You give them something to eat" (Matt. 14:16). It was an impossible task, but Jesus made it possible with only a few loaves and fishes: He "gave the loaves to the disciples; and the disciples gave to the multitudes" (v. 19).

John's account records the eventual outcome of this miracle. The crowd wanted to make Jesus their King, but He refused their demand and went away (Jn. 6:15). The multitude followed, seeking more handouts. When Jesus declined to deliver, they lost interest. "From that time many of His disciples went back and walked with Him no more" (Jn. 6:66). He was left with only a handful of followers.

Scholars call this event the collapse of Jesus' Galilean campaign. The most prodigious miracle Jesus ever performed marked the beginning of the end of His career. It was the turning point that eventually led to His death.

This event offers two take-aways for modern disciples of Christ. First, if grand spectacles and free food were not enough to convert the masses then, neither will they convert the masses today. We are mistaken if we think physical enticements will be sufficient to reach the lost.

Second, disappointment is a common companion among those who follow the Lord. Our work will not always be exciting and productive. Hard work may yield little fruit; great plans may collapse in disarray; dreams may be crushed by apathy and neglect. Like the apostles, our challenge is to cling to the Lord in faith, looking to Him for the final reward.

Crumbs, Please

Before we approach God to ask a favor, we must first examine our heart. Do we have the humility required to get God's attention?

Then she came and worshiped Him, saying, "Lord, help me!" But He answered and said, "It is not good to take the children's bread and throw it to the little dogs." And she said, "Yes, Lord, yet even the little dogs eat the crumbs which fall from their masters' table." Then Jesus answered and said to her, "O woman, great is your faith! Let it be to you as you desire." And her daughter was healed from that very hour (Matt. 15:25-28).

৩৯৫

This Syro-Phoenician woman holds the distinction of being the only person ever to beat Jesus in a debate. Her verbal "victory" was a setup, of course; Jesus lobbed a softball in her direction, knowing she would knock it out of the park. But her response to Jesus' refusal to heal her daughter reveals a lesson in humility that we all should take to heart.

This woman had multiple dings against her that should have dissuaded her from approaching Jesus with such a request. First, she was a woman—meaning, in that culture she had no rights, no influence, and no standing in her community. Second, she was a Syro-Phoenician (Mark's account calls her a Canaanite)—definitely an outsider who had no claims on this Jewish rabbi. Third, she was the mom of a "severely demon possessed" daughter (v. 22)—what we would call a special-needs child, a burden that came with its own set of social challenges and embarrassments. Finally, where is the husband in this story? We aren't told, but it is possible that, like so many fathers in this predicament, he had bailed on his family, leaving his poor wife to deal with the problem by herself.

So when Jesus called her a "little dog," she was not offended. She was already so far down the social ladder that the label fit—and she knew it.

And Jesus knew that she knew. His offensive remark was deliberately designed to draw out her reaction: "Yes, Lord, yet even the little dogs eat the crumbs which fall from their masters' table." There was no pride left in this woman; just a desperate plea for help to a Man she believed could give it. Jesus rewarded her faith with the greatest gift she could have hoped for.

The faith of this woman puts most of us to shame. How many times do we approach God with a request for help in dealing with some life situation—but only on our terms? We want to retain our social status and the approval of our peers. We don't want to sacrifice our lifestyle or the comforts we currently enjoy. We prefer to hold on to what we have—yet expect God to tweak the details to make our life even better. We treat God not as our Master, but as a butler whose job is to serve us.

Like this poor woman, our pleas for God's help must come from a heart that knows it has nothing left of which to boast. Until we can see ourselves as little dogs worthy of no more than crumbs from the Master's table, crumbs is all we will get.

But, oh, what a feast He will spread for us, if we will come to Him with this same kind of humble faith!

The Misunderstood Christ

The search for the real Jesus is obscured by a
flood of misinformation. We can find out the truth
about Jesus—if we really want to know it.

---

*When Jesus came into the region of Caesarea Philippi,
He asked His disciples, saying, "Who do men say that I, the
Son of Man, am?" So they said, "Some say John the Baptist,
some Elijah, and others Jeremiah or one of the prophets." He
said to them, "But who do you say that I am?" Simon Peter
answered and said, "You are the Christ, the Son of the living
God" (Matt. 16:13-16).*

૭∞ઌ

Long before George Gallup or George Barna began
polling Americans about their religious preferences, Jesus
conducted His own little survey to determine what people
thought about Him. The sampling base was not scientifically
selected, so the margin of error was undoubtedly large. But
the responses He got reflected the wide diversity of opinion
that existed among the populace: John the Baptist . . . Elijah
. . . Jeremiah . . . one of the prophets. The speculations were
all over the map. Actually, the disciples had likely skewed the
data, because these answers covered only the *favorable* opinions. We know that others believed Jesus to be a con artist
(Jn. 7:12), a demonic idiot (Jn. 10:20), or a servant of Satan
(Matt. 9:34). His own family believed Him to be delusional
(Mk. 3:21). Finally, of course, there were those who chose
the "no opinion" option (Jn. 9:25).

How did the people of Jesus' day arrive at such wildly
varying opinions of who He was? As in every culture, there

was a lot of apocryphal wishful thinking floating around that projected onto Jesus hopes for national glory. People were desperate for heroes, and—at least initially—Jesus qualified. On the negative side, blind prejudice kept many people from seeing Jesus as anything other than a simple carpenter of humble background. He did not fit their pre-conceived notions of what the Messiah should be, so they had to find something wrong with Him, even if they had to invent it.

But here is the key point: Whatever their opinion of Jesus, virtually everyone based their assessment of Jesus on *superficial evidence*. The brief glimpses that most people saw of His actual work and character were overwhelmed by the volume of rumors and tall tales that grew up around Him. For the vast majority of people, the real Jesus was obscured by a blizzard of misinformation. It's no wonder that so many of His contemporaries misunderstood who He was.

Today, the situation hasn't changed much. A wide variety of opinion exists about who the historical Jesus was. Some think Him to be just one in a long series of prophets sent to different cultures at different times. Others see Jesus as nothing more than a moral reformer who never intended to start a new religion. A few will deny that He even existed. Two thousand years later, the speculations are still all over the map.

But in the midst of all the confusion surrounding Jesus' identity, a few people have the courage to look past the noise surrounding the man and study the source evidence for themselves. Like Simon Peter, these people will discover in Jesus a man unlike any other, a unique character who was, in every sense of the word, the Son of God. These people will find in Jesus the solid foundation they can build their lives upon.

They understand Jesus perfectly—and their lives will be transformed as a result.

Is the Church of Christ a Denomination?

It's a valid question, but the answer depends on how we define our terms. Sloppy thinking results in sloppy terminology—and sloppy conclusions.

"And I also say to you that you are Peter, and on this rock I will build My church, and the gates of Hades shall not prevail against it" (Matt. 16:18).

৩৩৩

"My church" denotes possession. This church belongs to Christ; it is "of" Him. There are many people today who claim membership in this "church of Christ." Given today's religious landscape, an obvious question presents itself: *Is the Church of Christ a denomination?*

Like any other loaded question, the answer depends on how we define the key terms.

First, what do we mean by "the Church of Christ"? There are two possibilities. The first definition—and by far the more popular one, even among my brethren—is a loose confederation of local congregations that wear a common moniker, "Church of Christ." Using this definition, "faithfulness" is generally measured by how closely one aligns with the doctrines and practices of this group (for more information, subscribe to one of the leading brotherhood journals). The membership of this Church of Christ can be approximated by adding up the membership rolls of all the local congregations that belong to this metagroup.

The second, and more biblical, definition is quite different. The entity that Jesus called "My church" is nothing more or less than the sum of all those individuals who have been saved by His blood and are faithful to Him in their lives. Membership in this church is determined by Christ, not men ("The Lord added to the church," Ac. 2:47, NKJV). Consequently, the census of this group is tracked in heaven (Heb. 12:23), so it is impossible for us to know its true number. Certainly the New Testament speaks of "churches of Christ" (Rom. 16:16), referring to local congregations of believers. But one's membership in the heavenly "church of Christ" and in a local church of Christ are not necessarily the same thing.

The second term that we must define is "denomination." This word comes from the Latin *nomen*, meaning "name." So the simple dictionary definition is "a general name for a category." In religion, the word describes a religious organization comprised of congregations united in their adherence to a set of beliefs and practices, and identified by a common name.

So with these definitions before us, let's try to answer the question, "Is the Church of Christ a denomination?"

Look again at the two definitions of "the Church of Christ." If your conception of the church is a loose confederation of local churches, each one of which wears the name "Church of Christ" and adheres to a commonly recognized standard of "truth"; and if you believe that wearing this name and being a member of this group identifies you as "faithful," then, by definition, the Church of Christ that exists in your mental model is indeed a denomination. It certainly fits the dictionary definition.

If, on the other hand, your conception of the church of Christ follows the second definition, and you view the phrase as merely descriptive of the sum of all the saved; and you think of the church in terms of individuals, not local congregations; and that those who belong to this church are first and foremost faithful to the Lord, not to men; then the church of Christ that exists in your mental model does not fit the definition of a denomination. It transcends denominationalism.

Which of these definitions best fits *your* religious affiliation? Do you belong to the Lord's church—or to a "Church of Christ" denomination?

Doing Satan's Work

Peter's rebuke of Jesus was well-intentioned, but played into Satan's hands. Our own intentions can be just as destructive, if we are not careful.

From that time Jesus began to show to His disciples that He must go to Jerusalem, and suffer many things from the elders and chief priests and scribes, and be killed, and be raised the third day. Then Peter took Him aside and began to rebuke Him, saying, "Far be it from You, Lord, this shall not happen to You!" But He turned and said to Peter, "Get behind Me, Satan! You are an offense to Me, for you are not mindful of the things of God, but the things of men" (Matt. 16:21-23).

ॐ✦☙

This testy exchange between Jesus and Peter occurred right after Peter's famous confession that Jesus was the Christ (v. 13-19). Whatever pride Peter felt in that earlier incident was quickly smashed in this later episode, revealing the cleverness of our adversary.

First, consider this exchange from the perspective of Jesus. He not only knew how His life would end, He knew that it *had* to be that way—there was no other alternative for accomplishing God's plan. He began telling His apostles these details regarding His fate so they would be prepared for it when it happened. So when one of them responded with a rebuke, Jesus saw it for what it was: an attempt by Satan to discourage Him from finishing His mission. He came down hard on Peter, not out of personal animosity, but as a means of self-defense. If He allowed Himself to listen to too much of this kind of flattery, it would be even more difficult to finish His mission. He had to put an end to this kind of talk. So He set aside the personal friendship and dealt firmly with the temptation.

But if we look at this exchange from Peter's perspective, we learn another lesson. The apostle took Jesus aside (to avoid embarrassing the Master in front of the others—a noble gesture, no doubt), then proceeded to set Jesus straight. He was the Son of God (see v. 16); the idea of His work coming to such a humiliating end was unthinkable. Surely Jesus was being too pessimistic. Peter's rebuke was not intended to be hurtful, but instructive.

So when Jesus turned on him with such a sharp response, Peter was dumbfounded. "Satan"? "An offense"? "Not mindful of the things of God"? How those words must have stung Peter's ears! If he knew his own heart, Peter would never say or do anything to offend His Master. Yet here was Jesus turning Peter's admonition back on his head with uncharacteristic ferocity.

Peter did not argue back, so perhaps he took Jesus' words to heart. His later behavior at Jesus' arrest and trial, however, suggests that he still didn't understand what Jesus was talking about. When he tried to defend Jesus with a sword, he was once again rebuked by his Master. Peter loved Jesus dearly, but his ignorance was counterproductive to the ultimate objective to which Jesus was working.

Peter's clumsy loyalty should teach us a lesson about our own service in the Lord's work. When we feel compelled to set a brother straight, our words of sincere rebuke can end up doing Satan's work if we are not careful to understand the circumstances our friend is dealing with. Peter misspoke because he did not see the bigger picture. We, too, can cause a brother to stumble by not taking the time to understand the larger context.

Before we rebuke, we should take time to listen and understand.

The Value of a Soul

How we spend our life here and now will define what we value. And our life hereafter will be defined by what we value now. So live wisely.

"For whoever desires to save his life will lose it, and whoever loses his life for My sake will find it. For what is a man profited if he gains the whole world, and loses his own soul? Or what will a man give in exchange for his soul? For the Son of Man will come in the glory of His Father with His angels, and then He will reward each according to his works" (Matt. 16:25-27).

❧

In the original language, the word translated "life" in verse 25 is the same word for "soul" in verse 26. So the principle Jesus is teaching here can be summarized thusly: We can save our soul by expending it in the Lord's service, or we can lose our soul by expending it in the pursuit of selfish interests. Either way, our works define how our soul is spent in this life, and our eternal destiny will be set accordingly.

In these few words, Jesus reduces the entire sum of a person's life down to one fundamental question: What is my soul—my life—worth? God has given me one life to live, and I can use that life any way I wish. But in the end, how I use that life will determine the value I place upon it.

If I use my life in a drive to accumulate *worldly possessions*, I will reach the end destitute and empty. I will have squandered my one life on gaining things I cannot take with me when I leave, things that will not benefit me where I am going. No matter how comfortable I may live in this life, these worldly goods will be of no value to me when I am gone. I will have traded my soul for worthless trinkets.

If I use my life in a mad dash for *pleasure and fun*, I will probably find it, but the hangover will not be worth it. A life spent solely in the satisfaction of carnal appetites is like feeding a kid nothing but candy. It may taste good for awhile, but it leaves one malnourished, starved for something more substantial. For all the thrills and laughs, a life spent in the pursuit of pleasure is a soul wasted on one long drug trip.

If I use my life in a noble quest to gain *academic knowledge*, I will learn much, but never find the real answers to the most pressing questions of life. Even with all the degrees and honors, my great learning will, at best, be remembered by only a few people until the next latest and greatest theories come along. A life devoted to studying the philosophies of men is a soul tossed into a bottomless pit of endless and fruitless searching.

But if I use my life to *serve God*—that is, to improve my character, to spend my time helping, encouraging, befriending and serving others—then I will have used my life wisely. At the end of my life, I can look back with satisfaction, knowing that mine was a life well spent. Whatever possessions I might have accumulated, whatever experiences I might have enjoyed, whatever knowledge I might have gained, it will all pale in comparison to the real treasure I stored up in heaven.

I will have exchanged my soul—my life—for an inheritance that could not be obtained any other way.

The Value of Failure

Before we get down on ourselves for our failures,
we need to remember that we are not the first
disciples to disappoint our Master.

---

*"Lord, have mercy on my son, for he is an epileptic and
suffers severely; for he often falls into the fire and often into
the water. So I brought him to Your disciples, but they could
not cure him." Then Jesus answered and said, "O faithless
and perverse generation, how long shall I be with you? How
long shall I bear with you? Bring him here to Me" (Matt.
17:15-17).*

శ్రీ

This had to be an embarrassing moment for the apostles.
Jesus had given them the power to cast out demons (Matt.
10), but on this occasion, that power failed them. Jesus' frustration here—"How long shall I be with you?"—was not
directed at the crowd but at His own apostles. It is the closest
we ever see to Jesus becoming exasperated at the ineptitude
of His disciples.

We are not concerned here with the underlying cause of
their failure, but the more general topic of how their failures
played a role in their training.

Several years ago, a technology design expert named Peter Skillman conducted a series of studies to determine how
different types of people respond to challenges. He assem-
bled several four-person teams to tackle what he called "The
Spaghetti Challenge." Each team was composed of individuals from the same background and field, with each team being
completely different from the others. Each team was given

several strands of dry spaghetti, a short section of tape, a piece of string, and a marshmallow. Their objective was to create the highest structure possible, supporting the marshmallow on top—but do it in only eighteen minutes.

Predictably, teams comprised exclusively of engineers did quite well. Teams of CEOs and business school grads, not so much. But the teams that did the best were . . . *kindergartners.* Unlike their more educated and experienced competitors, the kids did not waste precious time drawing up plans or assigning duties. They just plunged into building. Their early prototypes were awful and failed; but by failing, the kiddos quickly learned what worked and what didn't. This iterative process enabled them to arrive at some clever and effective solutions within the time limit.

The apostles eventually learned from their mistakes, too. Lots of mistakes. The Lord did not expect them to be perfect. Rather, He wanted them to learn from their failures. It took several years, but by the time Jesus left them on their own, they were equipped to take on the world.

The path to success is open to us as well. Rather than waiting for the perfect conditions to act, or beating ourselves up over mistakes we make, or expending time on endless researching and planning, we should just jump in and learn as we go. Failures in life are not fatal, unless we choose to define our existence by them.

Try, fail, try, fail, try, fail . . . and eventually you'll be a winner.

Evaluating Christianity

Judging Christianity by the performance of its
adherents ignores the purpose of the enterprise.
It exists precisely because we are not perfect.

---

*Then Jesus answered and said, "O faithless and per-
verse generation, how long shall I be with you? How long
shall I bear with you?" (Matt. 17:17).*

৩০৫

Enemies of Christianity have a variety of measures by
which they attack the integrity of the faith. Their targets are
numerous: pedophile priests; money-grubbing faith-healers;
the embarrassing squabbles and divisions that have torn the
religion to shreds; the atrocities throughout history committed in the name of God; the sanctimonious co-worker in the
next cubicle who wears his religion on his sleeve. It's hard to
argue against this array of evidence. Christianity's historical
track record is indeed a sorry one.

But why stop there? We can go all the way back to the
Bible itself and see evidence of the failings of its practitioners
at the very beginning. The apostles of Jesus are portrayed in
the gospels as bumbling, narrow-minded simpletons who
drove Jesus Himself to exasperation. In this text, Jesus was
not addressing His enemies, but His own disciples, who had
embarrassed themselves by their failure to heal a demon-possessed boy (v. 14-16). Ours is not the only generation of
believers to be labeled "faithless and perverse"—by the
Founder of the religion, no less.

Evaluating Christianity by the failings of its followers is
like judging a book by its cover—it's easy to do, but over-

looks the real substance of the product. Christianity's quality lies not in its *people* but in its *message*. It is true and valid, not because its adherents are so perfect, but precisely because they are not. At its heart, Christianity is the story of what God has done for fallen humanity through Christ Jesus. The defects of those who flock to its message merely reinforce the need for that divine grace.

If you are troubled by the hypocrisy of those who claim to follow Christ, that's good; you ought to be troubled! But consider the standard by which you are judging them as hypocrites. There is a higher ideal by which all of us are judged, whether believer or unbeliever. That ideal is embedded in the foundation of Christianity, the story of a perfect Man who lived life as God intended it to be lived, and offered that life as a ransom for our faults.

It's a gift that compels me to evaluate myself by that perfect model of self-sacrifice, rather than by the faulty conduct of others. And in the process of fixating on that model, I find the best path to improving myself, despite the failings of others.

The World of a Child

"Child-like faith" is a powerful metaphor, but only if we allow ourselves the opportunity to once again view life through the eyes of a child.

"Unless you are converted and become as little children, you will by no means enter the kingdom of heaven. Therefore whoever humbles himself as this little child is the greatest in the kingdom of heaven" (Matt. 18:3-4).

"Let the little children come to Me, and do not forbid them; for of such is the kingdom of God. Assuredly, I say to you, whoever does not receive the kingdom of God as a little child will by no means enter it" (Mk. 10:14-15).

ço·ço

John the Baptist's mission was to "turn the hearts of the fathers to the children" (Lk. 1:17). Jesus likewise used children as role models for His disciples. We cannot reach heaven unless we are "converted and become as little children." There is something about little kids that makes them a perfect illustration of what God wants us to be.

But what is that special quality about children that we should emulate? Even though every one of us passed through that phase once in our lives, we struggle to appreciate this lesson because we have forgotten what it means to be a kid. We need to take the time to study children and learn again how they deal with life. Doing so will challenge our jaded grown-up outlook on things. Consider some examples:

Children are *inquisitive*. They are eager to learn, to grow, to explore their surroundings. Every new day promises new surprises, and they usually embrace these challenges with enthusiasm. Unlike adults, children have no concept of getting stuck in a rut.

Children *make no pretenses*. They are ignorant of much about the world, and they know it. That explains the exasperating "Why?" questions they're always asking. It doesn't bother them at all to admit they don't know everything, so they have no problem asking authority figures for help. Adults, by contrast, become quite good at pretending they know everything. When Solomon became the king of Israel, God offered him anything he wanted. Solomon responded with a most unusual request. More than wealth or power, he wanted wisdom to lead his people justly. His new role did not go to his head; instead, it filled him with trepidation. "I am a little child" was Solomon's confession of inadequacy (1 Kgs. 3:7, 9). But it was exactly the right attitude the young king needed. God granted Solomon's request, and the "little child" went on to become the wisest king who ever lived.

Children are *incapable of holding grudges*. Oh, sure, they can squabble with their playmates over the most trivial issues (see the definition of "childish"). But the issue is quickly forgotten and everyone is soon best friends again. When was the last time you saw adults do that?

Finally, children are *incurably positive*. They are naturally happy, cheerful, and playful. They have an exuberance about life that infects everything they do. The world may be a big, mysterious place, full of things they do not understand. But unlike adults, they do not waste time worrying about those things. They are too busy enjoying the things they do understand.

The world of a child is a fascinating place to live. We grown-ups would do well to return there—if we dare.

When You Marry

When asked about divorce, Jesus responded with a beautiful commentary on the origin of marriage. That should be our starting place, too.

"Have you not read that He who made them at the beginning 'made them male and female,' and said, 'For this reason a man shall leave his father and mother and be joined to his wife, and the two shall become one flesh'? So then, they are no longer two but one flesh. Therefore what God has joined together, let not man separate" (Matt. 19:4-6).

෨෬

When critics challenged Jesus on the topic of divorce, He did not immediately address the divorce question, but built His case on an appeal to God's original intent for marriage (Gen. 1:27; 2:24). That's a strong clue that our best response to the divorce crisis plaguing our society is more teaching on what God intends marriage to be.

God created Adam because He knew that "it is not good that man should be alone" (Gen. 2:18). To provide for this social need, He gave Adam not another man or a group, but a woman, a single human being who was different from him, yet uniquely suited to his nature. Throughout the history of humanity, this arrangement of one-man-one-woman-for-life has served as the foundation of every stable human society. Even as the institution of marriage is under attack in our culture, millions of young people continue to enter into this relationship, giving hope that marriage will somehow survive this latest assault. And it *will* survive, because the inherent benefits of the arrangement are indisputable.

When you marry, *you become more balanced as an individual.* Every person has his or her unique strengths and weaknesses. Men generally are more logical, practical, and detached, while women tend to be more emotional, idealistic, and intimate. When a man and woman enter into this relationship with each other, they must learn how to integrate their own qualities with the qualities of the other. Their differences, though difficult to reconcile at first, can merge to provide a strong, stable partnership in which both parties can thrive and be happy.

When you marry, *you enter into the most efficient social arrangement known to humans.* Marriage takes the biological and emotional strengths of a man and a woman and blends them into a social unit that provides the best economic benefits for all. Ideally, men contribute the hard work of providing the home and living expenses, freeing the woman to nurture the little ones. The woman contributes her skills as a domestic engineer, allowing the man to concentrate on what he does best. It's a beautiful symbiotic relationship.

When you marry, *you provide a nurturing environment for the raising of children.* The benefits described above combine to provide a warm, stable, and happy environment for any children that come into the picture. Children not only have their physical needs met and have the practical discipline they need to learn about life, but they also have role models showing them how to form well-adjusted and meaningful relationships of their own.

The superiority of traditional marriage has been documented by research, summarized in a recent book, *The Case for Marriage: Why Married People Are Happier, Healthier and Better Off Financially*, coauthored by sociologists Linda Waite and Maggie Gallagher (2001). The research reaffirms what mankind has instinctively known and practiced for ages, that traditional marriage is the best of all human relationships.

"Therefore what God has joined together, let not man separate."

God's Marriage Law

Jesus' teaching on marriage and divorce is one contribution to a larger treatment of the subject throughout the Bible.

"I say to you, whoever divorces his wife, except for sexual immorality, and marries another, commits adultery; and whoever marries her who is divorced commits adultery" (Matt. 19:9).

৽৽৵

Much of the controversy over what Jesus taught on the subject of divorce is concerned (as usual) more with what He didn't say than with what He actually taught. If we just stick with the text, we can better understand what Jesus was addressing—and learn a valuable lesson about how we should approach the divorce problem today.

The contemporary view of divorce in Jesus' day assumed that divorce was a divinely authorized means of ending a marriage. In both Matt. 5:31 and Matt. 19:7, it's clear that the Pharisees took Moses' "certificate of divorce" statement (Deut. 24:1) as divine approval to dump one's spouse and shop around for a newer model. In Pharisaical theology, therefore—especially according to the school of Hillel—marriage was a relationship of convenience that could be entered and ended at will, so long as the legal details were properly administered.

It's that casual view of marriage that Jesus was addressing in His divorce statements. By labeling as "adultery" any divorce and remarriage that does not involve infidelity, Jesus was reinforcing the sacred nature of marriage that God instituted at the very beginning. The divine order was one man and one woman for life, a principle that was established in the first two chapters of the Bible. "Therefore what God has joined together, let not man separate" (v. 4-6). Moses may have implemented protections to shield wives from impetuous husbands, but "from the beginning it was not so" (v. 8).

The strongest rebuke against divorce in the Bible was written by Malachi, some four hundred years before Jesus (Mal. 2:13-16). Curiously, everywhere Jesus addressed the topic of divorce, He never quoted Malachi's more direct statement of the divine view of divorce. That's because the real problem Jesus was addressing was not the Jews' view of *divorce*, but their view of *marriage*. So He passed over Malachi and went all the way back to the original model in Genesis 2, the divine leave-and-cleave one-flesh relationship between a man and a woman.

They err, therefore, who argue that Jesus introduced a new "law of Christ" on marriage and divorce. In His Sermon on the Mount, He carefully disavowed any intention of replacing or modifying the Law of Moses (Matt. 5:17-19). Whatever He taught on this subject (including in that Sermon, 5:31-32) had to be consistent with that Law, or His enemies could charge Him with blasphemy.

A fair reading of all the divorce passages in the Bible shows that God's marriage law has never changed throughout the ages. Jesus restated and reinforced that law. He did not introduce a new "law of Christ" on marriage and divorce.

Something else hasn't changed either: Hearts are just as hard today as they were in the days of Moses and in the days of Jesus, treating the marriage bond with callous indifference and reaping the same disastrous results. Our task today is to hold forth the beauty and sanctity of the marriage relationship as the divine alternative to the destructive behaviors that are tearing our society to shreds. We do that, not by parsing the words of Jesus in lawyerly fashion, but by promoting the lofty standard of sexual ethics taught consistently throughout the Bible and exalted by Jesus.

When You Divorce

Spouses in a bad marriage believe that divorce is the answer to their problems. In reality, divorce is Satan's lie—it only adds to their misery.

"I say to you, whoever divorces his wife, except for sexual immorality, and marries another, commits adultery; and whoever marries her who is divorced commits adultery" (Matt. 19:9).

"The Lord God of Israel says that He hates divorce, for it covers one's garment with violence" (Mal. 2:16).

৵৽৵৽

More than one-half of all marriages in America end in divorce, the highest divorce rate in the world. No-fault divorce laws and a declining moral standard have combined to create a vast population of divorce victims.

For "victims" is what they are. Every divorce—even a divorce initiated on "scriptural" grounds—leaves a trail of wreckage in its wake, quite unexpected by the people who saw it as an escape from a bad relationship. Consider these cold, hard facts:

When you divorce, *you increase the odds of you and other family members having long-term emotional and psychological problems.* Recent research indicates that children of divorce are more than twice as likely to suffer serious adaptive difficulties than children from intact families. Even in adulthood, long after the divorce of their parents, these children are more likely to avoid fulfilling, long-term relationships. When they do marry, their marriages are more than twice as likely to fail. The parents, too, struggle with persistent feelings of failure, tormented by the knowledge that they could not succeed in the most basic human relationship.

When you divorce, *you create a financial hardship for everyone involved (except the lawyers)*. This is not hard to figure out. When the combined incomes of two people (at best) must start supporting two households instead of one, the standard of living for everyone goes down. Men struggle to meet alimony and child support payments. Even when they get these payments, the financial status of women typically drops after divorce. And the children in these split families are more likely to live in poverty.

When you divorce, *you are contributing to the destablization of society.* Each of the consequences listed above, multiplied by a factor of a few million, creates a burden of social instability that no nation can survive. Divorce rates are directly linked to rates of welfare, productivity decline, mental illness, poor school performance, juvenile delinquency, illegitimate births and criminal behavior. No enemy could more effectively harm us than we are harming ourselves through our casual attitudes toward divorce.

Finally, when you divorce, *you offend God.* God wants us to be happy. That's why He gave us marriage, and that's why, in the words of Malachi, He "hates" divorce. There are few things in the Bible that God says He hates, and divorce is one of them. When we choose to dissolve our marriage instead of work out our problems, we spit in God's face. We will have all eternity to regret that decision.

Several years ago, a study published in the *Daily Mail* (UK) found that roughly one-half of divorcees believed they had made a mistake; they wished they had worked harder to save their marriages.

Think about that before you choose to end yours.

Difficult, But Not Impossible

When we accept God's calling, we sign up for
duties that will test our strength and endurance.
But they are achievable—if we really want them.

---

*Then Jesus said to His disciples, "Assuredly, I say to you
that it is hard for a rich man to enter the kingdom of heaven.
. . . With men this is impossible, but with God all things are
possible" (Matt. 19:23, 26).*

৽৽৹

When confronted with a challenge to liquidate his assets
and give the proceeds to the poor, the rich young ruler balked;
he just couldn't do it. Surely Jesus was asking the impossible
of this young man. Even His disciples winced at His order:
"Who then can be saved?" they asked (v. 25).

Each one of us faces similar challenges in our own faith
journey, decisions that require extraordinary levels of discipline and sacrifice. These decisions are hard, no doubt, but
not impossible.

Resisting temptation is hard. Whether breaking an addictive habit like alcohol or pornography or gambling; or
refusing to retaliate against an enemy who has wronged us;
or not allowing bitterness and envy to poison our heart when
passing through dark times, it's all hard—but not impossible.

Standing up for truth and right is difficult, especially in
an environment where anyone who does so is threatened and
attacked. Countless martyrs through the ages testify to the
price for staying true to one's convictions. It is painful—but
not impossible.

Building a happy marriage and raising children to be responsible adults is a challenge, especially in a culture that ridicules God and morality. The daily battles to keep integrity foremost in our families may grind us down and discourage us—but it is not impossible.

Jesus never asks us to do what is truly impossible. What the rich young ruler found impossible to do, the early Christians later did in large numbers (Ac. 2:44-45; 4:34-35). They did it, not because they possessed superhuman strength, but because they believed in a source of power that transcended their own human weakness. They saw in the life and teachings of Jesus a model of what humanity ought to be. That example inspired them to step out into a world they never knew existed. And by taking that step, they changed the world.

The next time you're faced with an obligation that makes you want to scream, "I can't do this!," step back and take a wider look at the scene before you. God has a reason for placing you in that moment, even if you can't see it. Yes, the task is hard He is calling you to do—but it is not impossible. Fix your eyes on Jesus, put your shoulder to the load, and press on.

You've got this.

Greatness in the Kingdom

In a world that measures greatness by raw power, God's kingdom operates on an entirely different paradigm. Even His own people struggle to get it.

"You know that the rulers of the Gentiles lord it over them, and those who are great exercise authority over them. Yet it shall not be so among you; but whoever desires to become great among you, let him be your servant. And whoever desires to be first among you, let him be your slave—just as the Son of Man did not come to be served, but to serve, and to give His life a ransom for many" (Matt. 20:25-28).

❧

These words of Jesus were prompted by an incident involving the mother of two of His apostles, James and John. She requested a special honor for her sons, a request that triggered a jealous response from the other apostles. Jesus had to remind His apostles that His mission was about *service*, not power. Sadly, they seemed not to grasp the idea. They were still engaging in these petty little power struggles right up until the night He was betrayed, when Jesus had to literally wash their feet to demonstrate the principle He was trying to teach them.

The lesson the apostles struggled to learn is the same lesson we need to learn today. We are accustomed to thinking of greatness in terms of authority over others. The bank president controls other people's money; the general has powerful armies under his command; the President wields power in guiding the nation; the CEO runs his corporation. The message the world sends us is unmistakable: The more people we are in a position to "look down" on, the greater we are.

But God's kingdom is not an ordinary human enterprise. Greatness here is measured by service, not dominance. That principle was displayed in the character of the King Himself. The One who could have summoned legions of angels to His aid, refused even to turn a few stones into bread to curb His hunger, choosing rather to use His powers for the benefit of others. He was great because He was so unselfishly good.

There is nothing glamorous about helping the poor, comforting the sorrowful, encouraging the weak, or being hospitable to strangers. Yet positions of prominence are meaningless compared to these expressions of nobility. Sadly, we often fail to recognize these lofty virtues and, like the apostles, begin elbowing for higher ranking.

- Denominations erect elaborate bureaucracies to exercise command-and-control over the congregations within their sphere.
- Preachers forget they are ministers (literally, "servants"), and use the pulpit as a pedestal from which they can promote themselves.
- Elders cease being shepherds, leading and feeding the flock, and become overlords, ruling their domain with jealous fists.
- Power struggles are fought by brethren who are driven by personal ambition or envy.
- Husbands and wives squabble over who "gets their way" in daily household decisions.

We are so busy elevating ourselves that we disgrace the very King we claim to honor. Meanwhile, a few obscure disciples are quietly doing the Lord's work. They seek no honor, get no earthly reward, and have no authority to flaunt. Yet the world is a better place because of them. In their own humble way, they are truly great.

Who is the greatest in the kingdom of God? If we have to ask the question, we probably still don't get it.

Serving Others or Self?

We might be shocked to know how much of our "serving others" work is contaminated by subtle distortions designed to serve our own interests.

"Whoever desires to become great among you, let him be your servant. And whoever desires to be first among you, let him be your slave—just as the Son of Man did not come to be served, but to serve, and to give His life a ransom for many" (Matt. 20:26-28).

୧∞ల

Thus did Jesus set His own example as the standard for determining greatness in His kingdom. The best and greatest are those who master the art of serving others, rather than themselves. The idea is expressed elsewhere using different words: esteem others as better than self (Phil. 2:3); submit to one another (Eph. 5:21); wash one another's feet (Jn. 13:12-14); and so on.

But as is the case with so many of Jesus' teachings, living up to this standard is a difficult challenge. Oh, sure, we grasp the basic message in His command, but too often we miss subtle opportunities to practice it. Like the Pharisees of old, we honor it with our lips, but our hearts miss the real meaning of the law.

Take, for example, the common practice of "keeping score." This is when we somehow keep track of the good deeds we've performed for others, and how others have returned (or failed to return) the favors. Many years ago, I knew an elderly sister who diligently wrote letters to numerous acquaintances. It was a laudable habit. She actually kept a little book in which she noted the dates and recipients of her outgoing letters. She also recorded the responses. And she ever-so-discreetly shared with others the fact that the balance was always in her favor. Clearly, she was so much more kind and caring than her acquaintances—and she had the receipts to prove it. Seriously now, for whose benefit was she writing those letters? Was she really serving others, or serving herself?

That's a pretty brazen example, but others are more difficult to detect in ourselves. Our relationships with family and friends can be poisoned by minor annoyances that fester and turn ugly. We get miffed because somebody said some little thing that hurt our precious feelings. We go off and pout because someone failed to acknowledge a good deed we performed. In every case, the formula is the same: My fragile ego got bruised, so somebody must bear the consequences.

After over half a century of life, I still am amazed at the absolutely silly things that can turn friends into enemies, brethren into strangers, families into warring camps. Real sin does enough damage; but all too often we add to the carnage by blowing our petty little grievances far out of proportion to their true gravity. If we really did treat others the way we wanted to be treated, would we nurse these grudges, or just shrug them off as the price we pay for living in an imperfect world? Are we serving others by being so critical of them, or are we serving ourselves? You figure it out.

More often than not, "serving others" consists not of the noble deeds of charity or sacrifice that grab headlines, but the small, simple acts of kindness and forgiveness that go unrecognized. Simply by doing good to others, expecting nothing in return, while being forgiving, patient, and longsuffering with the shortcomings of others, we demonstrate that we are serving them, not ourselves. That is the real measure of greatness in the kingdom of God.

By What Authority?

Respecting God's authority is essential. But also essential is an attitude of humility that views truth as more important than personal victory.

Now when He came into the temple, the chief priests and the elders of the people confronted Him as He was teaching, and said, "By what authority are You doing these things? And who gave You this authority?" (Matt. 21:23).

And when they had set them in the midst, they asked, "By what power or by what name have you done this?" (Ac. 4:7).

૭∞ર૭

To every serious Bible student, the idea of respecting divine authority is a given. How often do we read in the Scriptures, both Old and New Testaments, of the importance of following God's instructions (Deut. 6:1-3; 1 Jn. 2:3-5), neither adding to nor taking away from what He has revealed (Deut. 4:2; Rev. 22:18-19)? Those who presume to act outside of God's authority will incur His wrath (1 Sam. 15:22-23; Heb. 2:2-3). This basic principle is beyond dispute.

However, the two confrontations documented here present a disturbing variation on that theme. In both cases, the Jewish leaders—men who ostensibly represented the ultimate in respect for God—posed a test: "By what authority are you doing these things?" Of course, their challenge was a craven covering up of their own rebellion against God. For all their tough talk about authority, they had no intention of listening to any answer Jesus or the apostles gave them. (In fact, Jesus turned the question back on them, using the ministry of

John as an alternate test. They declined to commit to a position, thus exposing their duplicity.)

I can't help but think of these two incidents every time I hear a preacher badger his opponent with strikingly similar wording ("Where's your authority?!"). Some suggest the lesson here is that if even the enemies of Christ recognized the need for authority, how much more so should we. That's true, but I suspect the real lesson lies deeper—and much closer to home.

Jesus warned His apostles of enemies who "think that [they] offer God service" (Jn. 16:2). Saul of Tarsus was one of those enemies, who savagely attacked the early Christians because "I myself thought I must do many things contrary to the name of Jesus of Nazareth" (Ac. 26:9)—it was an "authority" issue. After his conversion, he bore his unbelieving brethren witness "that they have a zeal for God, but not according to knowledge" (Rom. 10:2). In each of these cases, intense devotion to God's word had morphed into a stubborn refusal to consider any new evidence that might challenge pre-existing beliefs and thus require changes.

It is important that we respect God's authority. But it is equally important that we maintain humble hearts that are willing to listen and consider other points of view. God looks upon the one who is "of a contrite spirit, and who trembles at My word" (Isa. 66:2). But that attitude of humble submission is lost when we reach a point where we think we have all the answers and our job now is to straighten out everyone else. Such a person is beyond God's help, even as he champions God's cause.

"By what authority" is a legitimate question to ask in religious discussions. But the first question should be, "Is this about God or about me?"

Hypocrites in the Church

Hypocrisy in the church is a huge turn-off to many. But letting hypocrites stand between us and God comes with its own downside.

"The scribes and the Pharisees sit in Moses' seat. Therefore whatever they tell you to observe, that observe and do. But do not do according to their works, for they say, and do not do" (Matt. 23:2-3).

૭∞ల

Of all the reasons offered by people for rejecting the religion of Christ, by far the most common is the complaint that "there are are hypocrites in the church." Christians claim to be so righteous and holy, but they are just as flawed as the rest of us. Their religion is just a pose, a disguise through which they look down their haughty noses at everyone else.

First, let's consider the legitimacy of that charge. Is it true that Christians are self-righteous zealots who delight in telling everyone else how to run their lives, while excusing misbehavior in their own? The sad answer is often "yes." In far too many cases, those who claim to be followers of Christ are pious frauds. They wear their religion on their sleeves, but do a lousy job of living up to what they preach. The inconsistency between their message and their behavior is a major turn-off to others.

But before we close the book on this question, we need to consider another angle. Is the fact that Christianity is tainted with hypocrites sufficient reason to reject it altogether? Could there be another, more appropriate, response to the problem, a response that salvages the good from the teachings of Christ, while avoiding the corrupting influence of the hypocrites?

Jesus understood the problem of hypocrisy in religion, and addressed it directly in His diatribe against the scribes and Pharisees. He railed against their self-important posturing, and the corrosive influence it had on the religion of His day. But in His view, the presence of hypocrites did not delegitimize the value of true religion. Notice the advice He gave His followers: "Whatever they tell you to observe, that observe and do. But do not do according to their works." Jesus made a distinction between what was *taught* and what was *practiced*. Clearly, the hypocrites did not live up to their claims. But their personal failure did not invalidate the truth of God's word. Jesus' response to the problem of the hypocrites was simple, but profound: We should center our attention on the divine standard, not on those who are imperfectly following it.

Actually, there is nothing all that unusual about this approach. Is there hypocrisy in politics? Of course! Do we encounter hypocrisy in the workplace? All the time. Yet we still vote in elections and go to work every day, in hope that our efforts will contribute to something better. Why should church be any different? Yes, there are hypocrites in the church. But instead of rejecting religion outright, why not get involved and show people how it should be done? After all, if we are qualified to pass judgment on those awful hypocrites, surely we can do a better job of living what we believe.

Of course, maybe "hypocrites in the church" is not the issue at all. Perhaps that's just a convenient excuse to avoid accepting the challenge of serving God. If so, then we are letting the hypocrites stand between us and God.

Which is another way of saying: The hypocrites are closer to God than we are.

Consistency Is a Jewel

Consistently understanding and applying the intricacies of God's word is a major challenge, requiring a generous dose of humility.

"The scribes and the Pharisees sit in Moses' seat. Therefore whatever they tell you to observe, that observe and do, but do not do according to their works; for they say, and do not do. For they bind heavy burdens, hard to bear, and lay them on men's shoulders; but they themselves will not move them with one of their fingers" (Matt. 23:2-4).

৵৽৵

The "heavy burdens" that Jesus condemns in this passage were the extensions of the Law that the Pharisees had created to help people properly apply the Law of Moses in their lives. It was not enough, for example, to teach people to honor God's instruction to "remember the Sabbath day" (Ex. 20:8). That instruction was insufficiently precise. So the Pharisees constructed a complex system of rules to micromanage every detail of what a person could or could not do on the Sabbath day. The result was an oppressive body of regulations that no human could possibly keep. A law that was intended to provide refreshment to the people was turned into a crushing burden.

Of course, as Jesus pointed out, even the Pharisees themselves could not keep the rules they had constructed. They laid burdens on others that they would not accept for themselves. There was a glaring inconsistency between their teaching and their own application of their teaching. That inconsistency rendered their credibility worthless.

This kind of capriciousness is a common danger among those who teach God's word. I recently heard a preacher expound on Romans 14, arguing that the chapter applied only to matters of "personal scruples" within the realm of "lawful liberties." Therefore, the chapter could not be applied to "sinful practices." What the preacher failed to address, however, is that by his reckoning, both the weak and strong brothers in this chapter would *first* have to agree that the issue over which they differed was a matter of indifference to God. Only then could they could apply Paul's principle of forbearance.

The preacher went on in his sermon to apply this principle to the thorny questions of military service and women's head covering in worship. The inconsistency here is glaring: Those brethren who refuse to serve in the military or insist that women wear a head covering in worship do not consider these positions to be "personal scruples" within "lawful liberties." They honestly believe these positions to be God's revealed will, and for them to violate those convictions would be a "sinful practice." So we make up a rule ("Romans 14 cannot apply to sinful practices"), then make arbitrary exceptions to that rule where it is convenient for us. Thinking people are not impressed with that kind of exegesis.

Our purpose here is not to thrash out the proper use of Romans 14, but to challenge us to face up to the inconsistencies that inevitably crop up in our efforts to understand and apply God's word. A key component of Bible study should include thinking through the logical implications of our conclusions, squaring them with our understanding of other Biblical principles and their applications. It can be a laborious and frustrating experience, but honesty demands nothing less. Spiritual growth cannot happen in an environment that shuts down examination of problematic interpretations.

"Consistency is a jewel," precisely because it is so difficult to achieve. The process of acknowledging and resolving our inconsistencies requires that we re-examine long-cherished beliefs, however difficult the struggle. We should not be ashamed to do so.

To Be Seen by Men

When our religion turns into performance art,
it loses any value as a means of improving our
character. In fact, it *destroys* our character.

"The scribes and Pharisees sit in Moses' seat. Therefore whatever they tell you to observe, that observe and do, but do not do according to their works; for they say, and do not do. For they bind heavy burdens, hard to bear, and lay them on men's shoulders; but they themselves will not move them with one of their fingers. But all their works they do to be seen by men" (Matt. 23:2-5).

ভক

The Pharisees no doubt accomplished much good during their glory days, but history does not remember them for that. The word "Pharisee" has become synonymous with "hypocrite," someone who does not practice what he preaches. Much of Jesus' career was spent exposing the hypocrisy of these men who put on a fine display of religion, but failed to live up to their own standards.

The Pharisees may have developed hypocrisy to an art form, but they certainly didn't have a lock on the market. Hypocrisy is still with us today. Wherever men profess religion, there will be those who say one thing, but do another.

Why is hypocrisy so widespread? How can people so eloquently preach one thing, yet so flagrantly violate the very thing they preach?

The answer lies in Jesus' description of what motivated the Pharisees. Their religion, Jesus said, consisted largely of a performance "to be seen by men." Like any good actor, the success of their religion was tied to the perception of their audience. In their minds, if people *observed* them as pious and holy, then they *were* pious and holy. So, despite lofty rhetoric about "honoring God," their religion became an exercise in manipulating what others thought of them. A whole range of behaviors were developed to help achieve the desired effect: special religious clothing, titles of respect, elaborate public ceremonies—whatever it took to build the image of "look at me, I'm religious!" This self-righteous posturing was further reinforced by participation in a tight network of similarly minded people, who sought honor from each other, rather than from God (Jn. 5:44).

But by emphasizing outward appearance, these men neglected the heart. They were so careful to maintain a good outward image, that they left the door open for deadly spiritual diseases such as pride, jealousy, lust, greed, and hate to corrupt their characters. And since behavior is always the child of attitude (Prov. 4:23), these sins of the heart eventually found expression in their outward lives. They became hypocrites—and never saw the discrepancy.

The root of the problem, of course, is that other men are not the judges of true religion. That's God's role. Instead of comparing ourselves to others, we must train ourselves to look at God. Other people see only a narrow slice of our behavior; God sees *every* detail of *every* behavior and *every* motive. Other people can be fooled; God can't.

Jesus laid out the cure for hypocrisy in the Sermon on the Mount. We should strive first to develop godly *attitudes*, not just behaviors (Matt. 5:20-48). When we exercise our religion, we should take care not to do so before others, "to be seen by them" (Matt. 6:1-18). Our religion should emanate from the heart, and be lived quietly, unobtrusively, without drawing attention to ourselves. If we focus on that objective, our public image will take care of itself.

And we'll never have to worry about falling into the trap of hypocrisy.

The High Cost of Hypocrisy

Jesus' fiery condemnation of hypocrisy in the
Pharisees should serve as a warning to all of us
to avoid its insidious influence in our own lives.

---

*"Woe to you, scribes and Pharisees, hypocrites!" (Matt.
23:13, 23, 27, 29).*

෨෬

Hypocrisy is not a simple moral blemish. It is a destructive behavior that imposes a steep price on everything and everyone it touches. In His diatribe against the scribes and Pharisees in this chapter, Jesus catalogs the high cost of hypocrisy.

Hypocrisy is costly *to its immediate victims*. Ask the widow whose meager resources are appropriated by a greedy con artist (v. 14), or the young proselyte who eagerly embraces the hypocrite's twisted theology, only to discover later that he has been sold a bill of goods (v. 15). Hypocrites cannot abide those who expose their duplicity, and will move to silence them with vicious fury (v. 34-35). That's a major reason why hypocrites are so despised.

As hypocrites grow in number and influence, *society in general will pay a price*. Justice, mercy, and faithfulness increasingly become scarce commodities (v. 23), destroying the trust and good will that are essential to a stable society. Hypocrites "shut up the kingdom of heaven against men"; that is, cynicism becomes the coin of the realm, and God becomes a distant abstraction. Everybody loses.

Ultimately, *the hypocrite himself* will pay a terrible price. "How can you escape the condemnation of hell?"

(v. 33). The hypocrite can enjoy his little shell game for a while, but in the end he will regret with bitter tears the double life he lived. He was only fooling himself.

If we read this chapter shaking our heads at the duplicity of those awful hypocrites around us, we're missing the real message in Jesus' words. The tendency to whitewash the truth about our own weaknesses is strong in every one of us. Hypocrisy is a constant threat to our character, requiring a continual commitment to honesty and transparency, not only in our dealings with others, but in our own self-assessment.

Integrity begins with me. If I am not addressing the hypocrisy in my own life, I have no grounds for criticizing it in others.

Jesus Loves Pharisees, Too

The Pharisees were enemies of Jesus, yet He loved them just as He loves all of us. We must follow that example in dealing with modern Pharisees.

"Woe to you, scribes and Pharisees, hypocrites! . . . O Jerusalem, Jerusalem, the one who kills the prophets and stones those who are sent to her! How often I wanted to gather your children together, as a hen gathers her chicks under her wings, but you were not willing!" (Matt. 23:13, 37).

୭∞୧

The verbal spanking that Jesus administered on the Pharisees in Matthew 23 contains some of the harshest language Jesus ever uttered. And for good reason. The Pharisees embodied all that was wrong with the Judaism of His day. In their zeal to honor God, the Pharisees had twisted His law into a jungle of oppressive regulations. Their self-righteous, hypocritical form of spirituality has become an ageless symbol of what can happen when a religion spends too much time reading its own press clippings.

Nevertheless, for all their faults, the Pharisees received a good deal of personal attention from Jesus during His ministry. The Pharisees had a curiosity about the Galilean, and on several occasions invited Him into their homes for meals. Jesus always accepted those invitations, using them as teaching opportunities (Lk. 7:36-50; 11:37-54; 14:1-24). One Pharisee, Nicodemus, was so impressed with Jesus that he sought Him out for a personal counseling session (Jn. 3:1-21). Nicodemus remained a secret disciple of Jesus until the end, assisting in His burial following His crucifixion (Jn. 19:38-42).

Most of the Pharisees were implacable enemies of Jesus. But true to His own teaching, Jesus loved them anyway. We remember the harsh denunciations of Matthew 23, but we forget that His rebuke ended with a tender desire to embrace them "as a hen gathers her chicks." That love reached its ultimate expression in the conversion of Saul of Tarsus, the most zealous Pharisee of his day (Phil. 3:5-6). Until the day he died, Paul marveled at the grace of the One who "loved me, and gave Himself for me" (Gal. 2:20). Jesus loved His enemy—and His enemy melted.

If the villains of the Bible serve as a warning to later generations not to repeat their mistakes, surely the Pharisees must rank high on that list. Even today, the greatest damage to the cause of Christ is inflicted not by His enemies, but by some of the very people who claim to be His disciples. Their condescending arrogance and self-serving hypocrisy sow discord among brethren and drive people away from the faith. The specific doctrines may be different, but the spirit of Phariseeism remains a very real threat today, and we must oppose it.

But therein lies a second, and more sinister, danger. While we must actively oppose the spirit and behavior of the Pharisees when it arises among us, we must take care not to allow that opposition to descend into contempt and hatred. If Jesus loved the Pharisees of His day, despite all the terrible things they did to Him, we must love the Pharisees among us today. Showing that love won't be easy; it certainly doesn't come naturally. But we never know if the recipient of that love might be another Saul of Tarsus, a confirmed Pharisee with a good heart who can become a tireless ambassador for the grace of God.

For Pretense

The revelations concerning the late Ravi Zacharias
remind us once again how easy it is to live one life
while professing another. It can happen to us, too.

*"Woe to you, scribes and Pharisees, hypocrites! For you
devour widows' houses, and for a pretense make long
prayers. Therefore you will receive greater condemnation"
(Matt. 23:14).*

୨୭୧

The evangelical Christian community was stunned this
week to see the final report on the charges of sexual miscon-
duct by the late Ravi Zacharias, a popular and effective
apologist for Christianity. The evidence indicates that he led
a private life that was a contradiction of his public persona. A
number of people, especially women, were victims of his
wrongdoing. The damage is incalculable.

The Greek word for actor is *hupokrites*, usually translated as hypocrite. Actors are people who make a living
pretending to be someone they are not. As a profession, acting is a perfectly legitimate artform. Everyone knows the
performance is just a put-on, and the actor is probably quite
different in real life. It's innocent fun, and nobody gets hurt.

But there is another form of acting that is more sinister,
and does hurt others. Hypocrisy is the hiding of our real motives with the intent to deceive others. The hypocrite puts on
an act to fool others into forming an opinion of him that is not
accurate. Like the scribes and Pharisees, he will "make long
prayers" and perform other acts of piety to show how righteous he is, and simultaneously "devour widows' houses" to

enrich himself. He puts on one face for public view, but privately he is another person entirely. If the evidence that has come to light is factual, Zacharias was such a man.

Hypocrisy is so common because it is so successful. A well-polished hypocrite can fool everyone into thinking he is the epitome of holiness, and keep up the charade throughout his entire lifetime. In some cases, his hypocrisy will not be revealed until after he is gone, if ever.

What is the cure for hypocrisy? It's *honesty*. Brutal, painful, humble, public honesty.

First, we must first *be honest with ourselves and with God*—two sides of the same coin. In the deepest recesses of our heart we must face up to our own imperfections and bad attitudes, not whitewash them with excuses. We must openly confess our weaknesses to God, acknowledging our struggles with temptation and ignorance. Without a conscience that is conditioned to feel the pain of sin, there is nothing to keep us from inflicting pain on others.

Then we must *be honest with others*. We should seek out close friends in whom we can confide, and enlist their help in fighting the battle. When we stumble, we should own up to our mistake, and seek to correct it with others as publicly as the sin is known. The purpose is not to curry sympathy, but to repair what is broken. This can be hard, even humiliating; but it is essential to maintaining a clean heart.

In the meantime, how can we deal with the impact of yet another revelation of hypocrisy by a prominent faith leader? As one observer explained it, we must remember that "I am not offering you Christians. I am offering you Christ."

We must keep our faith in Christ, not men—but keep it an honest faith.

Sons of Hell

Some of Satan's best allies are people who claim
to be God's best friends. Their destructive
behavior damages the very cause they espouse.

*"Woe to you, scribes and Pharisees, hypocrites! For you
travel land and sea to win one proselyte, and when he is won,
you make him twice as much a son of hell as yourselves"
(Matt. 23:15)*

ଚ∞ଏ

The phrase "son of" is a common Hebrew idiom meaning "to share the characteristics of" something. So "son of
perdition" in Jn. 17:12 and 2 Thess. 2:3 describes someone
who, by his rejection of God's authority, is doomed to destruction. By contrast, "sons of light" (Jn. 12:36) are those
who open their lives to the light of God's guidance. The fiery
temperament of James and John earned them the title of
"Sons of Thunder" (Mk. 3:17), while Barnabas ("Son of Encouragement") was known for his optimistic spirit (Ac.
4:36).

So when Jesus accused the Pharisees of turning a proselyte into "a son of hell," He was hurling the worst possible
insult at them. Read the rest of Matthew 23 and it's obvious
that Jesus viewed the Pharisees as embodying all the ugliness
of hell—deceit, selfishness, treachery, greed, pride. Anyone
who fell under their influence would be corrupted by their
faulty theology and do great harm to God's cause.

The irony, of course, is that the Pharisees considered
themselves to be the ultimate representatives of righteousness. They were defenders of God's holy law, practitioners of

the true faith, a tiny slice of humanity who truly "got it" when it came to morals and virtue. If you wanted to get a glimpse of heaven, the Pharisees said, "Look at us!"

But Jesus saw something more sinister at work in these people. Their very righteousness had become a stumbling block to achieving the most important virtue of all: humility. Their condescending treatment of others blinded them to their own imperfections, and turned them into insufferable snobs.

The "sons of hell" created by the Pharisees were not murderers, thieves, rapists, or idolaters. No, it was worse than that. They were hypocrites, pretenders who fooled no one but themselves by their sanctimonious preening. Satan has many allies, but none so effective as those who believe they are beyond his grasp. The Pharisees and their minions considered themselves too good for the sinners who surrounded them—and thereby erected a tall barrier that kept those sinners from ever finding God. What more does Satan need?

Holier-than-thou pride always produces the worst kind of evil. It cloaks itself in the mantle of godliness, but refuses to acknowledge the flaws and weaknesses that are common to all humanity. The result is a pretentiousness that is forever criticizing others while hiding or excusing its own faults—all in the name of God, of course. The damage inflicted by this kind of religion is incalculable.

Hell will be populated by legions of people who were confident they would never go there. If we want to avoid that fate, we must temper our loyalty to God with equal parts of humility and compassion, recognizing that our service to Him will always be imperfect and incomplete. It is only by displaying the same unselfish love for others that God has manifested toward us, that we can be called "sons of God."

Blind Guides

Knowledge of the Scriptures is a good thing, but it can get us into trouble if we misuse it to elevate ourselves above others.

"Woe to you, blind guides, who say, 'Whoever swears by the temple, it is nothing; but whoever swears by the gold of the temple, he is obliged to perform it.'... Blind guides, who strain out a gnat and swallow a camel!" (Matt. 23:16, 24).

✤

A guide is someone who not only possesses a superior level of knowledge about a course of action, but is also willing to help others navigate the terrain before them. Whether in academia, finance, or adventure trekking, a seasoned guide is a godsend to the ignorant.

But what if the guide is blind? What if the "expert" whom we trust to lead us can't see the terrain, or is just as ignorant of the subject matter as the one he is trying to help? The idea of a guide with such a handicap trying to help others is ludicrous: "If the blind leads the blind, both will fall into a ditch" (Matt. 15:14).

So when Jesus called the Pharisees "blind guides," He was leveling a serious charge against them. The Pharisees saw themselves as highly trained specialists in the Law, theological experts who helped the unwashed masses find God. But Jesus accused them of being just as lost as the people they were trying to lead. Why would He say such a thing?

One clue in this context is the fine distinctions the Pharisees used in their oaths. In their view, the binding force of an oath depended on whether the oath was based on the temple or the gold that encased the temple. Which is another way of saying, when you're making a deal with a Pharisee, you'd better read the fine print carefully, because he may have left an opening for himself to wiggle out of his obligations. Integrity was not a bedrock character trait for these people, but a legal game to be played at the expense of others.

Jesus summarized their approach to truth as "straining out a gnat and swallowing a camel." The Pharisees would expend enormous intellectual effort to tease out the tiniest distinctions in applications of the Law, yet let major indiscretions pass by unchallenged, depending on how it benefited themselves. They were religious frauds, people who preached respect for God's Law, but abused it shamelessly to suit their own selfish interests. "Hypocrite" was a label that Jesus used often in this chapter, because it best described who they were—scholars who did not practice what they preached.

Jesus' denunciation of the Pharisees should serve as a warning to the rest of us. It is good that we study hard and learn well the deep things of the word of God. But that learning carries a risk of feeding *pride*, a sense that our deeper knowledge has given us the ability to recognize distinctions where God intended none. The hypocritical behavior that grows out of this mindset can be seen by everyone except us. And that blindness makes us look foolish.

God's word is not a regulatory minefield that can be navigated only by experts with years of specialized training. It is a practical guide to life available to anyone who has the desire to know God's will. We can and should help each other along the way, but must never let our knowledge deceive us into thinking we're smarter than God.

Of Gnats and Camels

The details of God's law are important, but when we become so obsessed with the details that we neglect the major items, our religion is corrupted.

"Woe to you, scribes and Pharisees, hypocrites! For you pay tithe of mint and anise and cummin, and have neglected the weightier matters of the law: justice and mercy and faith. These you ought to have done, without leaving the others undone. Blind guides, who strain out a gnat and swallow a camel!" (Matt. 23:23-24).

Then the Pharisees and some of the scribes came together to Him, having come from Jerusalem. Now when they saw some of His disciples eat bread with defiled, that is, with unwashed hands, they found fault. For the Pharisees and all the Jews do not eat unless they wash their hands in a special way, holding the tradition of the elders (Mk. 7:1-3).

৵৵

Scenario #1: According to the Law of Moses, most insects were considered unclean and not to be eaten. Gnats are insects. It is possible for gnats to fall into drinking vessels. Therefore (concluded the Pharisees), all beverages must be strained before drinking to remove any possibility of eating a gnat. Non-strainers were obviously careless about their relationship with God.

Scenario #2: According to the Law of Moses, contacting anything (or anybody) that was unclean defiled a person. In the normal course of daily life, it is likely that some unclean object or person would be inadvertently touched. Eating food after contacting such an unclean source then makes the food unclean. Therefore (concluded the Pharisees), the hands must be washed before eating, lest one's food be ceremonially defiled. (According to Alfred Edersheim, the Pharisees carried this reasoning even further: After washing, the hands had to be held up for drying so that the water, which was now unclean, would drip off at the wrists; otherwise, it would flow back on the fingers and defile them again.) This was not a matter of mere hygiene; one's eternal destiny could be at risk if this was not done properly.

The Pharisees developed a mountain of complex rules like these from the Law of Moses, using this same kind of extended reasoning. Yet the same men who were so fastidious about *straining gnats*, were also *swallowing camels*. Their obsession with getting the details just right blinded them to "the weightier matters of the law": justice, mercy, and faithfulness (v. 23). They would go to great pains to tithe the tiniest herbs in their garden, yet defraud an aged widow (v. 14) or deny their aged parents support (15:1-9)—and never notice the contradiction. They forgot that the purpose of true religion was to train the human heart to love God and one's fellow man, not to create a religious freak show.

The lesson for us, the religious conservatives of our day, is sobering. It is right that we seek authority for all that we do. We must not neglect the details of the simple law by which God guides us ("without leaving the others undone," v. 23). But we must take care that our desire for religious purity does not descend into the same kind of self-righteous myopia that ruined the Pharisees. When we fail to recognize a hierarchy of importance in God's law, the result is always this kind of unbalanced religion. His Law turns into a theological jungle in which we can lose our way—and our souls.

If I Had Been There

Passing judgment on the villains of the past
is easy. The hard part is recognizing our own
mistakes in the history we are creating right now.

"Woe to you, scribes and Pharisees, hypocrites! Because you build the tombs of the prophets and adorn the monuments of the righteous, and say, 'If we had lived in the days of our fathers, we would not have been partakers with them in the blood of the prophets.' Therefore you are witnesses against yourselves that you are sons of those who murdered the prophets" (Matt. 23:29-31).

৵৽

Studying history can be like watching instant replays in a football game. Sitting in a cozy chair, we can analyze every move and pinpoint every flaw. Having the luxury of viewing the action from a distance, we know just what should have been done—and feel justified in criticizing the poor guy who's trying to play the game.

The scribes and Pharisees were excellent armchair quarterbacks. They could easily identify the good guys and bad guys in their nation's history. They knew exactly what should have been done in those bygone days. But their boast of what they would have done had they lived in those days was worthless, because they didn't live in those days. The only criteria by which their loyalty could be judged was how they treated the prophets of their own day. By that standard, they proved to be sons of their fathers, having rejected John the Baptist and Jesus for the same reasons their ancestors rejected the earlier prophets.

So the moral of the story is: The scribes and Pharisees were idiots, right? They should have seen the parallels between their behavior and that of their ancestors. Yeah, if we lived back then, we would not have been so blind. We would have recognized Jesus as the Son of God. We would have been faithful and loyal and . . . oh, wait a minute . . .

The hardest commandment God ever gave humanity was the duty to "examine yourselves" (2 Cor. 13:5). We are experts at identifying the faults of others, but remarkably blind to the same faults in ourselves. Like Walter Mitty, we create a fantasy world in which we are the heroes fearlessly standing for truth and justice, yet remain oblivious to the stumbles we commit in our own lives.

"If I had walked with the Israelites in the wilderness, I would not have grumbled against God." But I'll complain about the weather, the preacher, the economy, my job, my spouse, and anything else that doesn't suit my fancy.

"If I had been a first-century Jew, I would have listened to the gospel with an open mind." But don't try to push your wacky ideas off on me, buster; I'm not interested.

"If I had been a Christian in the church in Corinth, I would not have displayed the bad attitudes that plagued that church." But I will do whatever I feel is necessary to "defend the faith"—including stabbing my brethren in the back and assassinating their characters.

It's easy to be a hero when fighting yesterday's battles. But building castles in the long-distant past will not save us. We must wake up to the difficult duties of today, and fulfill our own role in history.

Notes from a Pastor-Eating Crocodile

Stories we read on the internet may catch our attention, but they're worthless if they aren't true, and may even be damaging to our faith.

"If anyone says to you, 'Look, here is the Christ!' or 'There!' do not believe it" (Matt. 24:23).

৵৽৽

No doubt you've seen the news item recently about the Zimbabwe pastor who was eaten by three crocodiles while attempting to walk on water in front of his congregation. The horrified parishioners could only look on as the poor man of God was devoured by the hungry crocs. All they found afterward was his underwear and sandals. One of his deacons wept, "We still don't understand how this happened because he fasted and prayed the whole week."

Now at this point, you probably expect me to launch into a lecture about the deadly consequences of false religion; how really believing in something doesn't make it true; how we should never follow a "man of God" just because he claims to be one; how the Bible is our only source of divine guidance, not latter-day carnival stunts; and so on and so on.

But I'm not going to do that here, for one simple reason: *This incident never happened.*

Do a little investigation online, and you'll find that the breathless reports about this tragedy all originated from a shadowy news source in Zimbabwe. Researchers have been unable to find anyone by the name of the deceased pastor, or the church he supposedly led. And the most telling evidence of all: There is no photographic record of the event (do you really think a pastor would stage a spectacle like this without a lot of cameras rolling?). In other words, it's just another piece of phony click bait.

But this story does open up another line of study for our consideration. In our internet-saturated world, a lie will spread just as quickly—in fact, more quickly—than the truth. It's sad that it must be this way, but we should remain skeptical of much that we read on the internet. We should check and double-check our sources before forwarding shocking stories like this to others. Otherwise, we are contributing to the spread of such junk. Whether intentional or not, we are peddling falsehood.

The same caution should be exercised when reading online commentary on the Bible or theology. The internet is a great tool for spreading the gospel, but it is equally effective at spreading falsehood. Religious hucksters have learned how to exploit cyberspace for their own nefarious purposes, and they're quite good at it. We must use caution when swimming in those waters (so to speak).

What is true of the internet is equally true of every other form of mass media to which we are exposed: newspapers, magazines, television, radio, billboards, movies, and so forth. This world is awash in misleading and destructive messages, all designed by Satan to bury the truth in a blizzard of counterfeits. Sadly, most people don't bother to look for the truth in this ocean of error.

When Jesus warned His disciples to "beware of false prophets," He wasn't talking about demons wearing horns and carrying pitchforks. Pious pastors and "trusted" news sources can just as dangerous.

Be Ready!

It is precisely because we do not know how much time we have remaining to us in this life that we should live it with deliberate care.

"Watch therefore, for you do not know what hour your Lord is coming. But know this, that if the master of the house had known what hour the thief would come, he would have watched and not allowed his house to be broken into. Therefore you also be ready, for the Son of Man is coming at an hour you do not expect" (Matt. 24:42-44).

❧

Chapters 24 and 25 of Matthew record the last discourse of Jesus to His disciples prior to the Last Supper. He first foretold the destruction of Jerusalem, which would be preceded by various omens (24:1-33) and would occur within their lifetimes (v. 34). Then He described His more distant Second Coming (starting with "heaven and earth will pass away," v. 35), an event that will come without warning to those who are alive to see it. He used two images to illustrate the sudden, unexpected nature of His coming: The flood that came upon Noah's generation (v. 37-39), and the stealthy strike of the thief who robs a house at night (v. 43).

Commentators disagree over which segments of these chapters cover which events, but we will not concern ourselves with that here. Our attention instead is drawn to the practical message that screams from both chapters: *Watch! Be ready! Don't let these events catch you by surprise!*

One of Satan's most effective strategies is to convince us that we have plenty of time to prepare for the end. Yes, I need to straighten up my life and change my ways—but I'm young and want to enjoy life while I can. Yes, I really should devote more of my time and resources to helping others—but first I have so much that I need to do to advance my career and feather my nest. Preparing my life to meet God in judgment can wait a little longer.

And a little longer . . . and a little longer . . . until suddenly the end comes and we are snatched away. We may not live to witness the Second Coming, but death serves the same practical purpose. It's the absolute end of our time on earth, the closing of the opportunity to do what we always knew we needed to do. Like the foolish virgins who delayed in preparing their lamps, then got shut out of the wedding (25:1-13), we will put off doing the more important things until that day when our lives come to a sudden end and we lose everything, including our souls. We were not prepared!

So what should that preparation consist of? Two things: First, we must *set our priorities correctly*. My time and resources in life are limited. I cannot do everything I would like to do, so some things must be left undone. What are the important things that must be done and the not-so-important things that can wait? Until we make a serious effort to prioritize the infinite options before us and concentrate on the most important priorities first, we will squander much of our time on trivia, and reach the end with empty hands.

Second, we must *attack life with a sense of urgency*. We do not know the number of days that remain to us in this life—but we do know that it's a frighteningly small number. What do we want to accomplish in that brief window of time that remains to us? The only way it will be accomplished is to get busy and work like there's no tomorrow—because there may not be one.

My time on earth will come to end someday, but I do not know the day. I must therefore watch and be ready!

Fearful? Or Lazy?

Failure can be a positive experience in our life,
if we're willing to learn from it. The first step
is to understand why we failed.

"'And I was afraid, and went and hid your talent in the
ground. Look, there you have what is yours.' But his lord answered and said to him, 'You wicked and lazy servant, you
knew that I reap where I have not sown, and gather where I
have not scattered seed'" (Matt. 25:26).

The lazy man says, "There is a lion outside! I shall be
slain in the streets!" (Prov. 22:13)

৵৽৻

The one-talent man in Jesus' parable of the talents is
often held up as an example of timidity. He allowed his fear
of making a mistake to hold him back from doing anything,
so he accomplished nothing. The moral of the story is clear:
Don't let your fear be a barrier to action!

That's a fair deduction. Like this servant, we have our
own fears that can paralyze us and keep us from using our
gifts. Fear of *failure* can paralyze us into not trying. Fear of
rejection or *ridicule* can prevent us from standing up to evil.
Fear of *exposure* can keep us curled up in our warm little co-
coon so others can't see "the real me." Or we may hold back
out of fear of the *unknown*; we prefer to stay sequestered in
the comfortable status quo that we know so well. Yes, fear
can be a powerful inhibitor to action.

However, if we read the rest of the parable we learn that
fear was not the real issue here. The master had distributed
his wealth among these men "each according to his own abil-

ity" (v. 15). He knew his servants well enough to know what they were capable of doing, and apportioned his wealth accordingly. The task assigned to the one-talent man was within his capabilities. So when the master confronted this servant, he charged him with a more serious offense: "You wicked and lazy servant." The master knew that the servant's claim of "fear" was merely a cop-out, a cheap excuse for a deeper moral defect.

Solomon captured the connection long before Jesus did: When people complain about the threat of lions in the street, they're usually just throwing out a flimsy alibi for their apathy. The fear may be real, but in almost every case, it is a cover for *laziness*. They just don't want to be bothered with the trouble of taking on the challenge that lies before them.

Even the most fearful people can muster the courage to overcome their fears—once they make up their minds to do so. Moses was afraid of confronting Pharaoh, but he did it anyway. Gideon was scared of taking on the Midianites, yet became a great hero. Esther was fearful of going before the King unannounced, but she barged in and spoke up ("If I perish, I perish."). The apostles were terrified of taking on the power structure of their day, yet look at what they accomplished! Fear was in the hearts of all these people, but with some coaching and prodding, they finally overcame their fears and achieved great victories.

It is good that we study our capabilities to know what we are good at and what tasks are beyond our limits. But even with that self-knowledge, we should not be afraid to step out of our comfort zone. Only by taking on new challenges will we learn new skills, develop new expertise, and grow new competencies.

The next time you are tempted to say "no" to a challenge out of fear of failure, reconsider your response. Could it be you just don't want to bother with the trouble of learning something new? The greatest fear of all should be the fear of giving back to God an empty bag, with nothing to show for the life He has given us. We must face our fears, and *try*.

Visiting the Sick

No act of mercy is more universally appreciated—
or accessible—than visiting the sick. Yet many of
us shy away from doing it. Why?

*"I was naked and you clothed Me; I was sick and you
visited Me; . . . Inasmuch as you did it to one of the least of
these My brethren, you did it to Me" (Matt. 25:36, 40).*

*. . . If she has brought up children, if she has lodged
strangers, if she has washed the saints' feet, if she has re-
lieved the afflicted, if she has diligently followed every good
work (1 Tim. 5:10).*

❧

As creatures of flesh in a cursed world, we navigate life's
journey with several unpleasant companions: illness, disease,
injury, old age. These afflictions are physically and mentally
exhausting—sometimes more than we can bear.

That's why a major component of a life of faith is helping the sick in their struggles. Whether providing meals,
watching the kids, doing laundry or other chores, or just sitting to chat, there is so much we can do to lift the spirits of
the sick and ease their discomfort. That is what God put us
here on this earth to do.

There is nothing especially newsworthy in these acts of
compassion, but they make a world of difference to the recipients. Their physical ailments may be beyond our ability to
cure, but our involvement at least conveys the message that
they are not forgotten, that they are not carrying their burden
alone. Indeed, Jesus views these acts of mercy toward others
as extensions of our love for Him.

We benefit from these visits, too. Helping others restores a sense of purpose in our lives, a realization that our presence in this world makes a difference. At a deeper level, helping the sick also leads us to reflect on our own mortality. We come away from these exchanges with an appreciation for the frailty of life, and a gratitude for the good health we enjoy.

Despite all these positive outcomes, some Christians shy away from visiting the sick. Why?

In some cases, sadly, people simply don't care. They shrug off the pain of others with a casual "that's too bad," nothing more. The only cure for this brand of selfishness is a recalibration of our faith. Remember, it's Jesus we are neglecting here.

Others claim they are too busy. Jobs, family obligations, household chores, and a host of other activities crowd out time that ought to go toward helping others. But we make time for whatever is important to us. If we recognized the value of this good work, we would find the time to do it.

Others avoid this work because they feel awkward in the presence of the afflicted, especially if the sickness is serious. "I don't know what to say" is a familiar refrain. But we learn what to say in these circumstances the same way we learn how to ride a bicycle—with practice. Just jump in and do it.

There is one more excuse I have heard several times over the years, especially when dealing with terminally ill friends: "I want to remember them the way they used to be." But think about it: Whose welfare are we looking after with that kind of response? *We're thinking only of ourselves, not the sick person,* and that attitude turns the whole affair upside down. Our duty is to help others in their affliction, not to protect our own comfort zone. Think about it: I'm concerned about how I will remember the dying person—*but how will the dying person remember me?*

Visiting the sick is, in every sense of the word, the Lord's work, a simple act of faith that all of us can perform. Let us be busy in this good work, with cheerfulness and enthusiasm.

Christianity in Contagion

Just as a light shines brightest in darkness, so the religion of Christ stands out best in times of gloom and despair. A pandemic is such a time.

"'When did we see You sick, or in prison, and come to You?' And the King will answer and say to them, 'Assuredly, I say to you, inasmuch as you did it to one of the least of these My brethren, you did it to Me'" (Matt. 25:39-40).

৵৽৵

During the first few centuries of Christianity's existence, its future hung in the balance. Few in number and hounded by their pagan enemies, the fate of the young religion was uncertain. But by the reign of Constantine (AD 306-337), its status as the dominant religious movement in the Roman Empire was settled. How did a new religion with no power, no money, and no political connections pull this off?

At least part of the answer lay in Christianity's emphasis on *social behavior* as a major component of its piety. Jesus taught His disciples to do good to others in their personal lives, to be generous, hospitable, and compassionate not only to one another, but also to their neighbors. In many of His teachings—His description of the final judgment, the parable of the Good Samaritan, the Sermon on the Mount, and so on—Jesus outlined the social contract that Christians sign up for when they embrace this new faith. Like their Master, disciples of Jesus are servants of humanity.

In those early centuries, that kind of big-heartedness had an impact on the pagan world in which the Christians lived. Twice in a hundred years—first in AD 165-180 and again in

AD 249-262—the Roman Empire was swept by deadly plagues that killed millions. In a series of books covering this period in history (*The Rise of Christianity* [1996], *Cities of God* [2006], *The Triumph of Christianity* [2011]), sociologist Rodney Stark documents the sharp contrast in the responses to these plagues among pagans and Christians. Among the pagans, the sick and dying were left to fend for themselves, which meant almost certain death for the victims. Among the Christians, however, the sick and dying—including many of their pagan neighbors—were tended to and cared for. Some of the Christian caretakers lost their lives in the process, but many more Christians and pagans were nursed back to health by their sacrifice. That kindness was not forgotten, and afterward resulted in widespread conversions to a religion that was clearly superior to paganism.

Today, as we all struggle to manage the impact of another contagion, we need to remember the teachings of our Savior and the examples of our predecessors. Rather than huddle in our homes in fear and anxiety, Christians need to be on the forefront of showing compassion to a population that is suffering. For all its danger, Covid is less of a threat than an opportunity. Let us not waste it.

Why This Waste?

When money becomes the primary measure by
which we evaluate our options, we lose sight of
what is truly important and make poor decisions.

*When Jesus was in Bethany at the house of Simon the
leper, a woman came to Him having an alabaster flask of very
costly fragrant oil, and she poured it on His head as He sat
at the table. But when His disciples saw it, they were indig-
nant, saying, "Why this waste? For this fragrant oil might
have been sold for much and given to the poor." But when
Jesus was aware of it, He said to them, "Why do you trouble
the woman? For she has done a good work for Me" (Matt.
26:6-10).*

∽∾

John identifies this woman as Mary, the sister of Martha
and Lazarus (Jn. 12:1-3). He also tells us that the fragrant oil
was a pound in weight—probably about twelve ounces by
our measure. This oil was rare, so such a large quantity of it
would have been very expensive. Judas pegged the value at
about three hundred denarii, roughly a year's wages (Jn.
12:5). So when Mary anointed Jesus with it, a lot of money
disappeared.

The apostles were shocked by this extravagance. Like
most men, they looked at this strictly from a monetary perspective. The oil could have accomplished much more if it
had been sold and the proceeds given to the poor. A year's
wages could have made quite a dent in the local poverty
problem. Mark's account says that "they criticized her
sharply" (Mk. 14:5).

Jesus, however, saw Mary's sacrifice through a different lens. "You have the poor with you always" (v. 11) is another way of saying, there will be other opportunities to help the poor. But with Jesus' departure drawing near, Mary would have only one chance to express her love for Him. In a culture where women were marginalized, there wasn't much she could do. But she did have this flask of precious oil (perhaps inventory from a family business?), so she "did what she could" (Mk. 14:8) and anointed Jesus' body with the entire amount. It is likely that a few days later at His trial, His body still gave off the fragrance from this generous gift. Mary was literally preparing Him for burial, and Jesus honored her for it (Matt. 26:12-13).

The reaction of the apostles—"Why this waste?"—speaks directly to our own skewed value system. When financial considerations are the only bottom line in our decision-making, we, too, will pass up opportunities to serve the Lord in favor of more mundane pursuits.

For example, the Lord wants us to spend time meeting with our brethren, encouraging and strengthening one another (Heb. 10:24-25). The man with his eyes on the world looks at that and says, "Why this waste? I could be working overtime or making progress on a DIY project!"

The Lord wants us to give generously to His work (2 Cor. 9:6-7). But too many people say, "Why this waste? That money could buy a better car or a nicer home or a more exotic vacation!"

A young woman decides to devote her life to service as a full time wife and mother. Her feminist sisters deride her, saying, "Why this waste? Your real potential is found in the workplace, not in the home!"

What is important in life is not always measured by money. We need to get our priorities straight by God's standard, and make our choices accordingly.

How to Forsake Christ

We do not have to publicly denounce our Savior
in order to forsake Him. Running away from our
convictions will serve Satan's purpose just as well.

---

*Then Jesus said to them, "All of you will be made to
stumble because of Me this night, for it is written: 'I will
strike the shepherd, and the sheep of the flock will be scattered'" (Matt. 26:31).*

*Then all the disciples forsook Him and fled (Matt.
26:56).*

ঙ৽ঌ

Following Jesus' arrest, the apostles did not denounce
Him. Unlike His enemies, they did not attack, curse, beat, or
spit upon Him. Instead, they simply ran away. When pressed
to identify himself as a disciple of Jesus, Simon Peter denied
that he even knew Him. The text bluntly summarizes their
behavior: They "forsook Him and fled."

The apostles were not evil men. They loved Jesus, and
were convinced that He was their Messiah. They were horrified at what was happening to Him. But none of them had the
courage to stand up and be counted when it really mattered.
Consequently, Jesus had to face His fate alone, abandoned by
those who were closest to Him.

In an age when being a faithful Christian is no longer a
resume enhancement but a badge of shame, we face a similar
dilemma. Cultural institutions are applying enormous pressure to force our faith underground. The most obvious
example is in the area of sexual morality. Christians are now
required, not merely to tolerate sexual depravity, but to cele-

brate it, endorse it, and promote it. Any word of opposition to this narrative will result in ridicule, censure, banishment from social media, loss of employment, even civil penalties. We are fast approaching a time when public defense of the Biblical model of sexuality will be criminalized.

We now stand where the apostles once stood: Do we openly defend our Lord and His teaching on this vital topic, whatever the cost? Or do we meekly go along with this cultural tsunami and thereby save our skins? Like the apostles, we do not have to denounce Christ or repudiate our faith to forsake Him. All we have to do is run away.

Following the resurrection, when the apostles finally realized the larger scope of God's plan, they redeemed themselves by becoming fearless apologists for the faith. Most of them died a martyr's death in defense of what they believed. The question that confronts us today is not, "What do we believe?" but rather, "Are we willing to stand up for what we believe?"

Jesus awaits our answer.

Silence of the Lamb

It is important that we defend our convictions, but sometimes it is a pointless exercise that serves no useful purpose. A dignified silence is better.

The high priest arose and said to Him, "Do You answer nothing? What is it these men testify against You?" But Jesus kept silent (Matt. 26:62-63).

And while He was being accused by the chief priests and elders, He answered nothing. Then Pilate said to Him, "Do You not hear how many things they testify against You?" But He answered him not one word, so that the governor marveled greatly (Matt. 27:12-14).

੭৽৻৶

Jesus was an articulate speaker, never at a loss for words. Whatever the occasion, whether among friends or critics, in small intimate groups or large multitudes, He knew exactly the right thing to say. During the week preceding His arrest and trial, Jesus again and again demonstrated His ability to embarrass His critics in debate.

But when Jesus was on trial for His life before the authorities, He remained silent in response to the scurrilous charges hurled against Him. If ever His sharp mind and golden tongue needed to be employed to good effect, surely this was the occasion. His rhetoric could have mopped the floor with these people. Yet He said nothing. Why?

There are some arguments we will never win—not because we do not have the truth, but because our antagonist does not have an honest heart. Trying to reason with such people accomplishes nothing except to raise our own frustration level. Not only are we wasting our time trying to press our point, we could be setting the stage for a catastrophic blowup that will hurt everyone involved. In that scenario, no one wins—not even truth.

We are not obligated to engage every squabble that is dumped in our lap. Sometimes the best course of action is to just walk away, especially when our critic has demonstrated that he has no interest in a fair and honest discussion, and is only spoiling for a fight. Solomon summed up the principle succinctly: There is "a time to keep silence, and a time to speak" (Eccl. 3:7). Wisdom is the ability to know the difference.

Jesus' silence on this occasion was not a sign of weakness, but of dignified strength. His fate was already sealed, and He knew it; nothing He could say in that moment would alter the outcome. He was confident in His convictions, and chose to let God sort out who was right and who was wrong. His enemies could gloat in their victory, but He knew that history would render a more honorable verdict. And Jesus would not have to say a word.

We should learn to do the same.

We Are All Barabbas

When Jesus died, a condemned man went free.
His pardon serves as a metaphor for the rest of us,
who must choose how we will use our freedom.

And at that time they had a notorious prisoner called Barabbas. Therefore, when they had gathered together, Pilate said to them, "Whom do you want me to release to you? Barabbas, or Jesus who is called Christ?" But the chief priests and elders persuaded the multitudes that they should ask for Barabbas and destroy Jesus. The governor answered and said to them, "Which of the two do you want me to release to you?" They said, "Barabbas!" . . . Then he released Barabbas to them; and when he had scourged Jesus, he delivered Him to be crucified (Matt. 27:16-21, 26).

§∾§

Matthew calls Barabbas "a notorious prisoner." Luke and Mark identify his crimes as murder and rebellion (Lk. 23:19; Mk. 15:7), while John adds that he was a robber (Jn. 18:40). These brief descriptions tell us everything we need to know about Barabbas. He was a man without scruples, a sociopath who deserved the punishment coming his way. He languished on death row, awaiting a hideous death on a Roman cross.

So when the Jews, appealing to an annual Passover tradition, demanded that Pilate crucify Jesus and release Barabbas, the governor was shocked. At worst, Jesus was a harmless crackpot, certainly not in the same league with a hardened criminal like Barabbas. By every measure of justice, Jesus should have been released, and Barabbas put to death. But the people were adamant that Barabbas be set free, and Jesus be crucified. So rather than preside over a riot, Pilate did the politically expedient thing and yielded to their demand. Jesus was destroyed, and a convicted insurrectionist/murderer/thief was released back into society.

When Barabbas awoke that morning, he was guilty and condemned. His fate was sealed, and he was powerless to escape it. Yet due to developments entirely outside his control, another man was executed in his place, and he was given his freedom. Pardoned. Exonerated. Officially declared "not guilty." He was a free man!

Did Barabbas have any appreciation for this remarkable turn of events in his life? Neither history nor tradition tells us what he did with his freedom. Did he return to his former life of crime, and die on a Roman cross somewhere else for a new set of offenses? Or did he use this act of mercy as an opportunity to start a new life? A 1961 epic film starring Anthony Quinn depicts Barabbas as a troubled man who, near the end of his life, finally recognized the role that God's grace had played in his life. But that's pure speculation. We simply don't know what happened to him.

Perhaps the end of his story is missing because we are the ones who must write it. *We are all Barabbas*—guilty, condemned, and doomed to face the wrath of God for our sins. Like Barabbas, with no input from ourselves, Jesus took our place and bore the punishment that should have fallen on us. God "made Him who knew no sin to be sin for us" (2 Cor. 5:21). He paid the price, and we got the freedom.

But what are we doing with that freedom? Has this gift of grace moved us to do something meaningful with our lives? Do we feel any sense of gratitude for the sacrifice that rescued us from divine judgment? Or are we indifferent to God's mercy, careless of the great debt we owe Him? Are we living our lives as though nothing has changed, still slaves to our passions?

We are all Barabbas—set free, yet owing so much.

The Power of Doubt

God wants us to believe without doubting. That confidence is possible, but ironically, it requires that we first struggle with serious doubts.

When they saw Him, they worshiped Him; but some doubted (Matt. 28:17).

৩৯৩

This account describes an incident in Galilee some time after the resurrection of Jesus (v. 16). We know that immediately following the resurrection, even His apostles struggled to accept the truth that He had come back from the dead. The response of doubting Thomas ("Unless I see . . . I will not believe," Jn. 20:25) illustrates the depth of their despair during those first few days (see also Mk. 16:11,13).

But at this late date described by Matthew, we would expect the disciples of Jesus to have already reconciled their minds to the reality of what had happened. Yet that was not the case. Even after numerous encounters with Jesus over several weeks, they still had trouble accepting the fact that He was really, literally, back from the dead.

It's easy for us who accept the resurrection as an historical fact—two thousand years after the event—to criticize these men as dense or slow-witted. But we did not personally walk with Jesus for three years as they did. We did not experience the shame and devastation of having all our dreams shattered by Roman nails as they did. The loss of faith these men experienced was total, and it was with great difficulty that they eventually came to believe again.

But they did believe again. And the new faith they found was not like the old. Before, they believed in a political Messiah who could save their nation. Now, they believed in a resurrected Son of God who could save the world. Their confidence sparked a spiritual revolution that swept the Roman Empire, and the same men who once had lost all faith would fearlessly challenge kings and rulers with the courage of their convictions: "We cannot but speak the things which we have seen and heard" (Ac. 4:20). The doubt was totally gone.

The metamorphosis of these men from timid losers to pillars of courage is one of the strongest evidences of the veracity of Jesus' resurrection. No other explanation can account for such an improbable change. The strength of their later conviction is underscored by the despair out of which it grew.

The story of the apostles' journey of faith illustrates the role that doubt can play in our own struggles to believe. Today, as in the first century, many people scoff at the idea of worshiping a crucified itinerant rabbi who supposedly arose from the dead. It is such a preposterous story upon which to build a religion. But that is precisely how the Lord intended it to be. Even those who eventually come to accept the story as true must struggle with the implications of that fact. It is through the process of dealing with these doubts that a real and lasting faith can emerge.

In all my years of watching people make this conversion, I have noticed a curious phenomenon: Those who quickly accept the message with a minimum of study or thought often don't stick around for long. In their hearts, they never really wrestled with the meaning of the new faith they embraced, so their conversion was shallow at best. But those who resisted the message, who fought against its demands before surrendering, usually become the strongest believers. Their faith was hardened in the furnace of doubt.

Holy Spirit Baptism

Holy Spirit baptism is a Biblical concept, but the evidence suggests it had a special purpose and limited application. No one experiences it today.

"I indeed baptized you with water, but He will baptize you with the Holy Spirit" (Mk. 1:8).

"John truly baptized with water, but you shall be baptized with the Holy Spirit not many days from now" (Ac. 1:5).

"Then I remembered the word of the Lord, how He said, 'John indeed baptized with water, but you shall be baptized with the Holy Spirit'" (Ac. 11:16).

෨෮

Baptism is an immersion, the act of being submerged or completely overwhelmed by something. So to be baptized with water is to be submerged or "buried" in water (Rom. 6:4). In the same way, to experience a baptism of suffering (Matt. 20:22) is to be overwhelmed with affliction.

The Holy Spirit is that aspect of Deity that embodies God's power in the physical world. The Spirit "moves" (Gen. 1:2), "speaks" (Matt. 10:20), and empowers human beings to do things they ordinarily could not do (Judg. 14:6; 1 Cor. 12:7-11). "Holy Spirit baptism," therefore, is an experience in which the Holy Spirit totally overwhelms a person with His power, providing convincing evidence of God's presence. John the Baptist promised that Jesus would extend that experience to some.

There are many references to the miraculous work of the Holy Spirit among the believers in the first century church (Ac. 8:6-7, 13; 1 Cor. 12-14; Gal. 3:5). But these widespread "spiritual gifts" were limited in scope, and were conveyed only through the laying on of the apostles' hands (Ac. 8:17-18; 19:6). A major part of the Spirit's work in these gifts was to reveal the message of salvation that the apostles and prophets preached (1 Pet. 1:12; Eph. 3:5; 1 Cor. 12:3).

There are only two cases in which a *baptism* with the Holy Spirit is said to have occurred. The first involved the apostles, shortly after Jesus' resurrection. Repeating John's promise, Jesus had told them they would "be baptized with the Holy Spirit not many days from now" (Ac. 1:5). His promise was fulfilled a few days later at Pentecost, when "they were all filled with the Holy Spirit" and began to speak in other tongues (Ac. 2:1-4f). The supernatural events of that day led several thousand Jews to respond to Peter's message.

The second case occurred several years later with the conversion of Cornelius and his household, the first Gentiles to obey the gospel. As Peter preached to them, "the Holy Spirit fell upon all those who heard the word" and they began to "speak with tongues and magnify God" (Ac. 10:44-46). Later, Peter explained to his colleagues in Jerusalem that "the Holy Spirit fell upon them, as upon us at the beginning. Then I remembered the word of the Lord, how He said, 'John indeed baptized with water, but you shall be baptized with the Holy Spirit'" (Ac. 11:15-16). Peter had to go all the way back to Pentecost to find something similar to what he had seen. This event demonstrated that the Gentiles were accepted by God through the gospel without first becoming Jews.

To summarize: Holy Spirit baptism occurred when the gospel was first offered to the Jews (at Pentecost), and when the gospel was first offered to the Gentiles (the household of Cornelius). Years later, Paul wrote that there is "one baptism" (Eph. 4:5), an obvious reference to water baptism (Ac. 2:38; Ac. 8:36-38; Ac. 10:47-48; Eph. 5:26; Heb. 10:22). We conclude, therefore, that Holy Spirit baptism was a temporary phenomenon with a targeted purpose: to open the gates of the kingdom to the Jews and to the Gentiles. Once that purpose was achieved, it never occurred again.

Do You Not Care?

It's well that we believe in Jesus as the Son of God. But unless that faith gives us peace and strength in the storms of life, it is shallow and worthless.

Now when they had left the multitude, they took Him along in the boat as He was. . . . And a great windstorm arose, and the waves beat into the boat, so that it was already filling. But He was in the stern, asleep on a pillow. And they awoke Him and said to Him, "Teacher, do You not care that we are perishing?" Then He arose and rebuked the wind, and said to the sea, "Peace, be still!" And the wind ceased and there was a great calm. But He said to them, "Why are you so fearful? How is it that you have no faith?" (Mk. 4:36-40).

လပ

In this little story of Jesus crossing the Sea of Galilee with His disciples, we find a metaphor for the voyage through life in which each of us is engaged. The storms of life are inevitable; but it is how we respond to those storms that makes all the difference.

First, consider the behavior of Jesus in the midst of the storm. The winds were howling, the waves were pounding, and water was already beginning to fill the boat; yet Jesus was sound asleep on a pillow at the rear of the boat, unfazed by the danger around Him. The disciples interpreted His casual demeanor as indifference: "Do You not care that we are perishing?" Of course, Jesus was not careless of the threat. The forces of nature were terrible, but Jesus had full faith in the power of God to deal with the situation as He saw fit. His life was in the Father's hands; what was there to fear? Armed with that comforting thought, He could sleep soundly through the worst storms. He had complete confidence that everything would turn out okay.

Now look at the behavior of the disciples. Of all the places in the world they could have been at that very moment, we would think they were in the best possible location—in the very presence of the Son of God Himself. That fact alone should have been enough to comfort them. Yet all they could see was the savagery of the storm around them. After Jesus stilled the storm, He analyzed their condition in two terms: they were "fearful"—terrified, overcome with anxiety and dread; and had "no faith"—no confidence, no trust, no expectation of divine help.

Theoretically, these disciples accepted that Jesus was the Son of God. But that belief was only an abstraction; their confession had not yet grown into a deep conviction that would transform their whole outlook on life. Jesus was all-powerful, yes—but not in their lives.

Did Jesus care whether or not they perished? Of course He did! With only three words (two words in the original language), He quieted the storm and removed the danger. But His greater contribution was His gentle challenge to His disciples to re-examine their faith in times of crisis.

If our faith in God will not allow us to sleep confidently through the storms of life . . . then do we believe at all?

Notes From a Carpenter's Workshop

Jesus spent His early career working as a carpenter. Working with wood can also teach us a great deal about working with people.

"Is this not the carpenter, the Son of Mary, and brother of James, Joses, Judas, and Simon? And are not His sisters here with us?" So they were offended at Him (Mk. 6:3).

৩৽৵৻

Have you ever wondered why, of all the possible options available to Jesus when He took on human form, He choose the occupation of a *carpenter*? I used to wonder that, too, until a mid-life career change landed me unexpectedly in the role of a finish carpenter. I spent over three years driving nails and breathing sawdust before moving on to another occupation, but the lessons I learned during that time have proven invaluable in my later years, especially in my dealings with people. Here are some examples:

A good carpenter project begins with a good foundation. The floors and walls of a house must be square, plumb, and solid. If they aren't, corrections must be made to shore up the deficiencies. Otherwise, the finished work won't look right and will likely not function properly. Likewise, working with people first requires a good relationship based on respect and dignity. (See Tit. 3:1-2.)

The right tool must be used for the right job. In some applications a scroll saw is more appropriate than a circular saw. In other situations, it's the reverse. A carpenter can create a real mess if he doesn't know the difference. In the same manner, working with people requires knowledge of a wide range of tools: private counseling versus public rebuke, incentives rather than punishments. Wisdom is knowing when to use the best approach for a given situation. (See Jude 22-23.)

Like different varieties of wood, different people must be handled differently. Oak is hard and can take a pounding to force it into place; pine is soft, and must be handled gently to avoid damage. Working with people involves dealing with all sorts of personality types and backgrounds, and the wise friend will treat every relationship as unique, and adapt accordingly. (See 1 Cor. 9:20-22.)

The most effective skills are learned through experience, not instruction. Working with wood requires a certain "feel" that can't be easily explained in words. Only by making thousands of cuts and driving thousands of nails can a carpenter develop that innate sense that tells him a job is going "right" or "wrong." Likewise, the best way to learn how to deal with people is to just plunge in and do it. A few verbal pointers along the way are helpful, but expertise is gained chiefly by spending time dealing with others and their issues. (See Heb. 5:14.)

Like wood putty, love covers a multitude of sins. Ideally, working with wood should involve zero mistakes—every joint is perfect, and every piece of wood is free of blemishes. But that ideal is not reality. Mistakes are inevitable, so even the best carpenter must occasionally use a little putty to mask flaws in his work. In the same way, even the best of friends understand that nobody is perfect. They know they must love each other despite their imperfections. (See 1 Pet. 4:8.)

As a carpenter, Jesus worked in an occupation that was best suited to His life's ultimate mission: "I will build My church" (Matt. 16:18). We don't have to be carpenters to learn the lessons that made His work so successful.

Jesus, the Blue Collar Guy

Jesus' working-class background gave Him a unique perspective on the lives of the ordinary people He came to save.

"Is this not the carpenter, the Son of Mary, and brother of James, Joses, Judas, and Simon? And are not His sisters here with us?" So they were offended at Him. (Mk. 6:3)

"Is this not the carpenter's son?" (Matt. 13:55)

৩০৫

We are accustomed to talking about Jesus the teacher, or Jesus the Savior, or Jesus the miracle worker, or Jesus the Son of God. But for the first fifteen years or so of his adult life Jesus labored as a carpenter, a trade that he learned from his earthly father, an arrangement that was typical of Jewish families. Jesus, in other words, was just an ordinary working-class guy who made a living with His hands. (Some commentators suggest that "carpenter" should be translated more generically as "builder," and that He was more likely a stone mason. Whichever trade He worked in does not materially alter the lessons that follow here.)

That detail in His background reveals a great deal about how Jesus was so successful in His later ministry. As a carpenter, He learned several important life skills. Consider a few examples:

He learned a strong work ethic. He knew what it was like to get up early, work hard, get His hands dirty, have his body caked with sweat and sawdust, and meet deadlines. When it came time to begin His ministry, His blue-collar work habits served Him well.

Jesus learned how to deal with people. He no doubt had frequent contact with customers, vendors, and co-workers. His work involved all the usual hassles that come with dealing with people, giving Him an appreciation for what others have to deal with in their daily lives. Jesus was no ivory-tower academic pontificating on things He knew nothing about.

As a carpenter, *Jesus learned patience.* Anyone who has worked with wood can testify to the frustrations that usually accompany that craft. Different species of wood have different properties requiring different techniques to shape. Splits, splinters, and smashed thumbs just come with the territory. Jesus learned how to put up with all those frustrations, always toward the goal of making something useful.

Jesus also enjoyed the satisfaction of creating things. We have no idea what He built. Houses? Carts? Furniture? Tools? Whatever His product line, Jesus knew the gratification of taking a stack of raw materials and creating something of value that others could use and admire.

It was the ordinariness of Jesus' occupation that offended so many people, especially among the ruling class. How could a man from such an humble background be an authoritative rabbi? So when they rejected Him, it seems fitting that He would die on a Roman cross—an implement of wood fashioned by a carpenter.

Even in death, Jesus' greatest construction project was yet to come. It was Jesus the carpenter who said, "I will build my church" (Matt. 16:18). Drawing on all the skills He learned as a carpenter, He built it, and two thousand years later it is still going strong.

What other craftsman can say that about his handiwork?

Come and Rest a While

Humans were created to work, but too much work will wear us down. God also intends that we give ourselves a little time off to relax and refresh.

He said to them, "Come aside by yourselves to a deserted place and rest a while." For there were many coming and going, and they did not even have time to eat (Mk. 6:31).

‿❦‿

Jesus gave this instruction to His apostles following the conclusion of the Limited Commission (v. 7-13). He had sent them out two by two to preach and heal the sick, and their work was so successful that they became overwhelmed with the multitudes that followed them. Their days were packed with activity, leaving no time to sit down to a leisurely meal. Jesus knew that this pace would wear His apostles down, so He ordered them to take a break: "Come aside by yourselves to a deserted place and rest a while." They needed a vacation, even if it was God's work they were doing.

Humans were created by God to be busy, active, and productive. The Bible stresses the value of work as the source of personal and societal success (2 Thess. 3:6-12; Eph. 4:28; Prov. 10:4-5; 12:11; 22:29; 27:23-27). Even in the perfect Garden of Eden, Adam had work to do ("tend and keep it," Gen. 2:15). The lazy man will find no sympathy from God.

But whatever rewards work provides us, it must never become our god. Like the apostles we need to occasionally take a break to recharge our batteries.

In ancient Israel, this was codified in the Law of Moses. The Ten Commandments instructed the Israelites to "Remember the Sabbath Day, to keep it holy" (Ex. 20:8). Contrary to a modern misconception, this was not a day of worship, but a day of rest: "In it, you shall do no work" (v. 10). The Law also mandated a variety of feast days, some lasting for a week or more, that involved taking a break from the normal work routine. Whatever the religious significance behind these holidays, the practical effect was to give God's people time off from the daily grind, and allow them opportunities to relax, enjoy their families, and refresh their physical and mental condition.

This principle was reinforced in the various Sabbath controversies that Jesus encountered during His ministry. The Pharisees had turned the simple Sabbath law into a byzantine set of regulations that became a burden rather than a blessing. Jesus rebuked their legalistic application of this law by reminding them of the original intent: "The Sabbath was made for man, and not man for the Sabbath" (Mk. 2:27). Stated another way, humans need a periodic day of rest.

Paul was a tireless ambassador for Christ, but he, too, recognized the need for taking a break. During his third missionary journey, he left his companions at Troas, and walked overland nineteen miles to Assos, where he rejoined his fellow travelers, who made the journey by ship (Ac. 20:13-14). The text gives no explanation for this personal detour, but those who have traveled this route say it's not hard to figure out. The road passes through beautiful coastal vistas, with the sea on one side and mountains on the other. Paul was simply using a couple of days to enjoy some much-needed R. & R., especially as he drew closer to Jerusalem and the crisis that likely awaited him there.

Whatever our occupation, it is in our best interest to balance work and pleasure in our lives. Schedule time to turn off the laptop, close the appointment book, put down the phone, and "rest a while."

A Fence Around the Law

In our eagerness to prevent people from violating God's word, we can go overboard and make laws where God made none. That does not honor God.

For the Pharisees and all the Jews do not eat unless they wash their hands in a special way, holding the tradition of the elders. When they come from the marketplace, they do not eat unless they wash. And there are many other things which they have received and hold, like the washing of cups, pitchers, copper vessels, and couches (Mk. 7:3-4).

৽৽

Mark, writing the gospel story for a Roman audience, offers this brief explanation of the oral Jewish legal system. But his summary does not do justice to the breathtaking scope of this law, or the immense burden it placed on the ordinary Jew trying to serve God.

To grasp the magnitude of the problem, we need to look at how this system developed. After the return from Babylonian captivity in the fifth-century BC, the rabbis set out to protect the Law from the careless attitudes that had caused the nation to neglect it in previous centuries. So they began compiling their deliberations on the meaning and application of the Law. These compilations, later known as the *Mishnah*, were believed to represent the intent of the original Law handed down at Mt. Sinai.

Their purpose was expressed in an early tractate entitled *Pirqei Avot* ("Sayings of the Fathers"):

"Moses received the Torah from Sinai, and he delivered it to Joshua, and Joshua to the elders, and the

elders to the prophets, and the prophets delivered it to the men of the Great Synagogue. They said three things: Be deliberate in judgment; and raise up many disciples; and make a fence around the Torah" (1:1).

Notice that last statement, "make a fence around the Torah." In order to protect the Torah (the Law of Moses) from violation, the rabbis erected a "fence" of additional regulations around it. In theory, these additional regulations would prevent people from even getting close to violating the Law. Over time, of course, this "fence" became indistinguishable from the Law itself.

Even by itself, the Law of Moses was a complex collection of civil and religious rules that was a challenge to any man (the apostle Peter called it "a yoke which neither we nor our fathers were able to bear," Ac. 15:10). But this fence erected by the rabbis was infinitely more complex, and hopelessly unobservable. The list of Sabbath regulations alone was a dense jungle of legalistic trivia that made the day of rest anything but. Mark's reference to the purification of utensils and furniture is another example of the bewildering burden that these traditions imposed on everyday Jewish life.

This is the legal system that Jesus challenged. He insisted that commentaries on divine law by pious men ("traditions") do not constitute God's law for everyone else. It's that distinction that got Him in trouble with the Jewish leaders.

The tendency to build a fence around the Law is still with us today. Devout men spend their lives studying every possible angle of every detail of the gospel, and seek to impose their conclusions on the rest of us. Their conclusions may be worth our consideration, but they should never be taken as God's Law. Whatever the good intentions of human fences, they obscure the beautiful simplicity of the gospel.

An Evil Eye

How we look at the good fortune of others says much about the condition of our own heart. We must train our hearts to appreciate what is good.

*"From within, out of the heart of men, proceed evil thoughts, adulteries, fornications, murders, thefts, covetousness, wickedness, deceit, lewdness, **an evil eye**, blasphemy, pride, foolishness. All these evil things come from within and defile a man" (Mk. 7:21-23).*

୬୭

In the NKJV, "an evil eye" is a literal translation of two Greek words. The expression is meaningless to the modern English reader, but to the original Jewish audience, it made perfect sense, because "evil eye" is a Hebrew idiom for *envy*. The same idiom is used in Matt. 20:15, where the master explains his reason for giving his eleventh-hour hires the same wages as the those who labored all day: "Is your *eye evil* because I am good?" In other words, "Are you envious because I was generous to those who were hired late?" For the sake of clarity, most modern translations simply drop the idiom and substitute the word "envy" in these passages (ESV, NASB, NIV, RSV, NLT).

Curiously, the Hebrew figure of speech is not all that different from the etymology of our English equivalent. "Envy" comes from the Latin word *invidia*, "to look against"; that is, "to look with ill will at another person because of what he is or has" (Hendrickson). To envy another is to view him with suspicion, ascribing dark motives to his good fortune.

Envy, to put it simply, describes *a harmful way of looking at those who are doing better than us*. With little or no evidence, we view their favored position as the result of some sinister motive. We see their good fortune as a threat to our own well-being. If we are suffering some adversity, then those who are doing better must be to blame somehow. The problem, of course, is that envy invents malevolence where none exists, and turns others into caricatures of who they really are. Our dark opinions of others are often lies that we conjure up in our own minds.

Both in our personal lives and in the broader culture, envy is the unspoken cause behind so many of our current social problems. Entire demographic groups are turning against one another because of a manufactured rage rooted in envy. Others have unfair advantages over me/us, so they must pay for their villainy! The end result is mutual destruction.

Jesus called envy an "evil thing" that defiles us. If we're serious about eliminating it from our character, we must replace it with something else. Paul gave the cure in 1 Cor. 13:4—"Love does not envy." We must train ourselves to look at others with eyes full of love and appreciation, even when their good fortune puts us at a disadvantage.

The only way to keep envy from corrupting our soul is to fill our heart with good will toward all.

What Do You Think?

Opinions about who Jesus was range from the crazy to the sublime to the indifferent. The most important opinion, however, is my own.

Now Jesus and His disciples went out to the towns of Caesarea Philippi; and on the road He asked His disciples, saying to them, "Who do men say that I am?" So they answered, "John the Baptist; but some say, Elijah; and others, one of the prophets." He said to them, "But who do you say that I am?" Peter answered and said to Him, "You are the Christ" (Mk. 8:27-29).

৩৯৵৶

I like to think of this account as the first public opinion survey in history. The survey consisted of only one question: Who do you think Jesus is? Of course, like most public opinion polls, the answers were all over the map. Some people believed Jesus was John the Baptist returned from the dead. Others thought He was Elijah, the prophetic archetype. Others pegged Him to be some lesser prophet. When you depend on public opinion to tell you the truth, this is the kind of incoherent drivel you'll get.

But Jesus' follow-up question to His apostles was more personal: "Who do *you* say that I am?" What everyone else thought about Jesus was irrelevant. Each man among the apostles had to decide for himself what he believed about Jesus.

The same challenge confronts every one of us today. It really doesn't matter what public opinion polls say about Jesus. It doesn't matter what our parents or grandparents thought about Him. What our church or elders or preacher think about Jesus cannot serve as a proxy for our faith. At the end of the day, each one of us has to make our own personal decision concerning who Jesus is and how He influences our manner of life.

For what we choose to think about Jesus indeed determines how we live. Is He the Son of God who deserves my complete allegiance, whatever the cost? Or is He a deluded impostor who should ignored? Or is He just a spiritual rock star whose poster hangs on my bedroom wall, but is otherwise ignored in my daily life?

Furthermore, what we believe about Jesus is shaped largely by the source to which we look for our beliefs. For many of us, our view of Jesus is based on the shifting winds of popular folklore. That's why the "faith" of many people is shallow, weak, erratic, inconsistent. Jesus-the-myth is a mere token, having little or no influence in charting the direction of their lives.

For Simon Peter, the answer was deeper: "You are the Christ." He still had some unresolved questions, but he knew enough to realize that he was in the presence of a Man unlike any other. What he believed about Jesus was forged in the furnace of intellectual struggle, and that conviction altered his destiny.

Who do *you* say Jesus is? Your life is your answer.

Self-Denial

The desire to follow Jesus is admirable, but that commitment comes at a cost. We cannot be His disciple without denying everything we have.

When He had called the people to Himself, with His disciples also, He said to them, "Whoever desires to come after Me, let him deny himself, and take up his cross, and follow Me" (Mk. 8:34).

৵৽৵

As humans, our interaction with the world around us is limited to what we experience with our physical senses. It is natural, therefore, that we evaluate everything in terms of how it impacts us. As we grow up we develop psychological filters that allow us to screen out anything that calls our performance into question, and highlight whatever makes us look good. Over time, we become skilled at promoting ourselves, honoring ourselves, enriching ourselves, protecting ourselves, pleasing ourselves. But the one thing we are not equipped to do well is to *deny* ourselves.

When Jesus walked among us, He challenged that paradigm, preaching a message that contradicts everything we thought we knew about life. We are here to serve, not to be served. It is more blessed to give than to receive. We are to esteem others as more important than ourselves. We must humble ourselves and exalt others. That message was as radical then as it is now. Few understood it then; few grasp it today.

But two thousand years of history has confirmed the wisdom of what Jesus taught. Every social environment populated by factions elbowing for advantage inevitably ends up quarreling and dividing, usually with somebody getting hurt. But on those rare occasions when a community comes together on the foundation that Jesus taught, something beautiful emerges: cooperation, compassion, healing, kindness, sharing, peace. This is what humanity ought to be! But those conditions can only flourish in a population that has learned the art of self-denial.

Denying self is not easy. Jesus said, "let him deny himself, *and take up his cross.*" That's the language of sacrifice and suffering. If we are going to take up Jesus' challenge, then something in our life has to go. What will it be? My income? My home? My investments? My comforts? My relationships? My pleasures? My time? Until we can identify something in our lives that we have sacrificed to serve the Lord's interests, we have not yet learned the meaning of self-denial. And if we have not yet learned the meaning of self-denial, we are not yet following Jesus. Oh, we may wear the label and sing the songs, but we're still the one sitting on the throne of our heart. Jesus is nothing more than a token that we flash now and then to signal party affiliation.

To be a disciple of Jesus is to change one's whole perspective on the purpose of life. Have I learned that lesson yet?

Questioning the Resurrection

Accepting the resurrection of Jesus as a real event in history can be a struggle for some. That's okay, so long as we are honest with the evidence.

Now as they came down from the mountain, He commanded them that they should tell no one the things they had seen, till the Son of Man had risen from the dead. So they kept this word to themselves, questioning what the rising from the dead meant (Mk. 9:9-10).

୨୦୧

Peter, James, and John had just witnessed the transfiguration of Jesus on an isolated mountain top. It must have been an awesome experience, but now Jesus was asking them to sit on the story until He had "risen from the dead." To us, Jesus' words make perfect sense, because we know what eventually happened. But to these disciples, this phrase was a riddle. They had no idea what was coming, so they assumed it must have some hidden meaning. A few months earlier, most of the crowds that followed Jesus became disillusioned and left; so perhaps Jesus was speaking of a "resurrection" of His popularity? Or maybe it was a code phrase for a new phase in His ministry? Whatever the meaning, it *couldn't* refer to a literal coming back from physical death. That was just impossible.

The disciples were honest, good-hearted men who can be excused for their ignorance of what was coming. It took them awhile, but they eventually learned what "rising from the dead" meant, and that which was once "impossible" became a bedrock truth for which they would gladly give their lives.

Today, however, there are still people who question what the resurrection means. These skeptics—some of whom still claim to be followers of Christ—argue that the resurrection did not really happen. Perhaps Jesus did not really die; He just fainted, and was resuscitated later. Or maybe the "witnesses" of His resurrection were so emotionally distraught that they only thought they saw Jesus. The real Jesus remained in His tomb, and is still there to this day. Whatever the explanation, this resurrection talk must have had some other meaning, because it's just impossible for someone to literally come back from the dead, right?

We can excuse the apostles for questioning the meaning of the resurrection, because it hadn't happened yet, and they had little information to go on. But these modern skeptics have the benefit of a collection of eyewitness testimony. The story of the transformation of a small group of defeated, disillusioned disciples into a disciplined cadre of shock troops that stormed the world, using nothing but words and good deeds, cannot be attributed to a lie. Something remarkable happened that profoundly changed these men.

In his defense before King Agrippa's court many years later, Paul challenged the skeptics' refusal to accept the resurrection: "Why should it be thought incredible by you that God raises the dead?" (Ac. 26:8). Why should the resurrection from the dead be any more incredible than the miracle of creation, or of conception and birth? We're dealing with God here; nothing is impossible for Him.

We do not criticize those who, when first confronted with the story of the resurrection, struggle with accepting it. Even the apostle Thomas had his doubts, and came to belief slowly (Jn. 20:24-29). But at some point, this struggle to believe can turn into mere stubbornness.

Jesus arose from the dead. That's a fact. Accept it, and let the implications of that fact change your life.

How Jesus Handled Frustration

If you get exasperated at the failures of others,
imagine how exasperated Jesus must have been.
His patience is an example for all of us.

---

*Then Jesus answered and said, "O faithless generation,
how long shall I be with you? How long shall I bear with
you?" (Mk. 9:19).*

ഏരു

Jesus had just come down from the mount of transfiguration, an experience that gave Him a rare insight into the glory
that awaited Him (v. 2-13). Now He was faced with an embarrassing PR disaster. His bumbling disciples had failed to
cast out a demon, and local scribes were making the most of
the failure. A large crowd witnessed the fiasco (v. 14-15).

Jesus' terse rebuke was not directed at the crowd, nor at
His critics, but at the disciples who had botched what should
have been a "routine" miracle. It was the closest Jesus ever
came to complaining about something that didn't go right.

We know the experience, don't we? A freak weather
event ruins what should have been a fun family outing. A co-
worker bungles an assignment that sets back an important
project. A spouse makes a dumb decision that hits the family
checkbook. Government incompetence. A broken shoelace. A
sister who sings off-key. Flat tires, mosquitoes, poor cus-
tomer service, messy kids—the list of things we complain
about could go on and on.

Jesus had plenty to complain about, too. The disappointment over disciples who were clueless or fickle—or both.
The injustice perpetrated by those in power, especially by

"experts" in the Law who should have known better. The ingratitude of people who received the benefit of His healing power, yet couldn't be bothered to tell Him "thank you." Most of all, the assignment of living and dying for a race of creatures who were too stupid and/or indifferent to appreciate what He was doing for them. And what did all this vexation earn Him? Death on a Roman cross.

Yes, Jesus had plenty to complain about. But He did not come to this world to complain about its imperfections. He came to save it. Whining about its faults would serve no useful purpose, so He patiently went about His work, trusting the final outcome to His Father.

In response to this disappointment, Jesus muttered, "How long shall I be with you?"—but He answered His own question with His life: However long it took to accomplish His Father's purpose. On this occasion, He channeled His frustration into useful action: He cast out the demon (v. 25-27), then used the experience as a teaching opportunity for His disciples (v. 28-29). And He kept on putting up with the frustrations until His task was completed.

As followers of Jesus, His example should influence how we respond to our own frustrations. They are opportunities to let the patience of God be seen in us. Let us follow His lead.

He Who Is Not Against Us

Party loyalty is a poor substitute for loyalty to
Christ. But it's easy to conflate the two, and
thereby lose sight of the real standard of faith.

---

*John said to Him, "Teacher, we saw someone casting out
demons in Your name, and we tried to hinder him because he
was not following us." But Jesus said, "Do not hinder him,
for there is no one who shall perform a miracle in My name,
and be able soon afterward to speak evil of Me. For he who
is not against us is for us" (Mk. 9:38-40).*

৵৽৻

We have no idea who this exorcist was, or how he came
to have his powers. Jesus occasionally met with people privately (for example, Nicodemus), so it's not unreasonable to
assume that Jesus had had some contact with this man in the
past. We just don't know. The apostles didn't know either,
and in their thinking, that was reason enough to put this impostor out of action. But the Lord saw things differently, and
set His apostles straight.

John and his fellow apostles were guilty of confusing
loyalty to the party with *loyalty to Christ*. They opposed the
exorcist because "he was not following *us*," not because he
was disobedient to Christ. The fact that the man was not
among the little group that traveled with Jesus—and was unknown by them—did not prove that he was a heretic. But the
apostles had developed a self-centered view of discipleship,
one that blinded them to the true standard of loyalty, namely,
faithfulness to the word of Christ. Had they bothered to
investigate the exorcist more carefully, they would have dis-

covered that he was not "against" them in any area of truth; thus, he was "for" them, just as they were for Jesus. They were co-workers for the Lord, laboring in different fields, unknown to one another.

The seed of the kingdom can sprout and take root anywhere there are honest people (Lk. 8:15). It is entirely possible today for individuals or even churches to exist as Christians, faithful to the Lord in every respect, yet have no direct historical link with the nineteenth-century Restoration Movement in America and the churches of Christ that sprang from that movement. If we were to stumble across such individuals or churches today, we would likely react to them the same way John reacted to the exorcist: "They are not following us." Our mistake would be the same as his. Other Christians do not have to be visibly linked to us in order to be faithful to Christ. True, their methods might be so different from ours that they would appear to be too radical to accept (no Wednesday night Bible study, song service *after* the sermon, raising hands in prayer, and so on). But our traditions are not the standard of truth. We should be willing to honestly investigate what others are doing in their service to the Lord. Who knows? We might learn that they are closer to the Lord's standard than we are.

God's people are an exclusive people (2 Cor. 6:14-18), but we must never use ourselves as the basis of exclusion.

Child-Like Faith

The innocent trust of little children can sometimes put them in danger. But on other occasions it can put the rest of us to shame.

Then they brought little children to Him, that He might touch them; but the disciples rebuked those who brought them. But when Jesus saw it, He was greatly displeased and said to them, "Let the little children come to Me, and do not forbid them; for of such is the kingdom of God. Assuredly, I say to you, whoever does not receive the kingdom of God as a little child will by no means enter it." And He took them up in His arms, put His hands on them, and blessed them (Mk. 10:13-16).

৩৹৶৹

Sometimes it takes the smallest encounter in life to teach us the most important lesson. The disciples of Jesus had one such encounter here.

As He approached Jerusalem for the last time, Jesus knew—and the disciples surely must have sensed—that a climax was drawing near. The tectonic pressures that had been building over the preceding months were reaching the breaking point, and this visit could trigger a final confrontation with the authorities. The very course of history could be altered by what was about to unfold.

So when some parents brought their children to Jesus for a blessing, the disciples saw them as a distraction. The Master had more important kingdom business to attend to; He couldn't be bothered with such a trivial matter. Like grumpy old men, they told the parents to get lost.

As usual, the disciples found out soon enough that *they* were the ones with distorted priorities. Jesus was "greatly displeased" with them. (That's not a good position to be in, is it?) He brought the whole show to a halt to spend some quality time with these kids. The foreboding thoughts that occupied the minds of the disciples were of no concern to these little children, nor to their parents. The sight of Jesus taking up these kids in His arms and blessing them—no doubt with the kind of smile that only toddlers can draw out of adults—must have perplexed the disciples.

Jesus used this occasion to teach His disciples—and us—an important lesson about the nature of faith. For all their innocent naivete, little children are the perfect model of *trust*. They exemplify the kind of whole-hearted confidence that ought to motivate us when we surrender our lives to God's control. Yes, this world is a cruel place; the storms of life can be harsh and bitter; there is so much we need to do, and so little time to do it. But we repose in the arms of One whose love washes away all our cares. Whatever the future may hold, He holds us in His care, and that is enough.

On those days when the burdens of life seem unbearable, we need to remember the image of Jesus in the shadow of the cross, holding those little children in His arms. That's you and me, brother, and we're in good hands. Believe it!

When Jesus Got Angry

Jesus' cleansing of the temple is a jarring image,
until we recognize *why* He took that action. There
is a time and place for righteous indignation.

---

*Then Jesus went into the temple and began to drive out
those who bought and sold in the temple, and overturned the
tables of the money changers and the seats of those who sold
doves. And He would not allow anyone to carry wares
through the temple. Then He taught, saying to them, "Is it not
written, 'My house shall be called a house of prayer for all
nations'? But you have made it a 'den of thieves'" (Mk.
11:15-17).*

❧

The popular image of Jesus as a sweet, gentle teacher
takes a hit when we read the story of Him cleansing the temple. Here is a man who was clearly angry at the crass
commercialization of the holy place, and took action to stop
it. How can we reconcile His behavior on this occasion with
His message of love and reconciliation?

First, we must understand the unique circumstances surrounding this event. The temple was a large complex of
courtyards with the Holy of Holies occupying the innermost
section. The area that Jesus cleansed was the Court of the
Gentiles, a large outer compound into which anyone could
come, even Gentiles.

But if any Gentiles came into this temple compound
seeking connection with the true God, it could not be found
in the cacophony of noise that overwhelmed the senses, especially during Passover week. Moneychangers, livestock

brokers and their animals, and thousands of hapless customers turned the house of prayer into a raucous trading exchange.

To make matters worse, the authorities who ran the temple grounds (the high priest and his underlings) took a cut from every transaction—and there was no SEC to ensure that consumers were being treated fairly. The whole operation had turned the temple of God into "a den of thieves," rather than a place of worship and reflection.

So when Jesus came into Jerusalem to trigger a final showdown with His enemies, the temple was the most obvious target. It was "My Father's house" (Jn. 2:16) in a manner that no one else could claim, and He exercised the right to purify it. That He performed this cleansing both at the beginning of His ministry (John) and at the end (the Synoptics) highlighted His claim to fix what was broken. No man or animal was harmed, and no property was taken or destroyed—but Jesus made His point: God was to be honored in His house, not mocked.

There is a place in this world for righteous indignation. When people act in flagrant defiance of the rules, love requires firm discipline, and Jesus knew when and how to administer it. Parents, employers, preachers, and elders must learn to do the same.

Forgive

In a world dominated by vengeance, the idea of unilaterally forgiving our enemies is revolutionary. That's exactly how Jesus intended it to be.

"Whenever you stand praying, if you have anything against anyone, forgive him, that your Father in heaven may also forgive you your trespasses" (Mk. 11:25).

Bearing with one another, and forgiving one another, if anyone has a complaint against another; even as Christ forgave you, so you also must do (Col. 3:13).

❧

To "forgive" another is to release them from their debt, to grant an absolution they do not deserve. God has done that for us, and in these passages we are instructed to pass that benefit on to those who have offended us.

In one sense, full forgiveness and reconciliation cannot be achieved unless the offender actively seeks it. Paul told the Corinthians to deal with the fornicator in their midst by removing him (1 Cor. 5:5-7). Only after he was restored could they forgive him and welcome him back to full fellowship (2 Cor. 2:6-8).

But in our opening passages, Jesus and Paul do not condition our forgiveness on anything the offender does. In fact, Jesus says that the forgiveness should be extended *while we are in the act of praying to God,* when the offender is nowhere around. So there is another sense in which we can forgive someone of offenses for which they have shown no remorse and offer no apology. It is this proactive approach to forgiveness that is essential to healing broken relationships.

Some take Jesus' words here to mean that we must "be ready" to forgive if and when the offending party begs our forgiveness. But too often this notion of being "ready" to forgive is simply a license to hold a grudge until my enemy surrenders and grovels at my feet.

Furthermore, we have examples of forgiveness being extended to wicked men who clearly were not seeking it. In the Old Testament, David refused to exact justice on King Saul, even though he was clearly the innocent victim in their strained relationship. Stephen prayed for those who were throwing the stones that were pummeling his body: "Lord, do not charge them with this sin" (Ac. 7:60). These men extended forgiveness to their most hardened enemies, even while suffering at their hands.

The forgiveness under consideration here is not a legal cancellation that is contingent on the offender's first move. Rather, it is an attitude of unconditional love toward the one who has offended us, the absence of any vengeful passion. It is a state of mind that takes the initiative in seeking reconciliation through unrequited acts of kindness.

This principle addresses the very foundation of who we are as children of God. Our relationship with God is defined by our willingness to model the same attitude toward sinners that He has displayed toward us. God desires reconciliation with those who have wronged Him, and has taken unilateral action to initiate it, without any input from us. He sacrificed His very best to make it happen, even while we were still enemies.

In demanding that we forgive those who harm us, Jesus was not speculating on abstract theology; He practiced what He preached. As He hung dying on the cross, His prayer for His executioners was, "Father, forgive them, for they do not know what they do" (Lk. 23:34). And remember, these people had never asked for His forgiveness.

If you claim to wear the name of Christ, you must follow His example. Forgive those who have wronged you. Period.

The End Is Not Yet

When overwhelmed by adversity and grief, it's tempting to give up hope. But we can't see the end that God has in store for us.

"But when you hear of wars and rumors of wars, do not be troubled; for such things must happen, but the end is not yet" (Mk. 13:7).

৵৽৽

In the lead-up to the destruction of Jerusalem in AD 70, Jesus' disciples would encounter many hardships. But whatever their travails, Jesus promised that they were only temporary troubles leading to a greater glory. God's plan was not finished, and hope remained.

Throughout history, it has always been thus. When Adam and Eve were expelled from the garden of Eden, their pleasant life was turned into one of drudgery—but it was only the beginning of a long adventure for humanity. The end was not yet.

When God destroyed Noah's world in a great flood, it was the passing of one world for Noah's family and the beginning of a new. Life in this new world would not be perfect either—but the end was not yet.

The Israelites who toiled in slavery in Egypt could see no hope of relief from their misery. But neither could they see the plans God had for His people. Their suffering had a purpose, and God was slowly turning the wheels to bring that purpose to a climax. They couldn't see it, but the end was not yet.

As David fled from Saul, he had to wonder what had become of God's promise. Betrayals, disappointments, setbacks —would this fugitive life never come to an end? Yes, it would—but not yet.

To the Jews carried away into Babylonian exile, it seemed that their destiny as the people of God had come to an ignoble end. All their dreams of grandeur were dashed, and there could be no possible revival of their fortunes. But they had no idea what the future held for their nation. The end was not yet.

The crucifixion of Jesus marked the end of the messianic hope of the apostles. They thought He was the One; how could they have been so deceived? He could heal the sick, feed the multitudes, and raise the dead, but was powerless against the might of the Roman Empire. They couldn't see it, but the end was not yet, and three days later . . . .

Friend, whatever discouragement you're going through right now, know that your story is not over either. Whatever your burden, don't give in to despair. Whatever the struggle, don't quit. Whatever the treachery, don't become bitter. Your journey is not over, and God has a surprise for you that you can scarce imagine. You have every reason to look to the future with optimism and good cheer.

Because the end is not yet.

Is It I?

It's easy to criticize the apostles for their cowardice, but we have our own failures to answer for. That should humble us.

Now as they sat and ate, Jesus said, "Assuredly, I say to you, one of you who eats with Me will betray Me." And they began to be sorrowful, and to say to Him one by one, "Is it I?" And another said, "Is it I?" He answered and said to them, "It is one of the twelve, who dips with Me in the dish" (Mk. 14:18-20).

৩৩৩

For a long time, Jesus had known that one of His disciples would betray Him. He even knew the identity of the betrayer. So at the Last Supper, when Jesus told His apostles there was a traitor in their midst, it was a bombshell revelation. Betrayal? By one of His closest disciples? As the men looked around the table at each other, their minds must have been racing with speculation.

Each one of these men knew perfectly well his own shortcomings. How many times had they disappointed their Master? How often had He chided them for their slowness of heart? Yes, they had a track record of failure. But *betrayal*? Each one must have wrestled with the thought, Am I capable of such treachery? Could it be me? Almost on cue, their fears erupted into an argument over which of them was the greatest (Lk. 22:23-24). Bravado is a convenient mask to cover up insecurity.

Jesus did not reveal the identity of His betrayer to the group, because He wanted each man to face his own potential for selling out. "Is it I?" reflected the anguished searchings of a heart that knows its own weakness. Inside every one of us is a monster that could wreak unspeakable horror if unleashed, and we do not know the trigger that might allow the monster to break free. Each apostle was struggling with his own monster at this point.

Soon enough, the identity of the betrayer, Judas, became known. But as the events of the night unfolded, the rest of the apostles betrayed Jesus, too, each in his own way. When the soldiers apprehended Jesus, they all fled in terror, abandoning Him to his fate. One of them, when challenged as a disciple, denied that he even knew Jesus.

For every one of the apostles, "Is it I?" turned into, "Yes, it's me."

It's me, too. How often have I shirked an unpleasant duty that the Lord placed in my path? How often have I remained quiet as others mocked my Savior? How often have I clung with miserly fingers to wealth that could have been used to alleviate the want of a brother? Betrayal comes in many forms, and I have committed my share.

Except for Judas, all the apostles eventually learned from their failure and were restored to the Lord's service. We need to learn from our failures, too, and look to the resurrected Jesus for the strength we need to stay the course.

When the Proud Fall

Pride goes before a fall, and the story of Peter's denial of Jesus illustrates that truth. We cannot afford to get cocky in our faith.

Peter said to Him, "Even if all are made to stumble, yet I will not be." Jesus said to him, "Assuredly, I say to you that today, even this night, before the rooster crows twice, you will deny Me three times." But he spoke more vehemently, "If I have to die with You, I will not deny You!" (Mk. 14:29-31).

A second time the rooster crowed. Then Peter called to mind the word that Jesus had said to him, "Before the rooster crows twice, you will deny Me three times." And when he thought about it, he wept (Mk. 14:72).

∽∾

The story of Peter's denial of Jesus stands out as one of the epic failures in the Bible. It's easy to criticize Peter for his cowardice, but we would do well to analyze this incident more closely and notice some details that strike uncomfortably close to home. Peter's experience is a warning of the danger of *pride* in the life of the disciple of Christ.

First, we notice that pride inflated Peter's self-confidence to a dangerous level. His cocky boasts—"I will not stumble! . . . I will not deny You!"—are almost laughable in view of what he actually did just hours later. Surely when he uttered those promises he meant every word of them. But his bragging involved a situation he had never encountered before. He had no basis for making such a bold declaration, especially in view of the prediction Jesus had just made about all of them forsaking Him (v. 27). Rather than crow about how loyal he was, Peter should have looked inward at his own heart and prayed for strength to endure the challenge that was coming.

Second, we see that Peter's pride led him to blend in with the crowd rather than stand for his convictions. Peter could talk a big game among friends, but in the midst of a hostile audience all the bluster melted away and he chose to fit in rather than stand out. If our faith makes us look like an oddball, any pride lurking in our heart will suddenly take over and "fix" the problem. That's how an unfriendly environment can quickly strip away our pretensions and expose the weaknesses we cannot see in ourselves. It is possible to stand up to a crowd of critics, but it requires a great deal of self-reflection in advance to prepare for it. Idle boasts only hide the danger.

Finally, we learn that pride blinded Peter to even the possibility that he could do the unthinkable. Peter committed this embarrassing blunder, not as a turncoat who renounced his association with Jesus, but as a loyal disciple who desperately wanted to see what would become of his Master. He had good motives for being in that courtyard; what could go wrong? Actually, a lot could go wrong, and Peter never paused to consider the risks. He walked blindly into a trap that Satan had cleverly laid for him, and his good intentions became the very means of his downfall.

Peter "wept bitterly" when he realized what a terrible thing he had done (Lk. 22:62). Ever patient with His own, Jesus later restored and forgave His apostle (Jn. 21:15-19). But the experience chastened Peter, teaching him a valuable lesson in humility.

We, too, are never more vulnerable than when we think we have everything figured out. Wisdom dictates that we acknowledge our weaknesses and prepare accordingly.

Following Jesus . . .
from a Distance

Peter's loyalty compelled him to follow Jesus at His trial—but in a manner that did not expose him. Is our loyalty to the Lord any different?

But Peter followed Him at a distance, right into the courtyard of the high priest. And he sat with the servants and warmed himself at the fire (Mk. 14:54).

କ୬୭

When Jesus was arrested in Gethsemane, all the apostles "forsook Him and fled" (v. 50). We don't know the whereabouts of most of the disciples from that moment on, but we do know what Peter did. After the initial panic, he collected his senses and continued to follow Jesus. But only from a distance.

Peter still loved his Master. A few hours earlier he had vowed to die for Jesus if necessary. He had even tried to defend Jesus with a sword at His arrest, but had been rebuked for his effort. Now that Jesus had been formally taken into custody and carried away to be interrogated, Peter could not bear the thought of Jesus going to His fate alone. Confused and fearful, he followed Him into the courtyard of the high priest's house. But he kept his distance.

As he gathered with the servants around the fire in the courtyard, several bystanders thought they recognized Peter as one of Jesus' disciples. But Peter denied that He even knew the accused. With cursing and swearing he repudiated any affiliation with Him (v. 71). In his heart he yearned to know what would become of His master, so he got as close to the action as he could get. Yet even in his language, Peter was careful to maintain his distance.

Whatever his inner convictions, Peter's outward behavior betrayed the weakness of his faith. He was willing to follow Jesus, but only if it didn't cost him anything. So at the critical moment when Jesus most needed a friend, Peter remained conveniently hidden. Jesus had to face His fate alone.

The one apostle who vowed to defend Him to the very end, chose to remain at a distance.

Following Jesus comes at a price. We must forsake all, and commit our body, soul, and spirit to His service. We make that commitment knowing that we live in a world that despises everything Jesus stands for. His fate is our fate. The abuse that was hurled at Him will be hurled at us. If they hate Him, they will hate us.

Of course, we can avoid that trouble if, like Peter, we elect to follow Jesus from a distance. In our lifestyle and our speech, we can conduct ourselves in a manner that signals little or no enthusiasm for the Master. The people around us will never know.

But if we try to follow Jesus from a distance—leaving just enough space to disguise from others what we really believe in our heart—we will regret it on that day when we hear Him say, "Take him away, and cast him into outer darkness; there will be weeping and gnashing of teeth."

We wanted distance . . . and we got it.

Betrayed by Our Speech

Whatever claims we make about our loyalty to God, our daily speech habits provide a far more accurate gauge of where our heart is.

A little later those who stood by said to Peter again, "Surely you are one of them; for you are a Galilean, and your speech shows it." Then he began to curse and swear, "I do not know this Man of whom you speak!" (Mk. 14:70-71).

৵৽৹

When the pressure was on and Peter was in danger of being outed as a disciple of Jesus, a simple denial was not enough. Somehow he had to convince his interlocutors that he was in no way connected to the Galilean. So he pulled out the most effective weapon available to the purpose: He began to curse and swear.

Peter knew—and his critics knew—that profanity was incompatible with the message and life of Jesus. Jesus promoted a high standard of moral and ethical excellence. Cursing and swearing did not fit that standard. By getting down in the gutter with his language, Peter provided the strongest possible evidence that he was not a disciple of Jesus. It was a betrayal just as diabolical as what Judas had done a few hours earlier.

This was the same man who earlier had given such a noble response to Jesus' question about His identity: "You are the Christ, the Son of the living God" (Matt. 16:16). Given the religious and political winds of the day, it took a lot of courage for Peter to make that confession. But it was all undone by a foolish lapse of judgment during Jesus' trial.

When we make a commitment to exalt Jesus as the Lord of our life, our tongue is included in the deal. Our speech must henceforth "always be with grace, seasoned with salt" (Col. 4:6; and notice, this is in a context of how we should behave "toward those who are outside," v. 5). Our changed lifestyle must include putting away "filthiness . . . foolish talking . . . course jesting" (Eph. 5:4). James reduces the matter to a simple either/or equation: "Out of the same mouth proceed blessing and cursing. My brethren, these things ought not to be so" (Jas. 3:10). We can act like an angel or talk like the devil, but we can't do both. Whatever our intentions, our speech sends a strong signal to others about our character.

So why do people have such a struggle with inappropriate language? There are a couple of reasons: For many, crude language is simply a long-standing habit, especially if they come from a rough background. Others use profanity for the same reason Peter used it: They want to fit in with the crowd around them, and tossing in the occasional swear word is an easy way to pay the club dues. Either way, we are not thinking about the message our speech is communicating to others —not the words themselves, but the *character* those words represent.

Jesus said, "For every idle word men may speak, they will give account of it in the day of judgment. For by your words you will be justified, and by your words you will be condemned" (Matt. 12:36-37). If we have any fear at all of a final judgment, we should be very careful every time we open our mouths.

There are many sins we can commit with our tongue (like anger, slander, gossip, and boasting), but cursing is the least excusable of them all. What does *your* speech show?

Mock Worship

We should worship Jesus as our King. But if we're not careful, our "worship" can degenerate into a pose that mocks everything He stands for.

Then they struck Him on the head with a reed and spat on Him; and bowing the knee, they worshiped Him (Mk. 15:19).

ço∞

Of course, the Roman soldiers who kneeled before Jesus were not offering genuine worship. This was mockery, a taunting gesture by which they displayed their contempt for Him. To their thinking, Jesus was just another piece of Jewish trash to be played with, then thrown away.

But the language Mark uses to describe their behavior carries a more ominous message. It captures perfectly the behavior of many today who claim to be followers of Jesus. Like these Roman soldiers, they also worship Jesus *while spitting on Him*.

How many people today listen to Christian music on their electronic devices, wear crosses around their necks or on their clothing, and say, "Thank you, Jesus!" for every little blessing that lands in their lap—yet never set foot in a church building or get involved in a group of fellow believers?

How many people on Sunday morning sing, "O How I Love Jesus," then through the rest of the week verbally stab their family members, neighbors, and co-workers in the back —the very people for whom Jesus died?

How many people preach vociferously about doing everything in religion by the authority of the Lord Jesus Christ, while mired in toxic relationships with their brethren and their families, blind to their own personality flaws that fuel the drama?

How many people complain loudly about the atheists, radicals, and homosexuals who are selling our country down the river, while their own addiction to the demons of anger, lust, and greed are contributing just as much damage to society as those they condemn?

These people put on a show of worshiping Jesus, but in their personal lives they spit on everything He represents. Their mockery may not be as intentional as the soldiers who executed Jesus, but it's just as despicable. The only ones they are fooling are themselves.

If we do not worship Jesus in *every* area of our lives, with all our heart, soul, strength, and mind, we are not worshiping Him at all; we are mocking Him. A day is coming when "every knee shall bow" before Him (Isa. 45:23; Phil. 2:10). There will be no mocking then, only fear and trembling. On that day, the counterfeit worshipers will be separated from the genuine, and given their just reward.

What kind of worshiper are you?

The Message and the Audience

Effective evangelism begins, not with a well-crafted message, but with a clear understanding of those whom we are trying to reach.

And He said to them, "Go into all the world and preach the gospel to every creature" (Mk. 16:15).

ഇൻ

A major component of the mission of the Lord's church can be summarized in the simple command, "preach the gospel to every creature." We are the instruments through which God's message of salvation is proclaimed to a lost world, and we must be busy in that good work.

But the execution of that task has proven to be not so simple. The obstacles of prejudice, ignorance, and even persecution stand in the way of getting the message into open hearts. We are competing against a host of alternate belief systems, and our approach to every audience must be tailored to address that audience's belief system.

This challenge can be illustrated by looking at two sermons from the book of Acts.

When Peter preached the first sermon on the day of Pentecost (Acts 2), his theme was devoted exclusively to the resurrection of Jesus. He made extensive use of the Hebrew Scriptures (Joel and Psalms) to build a compelling case for what happened to the missing body of Jesus.

Years later, when Paul preached in the city of Athens (Acts 17), his message was entirely different. His main topic was the nature of God, not the resurrection of Jesus. He did not quote a single Scripture, but quoted two ancient Greek poets, Aratus and Epimenides, to buttress his case (consult a commentary for the details). His argument for God was based, not on Scripture or revelation, but on his audience's existing knowledge of nature and history.

Why did these two preachers preach such different sermons? *Because their audiences came from entirely different backgrounds.* Peter was speaking to Jews who already believed in the true God, accepted the authority of the Old Testament, and knew about Jesus. They just needed to be convinced of Jesus' real identity. Paul was addressing pagans who knew nothing of those details. They first needed to get their thinking about God straightened out. Both Peter and Paul were working toward the same end—repentance (compare 2:38 and 17:30)—but they had to take different routes to get there.

The contrast between these two sermons offers an important lesson in evangelism: Before we can teach someone the gospel, we first need to understand where they are at in their spiritual lives, and adjust our message to fit their circumstances. If we take a one-size-fits-all approach to teaching the gospel, failing to account for the peculiar background of each listener, we will likely be disappointed in the results.

In years past in American culture, we could assume that most people we encountered were loyal to some form of sectarian Christianity, and approach them on that basis. That assumption is no longer valid. Today, we are more likely to encounter people who know nothing about the Bible, or are involved in a non-Christian religion, or no religion at all. Our teaching must be geared to reaching these people where they are at. Preparing for such diverse audiences will require a great deal of study, research, and listening on our part, but there is no other way to effectively connect with them.

But be careful! No matter the audience, the end goal of all our teaching is to bring people to repentance through faith in the resurrected Christ. Whatever our beginning point, all our teaching must arrive at that common destination.

The Significance of Baptism

The role of baptism in the believer's life is
not hard to understand, if we let the Scriptures
define that role for us.

---

*"He who believes and is baptized will be saved; but he
who does not believe will be condemned" (Mk. 16:16).*

*Then Peter said to them, "Repent, and let every one of
you be baptized in the name of Jesus Christ for the remission
of sins; and you shall receive the gift of the Holy Spirit" (Ac.
2:38).*

∽∾

Baptism was a big deal in early Christianity. Everywhere
the early apostles and evangelists went preaching the gospel,
baptisms immediately followed (Ac. 2:41; 8:12-13; 8:36-38;
9:18; 10:47-48; 18:8). Jesus Himself associated it with becoming His disciple (Matt. 28:19), and the "body" of
Christ—His church—was comprised of baptized believers
(1 Cor. 12:13).

Yet today baptism is treated as little more than a
ceremonial initiation rite that can be performed at one's convenience—or not at all.

Why do churches of Christ make such a big deal of baptism? Framing the question more accurately, why does the
New Testament place so much emphasis on it?

First, let's address a common misconception. There is
nothing magical about the water. The act of getting dunked
carries no significance by itself. No one will wave a bap-
tismal certificate in God's face on judgment day and get a
free pass through the pearly gates. It doesn't work that way.

First and foremost, baptism is *an act of faith*. Like Abraham offering up Isaac, or the Israelites crossing Red Sea, or Naaman dipping in the Jordan River to be healed of his leprosy, this act of obedience is a test of our willingness to submit to God's authority. The Pharisees and lawyers who refused to be baptized by John (Lk. 7:30) were in defiance of God's instructions. Their failure to submit to this ordinance revealed the true state of their heart. So for starters, we need to think of baptism as a simple test of our faith in God; will I submit to Him or not?

What makes that submission such a challenge for many is that baptism is also *an expression of humility*. Let's face it, allowing someone to plunge us in a large tub of water is somewhat humiliating. That's because it's *meant* to be humiliating. By surrendering to this ordinance, we are acknowledging our inability to save ourselves, and are "calling on the name of the Lord" to save us (Ac. 22:16).

Finally, baptism is *symbolic of a deeper transformation*. The water does not save, that's true. But the New Testament writers frequently connect baptism with belief and repentance, leading to forgiveness of sins (Ac. 2:38; Ac. 22:16; 1 Pet. 3:21). Just as Jesus' burial and resurrection marked a radical change to a new life, so baptism (a "burial" and "raising" from water) marks our own transition into a new life (Rom. 6:4). We can argue hypothetical cases of people who get killed on their way to the baptistery and so forth, but we'll let God handle those situations. Our task is to accept what He has written.

Have you been baptized? If not, why not?

Christmas Mythology

Much of the Christmas story is, in fact, mythology that has grown up around the original account. What does the Bible tell us about Jesus' birth?

So it was, that while they were there, the days were completed for her to be delivered. And she brought forth her firstborn Son, and wrapped Him in swaddling cloths, and laid Him in a manger, because there was no room for them in the inn (Lk. 2:6-7).

༺✦༻

Christmas is a celebration of the birth of Jesus, an historical event based on solid evidence. But surprisingly, much of our modern Christmas story is pure myth, having no basis in the original accounts. Consider some details:

Jesus was born on December 25. The Bible doesn't tell us when Jesus was born. In fact, the evidence suggests a date more likely in the spring, when the shepherds would be staying in the fields with their flocks (Lk. 2:8). The December date grew out of a later desire to compete with pagan celebrations of the winter solstice.

Jesus was born in a stable because there was no room in the inn. The common English translation of Luke 2:7 leaves the impression that the local Motel 6 was full, so Joseph and Mary had to find shelter in a nearby barn. Not exactly. "Inn" is a weak translation for "guest room" (see the same word in Mk. 14:14; Lk. 22:11)—in this case, probably a spare room in a relative's home. The manger would have been an attached shelter where the host family's stock was kept at night.

Joseph's little family was not homeless, just squeezed in tighter than usual.

Three kings visited the baby Jesus in the manger. This one is so off-the-charts wrong on multiple levels. First, the original language identifies these visitors as "magi" or "wise men" (Matt. 2:1), which refers to magicians or sorcerers, not kings (see the same word used in Ac. 13:6, 8). They were likely Persian astrologers to whom God had revealed a sign of the Messiah's birth. Next, we have no idea how many of these magi were in the group. The number "three" is based on the three gifts they brought, but it tells us nothing about the size of the party. Finally, the magi did not arrive in Bethlehem until many months after Jesus was born. That's why they visited Jesus in "the house" (Matt. 2:11), not in the manger. It's also why, when Herod heard of their search, he had all the infant boys in Bethlehem killed, "from two years old and under" (Matt. 2:16). So the typical nativity scenes featuring the kings surrounding the manger has no basis in the Bible.

Christmas is one of Christianity's two major holy days. Sorry, but not in God's book. Setting aside one day a year as a holy day to honor Jesus' birth is a human invention, without a shred of Biblical support. In fact, we are warned not to adopt a calendar of man-made holy days (Gal. 4:9-11). It's laudable that people want to remember the birth of Jesus, but why limit it to one day a year? We should rejoice every day that God's son came to live among us.

It is not my intention here to be a Scrooge and depress the spirit of the season. I'm grateful for any occasion in which people turn their attention to our Savior, even if only once a year. And there is nothing wrong with enjoying all the purely cultural traditions that accompany the season—the decorated tree, the lights, exchanging gifts, and so forth. But if we really want to honor Jesus, we would do better to focus on what He taught, rather than how He got here.

What Does Repentance Mean to You?

God's command to "repent" is universal, but the specifics vary from person to person. Each of us must identify the sins of which we should repent.

"Bear fruits worthy of repentance" (Lk. 3:8).

"Repent now everyone of his evil way and his evil doings" (Jer. 25:5).

❧

Like the Old Testament prophets before him, repentance was a major theme in the preaching of John the Baptist. His challenge to repent ("change the heart") and bear fruit consistent with that repentance has always been at the top of God's to-do list for humanity. But what does repentance mean for each one of us? How do we translate it into actionable behavior?

In the verses that follow, at least three different groups posed that very question to John: "What then shall we do?" (v. 10, 12, 14). The responses of John to each group are quite different. He told the common people to share their tunics and food with others (v. 11). To the tax collectors he warned, don't cheat the public (v. 13). The soldiers were told to treat their fellow citizens with justice, and be content with their wages (v. 14).

Three different groups of people, three different actions. Why the variations? *Because their sins were different.* Each group had their own unique circumstances to deal with, with their own unique temptations. Consequently, repentance meant different things to different people. John's different instructions to the three groups were entirely appropriate.

Allow me to share a personal perspective on this topic. I do not need to repent of the sin of drunkenness. I have never taken a drink of alcohol in my life, and have no desire to do so. Drunkenness poses a serious threat in lives of many people, but I'm not one of them. There is in me not the slightest temptation to go down that path. No temptation, no sin—and no repentance required.

But there is another sin of which I do need to repent . . . often. It's the sin of *pride*. In my role as a preacher and elder, it's easy to slip into a mode of thinking that I'm, well, better than others. After all, I'm more knowledgeable than others, more disciplined, more experienced, more wise, more proficient, more . . . . uh, oh, there I go again. Lord, forgive me! (Not to mention, I'm not nearly as good in any of those areas as I like to think I am.)

Repentance means different things to different people because we all have different temperaments and life experiences that expose us to different temptations. Pointing an accusing finger at the failures of others does not get us off the hook for our own weaknesses. It's just as easy to throw stones at a self-righteous Pharisee as it is to cast insults at an alcoholic—and anyone throwing stones at either of those two parties needs to repent, too. *All of us need to repent*, but for different reasons.

What are the sins that *you* struggle with? More importantly, what steps are you taking to genuinely repent of them?

Satan's Opportunities

Satan is a cunning adversary who knows exactly
how to exploit our weaknesses. Resisting him
requires that we first respect his tenacity.

---

*Now when the devil had ended every temptation, he de-
parted from Him until an opportune time (Lk. 4:13).*

ဢ

Thus ended the wilderness temptation of Christ at the
outset of His ministry. Jesus defeated Satan on all three temptations, so it was all downhill from there, right?

Wrong. Satan may have lost a battle, but he was not
about to give up the war. There would be another "opportune
time," and another, and another. He would not give up until
he had succeeded in his mission to thwart God's plan by en-
ticing His Son to commit sin. Any sin would do. If he could
trip up Jesus just once, His perfect character would be ruined,
and God's plan would come crashing down.

Satan had numerous other opportunities to entice Jesus
into sin. When Jesus foretold of His impending arrest and
crucifixion, Simon Peter rebuked Him for His negativity.
Peter no doubt had good intentions, but Jesus saw a more sinister hand at work: "Get behind me, Satan! You are an offense
to Me, for you are not mindful of the things of God, but the
things of men" (Matt. 16:22-23). It was a harsh put-down, but
Jesus was dealing with a master strategist who knew how to
use even His closest friends as instruments to bring about His
downfall.

Near the end, after Jesus had successfully beaten back
every attempt of Satan to distract Him from His goal, He en-

countered Satan's last and best temptation. Like any human, Jesus did not want to die, especially the kind of painful death that He knew awaited Him. So He was tempted to simply quit. All He had to do was call on God to save Him, and legions of angels would swoop down to deliver Him from the fate that awaited Him (Matt. 26:53). So with that option dangling in front Him, Jesus agonized with a temptation unlike any He had faced before. He prayed so intensely that His sweat became "like great drops of blood falling down to the ground" (Lk. 22:44). If Jesus had any weak spot, surely this was it. Satan knew exactly how to work it to his advantage. Thank God, Jesus resisted this last temptation also and finished His mission.

This review of Satan's tireless efforts explains much that happens in our own lives. Satan knows our every weakness, and can craft schemes that employ perfectly benign agents— even our best friends—to entice us to stray from God. With Adam and Eve, it was a simple piece of fruit. With King David, it was a beautiful neighbor. With Simon Peter at Jesus' trial, it was his desire to stay close to his Master that put him in a difficult position—ironically, a situation that led him to deny that he even knew Jesus. Oh, yes, Satan can use even our loyalty to the Lord as a weapon to bring us down.

The point of this study is that we can *never* become complacent in our struggle against sin. Resisting one temptation or a dozen proves nothing, for Satan has a bottomless bag of tricks to use against us in his determination to destroy us. This does not mean that we should go through life terrified of being ambushed. We can be confident and happy in our faith. But while enjoying life, we should keep alert for danger. "Let him who thinks he stands take heed lest he fall" (1 Cor. 10:12).

The Amazing Jesus

We can't duplicate the awe experienced by Jesus' original audiences, but with the right approach to His story, we can come close.

*So all bore witness to Him, and **marveled** at the gracious words which proceeded out of His mouth. . . . And they were **astonished** at His teaching, for His word was with authority. . . . Then they were all **amazed** and spoke among themselves, saying, "What a word this is! For with authority and power He commands the unclean spirits, and they come out" (Lk. 4:22, 32, 36).*

જ્જ

In the space of a few verses, Luke uses several words to describe how people reacted to the early ministry of Jesus: they "marveled . . . were astonished . . . were amazed." Jesus' teaching and miracles were unlike anything these people had seen before, and they reacted accordingly.

Today, that spirit of amazement at the life of Jesus is more subdued. We are so far removed from His life that many people respect Him as merely a wise teacher or social reformer, but nothing more. Some shrug off the details of His story as pure mythology. Even among those who embrace Him as the Son of God, there is a struggle to feel that same sense of wonder at what He did. We have heard the story so many times that we've become desensitized to the revolutionary nature of His work.

How can we moderns recapture the sense of amazement that these early audiences felt? Or is it even possible? It is possible, but it requires that we take the right approach.

Have you noticed that we tend to gravitate to the epistles as the more important "how to" part of God's revelation? But the epistles point us back to the gospel story as the foundation of our faith. So restoring our awe at the Jesus story begins with *spending more time in the gospels.* When we read those accounts of Jesus' work, we're looking at people who personally spent a good deal of time with Him. They heard His teaching with their own ears and witnessed the miracles with their own eyes. They were totally immersed in His work. If we would read the gospels more often and with greater intensity—not as dry pedagogy, but as eyewitness accounts of an extraordinary moment in history—we would begin to feel the same "wow" factor as those who originally experienced it. Our exposure takes a different form than that of the original witnesses, but the impact can be just as dramatic, once we open our eyes to see it.

Then as we become more familiar with the story of Jesus in the gospels, we should *personalize the message in our own lives.* Those early witnesses were captivated by what they saw and heard because it exposed their lives to closer scrutiny. Jesus opened their eyes and hearts to a new perspective on how the life works, giving them insights that rocked their world. In similar fashion, we should be asking ourselves constantly: How does this teaching or that interaction apply to me? How does this information help me understand similar experiences in my own life? What weakness does this story expose in my character? Once we begin to see the influence of Jesus reshaping our thinking and behavior, a sense of excitement will begin to emerge. And the impact on our hearts and lives will be exhilarating.

Jesus can still amaze people today—but only those who are willing to open their eyes to appreciate what He did while He walked among us.

At Your Word, I Will

One reason the teachings of Jesus are so barren in our lives is because we're not convinced they will work. We must repent of our skepticism.

But Simon answered and said to Him, "Master, we have toiled all night and caught nothing; nevertheless at Your word I will let down the net" (Lk. 5:5).

৩৹৵

Like any experienced fisherman, Peter knew when the fish just weren't biting—and the empty nets from the previous night's work told him everything he needed to know about his chances of success. So when Jesus walked up and told him to try one more time, Peter was skeptical. This would be a waste of his time. However, Peter already had a degree of respect for Jesus, so "at your word" he went out into deep water and cast his net again.

This time, the net caught so many fish that it almost capsized Peter's boat, and he had to call another boat over to help haul in the enormous load. Everyone "was astonished at the catch of fish which they had taken" (v. 9).

This episode taught Peter that Jesus knew what He was talking about. But the lesson would have been lost if Peter hadn't followed through on the Lord's instruction, despite his misgivings. Whether eager or grudging, Peter's compliance validated what seemed like a pointless order.

There are so many of Jesus' instructions that have the same potential for astonishing results, but are often greeted with skepticism. Some examples:

Jesus says, "Love your enemies . . . do good to those who hate you" (Matt. 5:44). That directive runs counter to everything we think we know about human relations. We love our friends and hate our enemies. We do good to those who do good to us. Is it even possible to generate positive emotions toward those who abuse us? Jesus says: Just do it, whether it makes sense or not.

Jesus says, "It is more blessed to give than to receive" (Ac. 20:35). From our earliest experiences around the annual Christmas tree, we are conditioned to believe the opposite: we're happier when we receive. But Jesus insists that there is something about radical generosity that satisfies our souls in a way that we can never achieve by getting, no matter how much we get. Jesus says: Give, give, and keep on giving, and you'll be glad you did.

Jesus says: "If you have anything against anyone, forgive him" (Mk. 11:25). Anything? Anyone? That's a sweeping statement that can't possibly hold water. There are some offenses that are so serious, some scoundrels who are so evil, that forgiveness is simply out of the question. Nevertheless, Jesus insists: Forgive anyway.

We could go on and on with these kinds of injunctions. They all seem so counterintuitive, but people who muster the courage to comply are usually astonished at the outcome of these behaviors. Like Peter, they discover that Jesus knows what He's talking about.

The life that Jesus calls us to live is not easy, but it is not our place to second-guess His orders. Whether or not we understand, appreciate, or agree with all the mandates He lays upon us, our response must be the same as Peter's: "Nevertheless at Your word I will."

Prayer and Decision-Making

Jesus' choice of The Twelve was guided by a whole night of intense prayer, seeking God's guidance. What role does prayer play in our life decisions?

Now it came to pass in those days that He went out to the mountain to pray, and continued all night in prayer to God. And when it was day, He called His disciples to Himself; and from them He chose twelve whom He also named apostles (Lk. 6:12-13).

৵৽৽

In the early stages of His ministry, Jesus had many disciples. But His long-term plan was to handpick a dozen men—"apostles"—who would form the foundation of His enterprise in the years following His departure. A lot was riding on His choice. The men He chose would face enormous pressures in their work, and almost certain death by martyrdom. Could they bear that burden? Would they be faithful representatives of the life and attitudes He taught them, especially in the midst of a hostile world? Among all His disciples, which ones were the best qualified for this role?

There was only one thing to do: One evening He went up alone to a deserted mountain top and spent the entire night in prayer. There were scores, perhaps hundreds, of available candidates, and Jesus mentally reviewed each man for his suitability in this role. More importantly, He held each one up to His Father, seeking wisdom to know how to judge the character of each individual.

When the first faint rays of light began to dawn across the eastern sky, Jesus had His final list. He was tired and weak, but He could return to His disciples with assurance that He had chosen the best men for the job. (And, yes, He knew which one would later betray Him. He knew how all this would work out, and that was likely a major part of His prayer struggle.)

We see this pattern often in Jesus' career. He prayed at the outset of His Galilean campaign (Mk. 1:35), and in the aftermath of its collapse (Mk. 6:45-46; Jn. 6:15, 66). He spent the night before His crucifixion in the garden of Gethsemane, pleading with His Father for the strength to endure the ordeal that lay before Him (Lk. 22:39-44). Every major decision or crisis that Jesus faced in His life, He met with intensive prayer.

If the Son of God needed to pray often and in depth, how much more do we need it when we face critical situations in our own lives? We must learn to dedicate time to clear away the mental clutter of daily living; to concentrate our minds on the challenge at hand; to sort through all the options before us, relying on God's word rather than our emotions for direction; and to seek God's wisdom in making our final decisions.

God will not make our decisions for us. But He will influence our choices—if we will humble our hearts to Him in fervent prayer.

The Apostles

Jesus trained a small handful of men to carry on
His work after His departure. We are still
benefiting from the work of these men today.

---

*And when it was day, He called His disciples to Himself,
and from them He chose twelve whom He also named apostles (Lk. 6:13).*

৽৵৹

While Jesus was upon this earth, He had many disciples,
but only a small handful that were designated "apostles."
What was unique about these men that set them apart from
the other disciples?

The word "apostle" means "one who is sent." The word
is sometimes used in a general sense to describe anyone who
is sent on a mission, but we are more familiar with that small
group whom Jesus designated as His personal emissaries, beginning with the original Twelve and ending with Paul.

None of the men who occupied the office of apostle actively campaigned for it, nor were they recruited by other
men. Rather, they were personally chosen by Jesus Himself
(Jn. 15:16). In Paul's case, that choice was a dramatic event
that changed his life (1 Cor. 1:1; 1 Tim. 1:12). Indeed, one of
the qualifications of an apostle was having witnessed the resurrected Lord (1 Cor. 9:1).

As ambassadors of Christ, the primary task of the apostles was to reveal and teach the word of God (Eph. 3:5; Ac.
5:42; Ac. 6:2-4). This preaching and teaching of the word
was accompanied by an extraordinary range of miraculous
powers (Ac. 2:43; 4:33; 5:12). These "signs of an apostles"

validated the message they taught (2 Cor. 12:12; Heb. 2:3-4). While other disciples had this or that miraculous gift, only the apostles had the full complement of gifts and the ability to bestow these gifts on others (Ac. 8:14-18; 1 Cor. 12:4-11).

The apostles were the unquestioned leaders of the early church. It was the apostles to whom the disciples looked for guidance, instruction, and leadership (Ac. 2:42; 2 Pet. 3:2). That's why Paul describes the church as being built "on the foundation of the apostles and prophets" (Eph. 2:20). Their work, now recorded in the New Testament, serves as the foundation upon which everything else rests.

This exalted position might make most men haughty, but in fact, being chosen as an apostle proved to be a death sentence for most of these men. Their lives were dedicated to a cause much higher than themselves, and sacrifice and suffering was their way of life.

Even in the first century, there were those who, conveniently ignoring the sacrificial element, sought to maneuver themselves into a position where they could enjoy the prestige of apostleship. These "false apostles" (2 Cor. 11:13) did a lot of damage in their day, as false prophets have always done.

Do we still have apostles today? Catholics, Mormons, and others insist that the apostolic office has been handed down to men today. However, the very fact that so many conflicting religious bodies claim apostolic authority tells us right away that somebody is falsifying the truth. Furthermore, the fact that no one today has seen the resurrected Lord, nor is performing the kind of miracles we read about in the New Testament, confirms that the only apostles we still have today are false apostles.

But the real apostles are still working among us, as we read and follow their revelation in the New Testament. For that, we can be grateful.

The Tax Collector and the Zealot

Two of Jesus' first apostles posed a serious threat to the unity of His team. But Jesus made it work, proving that prior biases are not insurmountable.

When it was day, He called His disciples to Himself; and from them He chose twelve whom he also named apostles. . . . Matthew . . . and Simon called the Zealot (Lk. 6:13, 15).

ఌఞఴ

The twelve men whom Jesus chose to be His apostles make an interesting study, but we want to single out two of them for closer scrutiny: Matthew, a tax collector (Matt. 10:3), and Simon the Zealot.

These two men represented opposite extremes in the political landscape of first-century Judaism. The tax collectors were local Jews who contracted with the Roman government to collect tribute from the local populace. Their collection methods provided ample opportunity for skimming excess profits for themselves. The Jews considered them traitors to their people. The Zealots, on the other hand, were the right-wing extremists of their day. Their hatred of the Romans extended even to advocating open rebellion against Rome (which actually happened in AD 66, leading to the destruction of Jerusalem four years later).

Under normal circumstances, there was no way Matthew and Simon could work together harmoniously. Had these two men been left together alone in the same room, only one of them would have walked out alive. Yet Jesus chose these two men to work alongside each other as fellow apostles under His oversight. Why did Jesus take such an enormous risk?

Having these two on His staff had a potential for a disastrous blow-up. But Jesus did not make a mistake. Remember, He spent the whole night in prayer before choosing these two. He knew what He was doing.

In fact, Jesus' gamble paid off. If there was any friction between these two over their political beliefs, we have no record of it. As far as we know, these two men spent the remainder of their lives in harmony, working for a common cause higher than their original allegiances.

How did it happen? The answer is not hard to figure out: Both men had a loyalty to Jesus that exceeded their political biases. They both found in Jesus a purpose in life that was greater than their earlier calling.

This same phenomenon was demonstrated repeatedly in the early days of Christianity. The church in Corinth included a former leader of the local Jewish synagogue (Ac. 18:8)—a paragon of virtue—along with former drunks, crooks, homosexuals, idolaters, and other assorted riff-raff from among the pagans (1 Cor. 6:9-11). Can you imagine how awkward their church services must have been, especially at the beginning? But again, the unifying factor here was a commitment to a common Savior. When they came to Jesus, they found the power to overcome their prejudices and suspicions, and forged a new relationship based on a higher calling. To be sure, both parties had to make changes to adapt to this new role, and those changes did not come easily. But they did it, and it worked.

The story of Matthew the tax collector and Simon the Zealot holds a powerful lesson for us today. It is possible for people from wildly different backgrounds to work together in harmony—but only if they all are *first* willing to submit to the rule of Christ.

Love Your Enemies

"Love your enemies" is dismissed as unrealistic,
but until we seriously commit to doing so, we will
never grasp what the religion of Jesus is about.

---

*"Love your enemies, do good to those who hate you,
bless those who curse you, and pray for those who spitefully
use you. To him who strikes you on the one cheek, offer the
other also. And from him who takes away your cloak, do not
withhold your tunic either. Give to everyone who asks of you.
And from him who takes away your goods do not ask them
back. And just as you want men to do to you, you also do to
them likewise. But if you love those who love you, what credit
is that to you? For even sinners love those who love them.
. . . But love your enemies, do good, and lend, hoping for
nothing in return; and your reward will be great, and you will
be sons of the Most High. For He is kind to the unthankful
and evil. Therefore be merciful, just as your Father also is
merciful" (Lk. 6:27-36).*

ꙮ

Of all the ethical teachings of Jesus, none draws more
attention than His command to "love your enemies." Skeptics
dismiss it as hopelessly unrealistic and unworkable. Disciples struggle with it, looking for ways to weaken its meaning
to render it less onerous. The idea of showing active, unconditional kindness to one's enemies seems so unnatural that it
strains credibility.

There are three reasons why we ought to take this lofty
ethical ideal at face value and incorporate it into our personal
relationships.

First, *what is the alternative?* The history of the human race is a long, sorry tale of hate, revenge, and getting even. Treating our enemies as enemies has done nothing but spawn more bloodshed and suffering. After thousands of years of this behavior, maybe it's time to try something different. The results couldn't be any worse than what we're already doing to one another.

Second, although it seems counter-intuitive, this approach to relational conflict *resonates with our nature.* There is something in the human psyche that responds positively to kindness, especially when it is undeserved. We cheer the hero who sacrifices himself for strangers, and for the athlete who treats his opponents with sportsmanlike dignity. What Jesus taught simply broadens that principle to cover those who mistreat us. The power of love to tear down walls of hatred has been demonstrated again and again throughout history.

Finally, Jesus was not merely theorizing about an abstract ideal—*He lived by this principle in His own life.* He embraced it fully, even in the face of a hideous death. His uncompromising love for His enemies has transformed the lives of millions of people, and changed the course of history.

So how do we incorporate this ethic in our lives? Notice that in His lengthy commentary on this rule, Jesus never addressed how we should *feel* about our enemy. Instead, He spoke only about how we should *behave* toward our enemy. He counsels us to treat our enemy *as if* he is our friend, even though he is not. It's hard to implement at first, but a lifetime of practice will gradually reshape our minds to the point that we really can love our enemies—from the bottom of our heart.

Loving our enemies is not an unrealistic ideal, but a practical approach to making the world a better place for all. We just have to make up our minds to do it.

Nothing in Return

Doing good to others is easy, when we receive some payback for our kindness. The real test is when there is no possibility of recompense.

"But love your enemies, do good, and lend, hoping for nothing in return; and your reward will be great, and you will be sons of the Highest. For He is kind to the unthankful and evil" (Lk. 6:35).

"But when you give a feast, invite the poor, the maimed, the lame, the blind. And you will be blessed, because they cannot repay you; for you shall be repaid at the resurrection of the just" (Lk. 14:13-14).

తళ

The religion of Christ is based on the principle of active love, that is, doing good to others whether they deserve it or not. But there is a corollary principle that seldom gets attention, addressed in both these verses: Our good deeds must not be tied to whatever selfish gain we might receive in return.

We might, for example, do a favor for someone we don't particularly like because they are in a position to return the favor in a manner that will advance our own agenda. But is that really a "good deed," or is it just political cronyism?

We could make a generous donation to a favorite charity, and feel good about the fine work it will accomplish. Of course, we might feel even better about the sizable tax deduction we get in return, or the reputation we gain in the community as a philanthropist.

Good deeds are really not all that good if they are performed with an expectation of getting something in return. As

Jesus reminds us in the Sermon on the Mount, even the irreligious and immoral people of the world are capable of doing good to each other when there is some exchange in the deal (Lk. 6:32-34). That kind of conditional generosity doesn't do much to advance God's cause in the world.

What really causes people to sit up and take notice is when good is performed where there is no possible gain to be achieved from it. Such goodness comes only from an unselfish desire to help others. That's why Jesus advises us to perform our charitable deeds quietly, without fanfare (Matt. 6:1-4). The purest form of charity is that which is performed anonymously, when payback is impossible.

The finest example of this kind of charity, of course, is the ultimate good deed performed by Jesus in His sacrificial death on the cross. Jesus gave Himself for us, knowing there is nothing we can give Him in return that can equal the value of what He has given us.

This does not mean we should refrain from doing good if there is any possibility of the favor somehow being repaid. We reap what we sow, and goodness will often naturally return more of the same. But the point of this lesson is that we must not manipulate this sowing-reaping principle to selfish advantage. We must train ourselves to view our goodness strictly as a means of extending God's grace to others, expecting nothing in return for ourselves.

Attitude Is Everything

God wants us to live transformed lives, but changing our behaviors is meaningless—even unlikely—in the absence of a changed heart.

"A good man out of the good treasure of his heart brings forth good; and an evil man out of the evil treasure of his heart brings forth evil. For out of the abundance of the heart his mouth speaks" (Lk. 6:45).

ഇരു

In the perpetual struggle to find genuine happiness in life, people look in all sorts of places to find it: work, travel, therapy, drugs, hobbies, a variety of relationships (or the absence of any relationships), and a plethora of philosophies or religions. But in most cases, the goal remains as elusive as ever. Despite the search, happiness is never really achieved, and life grinds them down.

The problem, of course, is that people are looking in the wrong places for meaning in their lives. Personal fulfillment does not come from rearranging the external furniture that clutters one's life. It is generated from within, as a product of a heart that chooses to think properly about one's place in this world.

The children of Israel who crossed the wilderness were not miserable because of the tiring march, hot sand, boring food, or nagging enemies. They were miserable because they had "gone astray in their hearts" (Psa. 95:10). Instead of looking at the positives in their situation, they chose to dwell on the negatives, and that negative mindset eventually destroyed them.

Conversely, the apostle Paul suffered more persecution and disappointment in his career than any of us could ever imagine. Yet the guy was an incurable optimist. His epistles are loaded with references to joy, hope, thankfulness, and confidence. The secret to Paul's unflagging optimism was his state of mind; he served God "with my spirit" (Rom. 1:9). Everything else flowed out of that fixed starting point. With that anchor firmly set, no disappointment in life could shake him.

This is a theme that is repeated again and again in the Bible. We are instructed to "keep your heart with all diligence, for out of it spring the issues of life" (Prov. 4:23). A transformed life begins with "the renewing of your mind" (Rom. 12:2). Paul promised that the peace of God will be upon those who train their hearts to meditate on things that are true, noble, just, pure, lovely, and so forth (Phil. 4:7-9). Ezekiel urged the downcast exiles of his day to "get yourselves a new heart and a new spirit" if they wanted to improve their situation (Eze. 18:31). We could go on and on with such references.

The central requirement of anyone who seeks a right relationship with God, whether unregenerate sinner or fallen saint, is *repentance*, a change of heart (Ac. 2:38; 8:22). That repentance will result in a changed life; but more importantly, it will result in a changed perspective on one's purpose in life, and a new appreciation for life's beauty. Without that inner recalibration of thinking, trying to change the outside will be a futile struggle.

There are many external details in our lives concerning which God has given us guidance, and we cannot shrug these off as unimportant. But before we start tackling these external behaviors, we need to get our minds straightened out. In the pursuit of life's meaning, attitude is everything. Train yourself to *think* right about life, and life will become so much easier to handle.

To Follow Jesus

Following Jesus can often take the form of a fad, highlighting the glitter but ignoring the sacrifice. Jesus doesn't need that kind of follower.

"Why do you call Me 'Lord, Lord,' and not do the things which I say?" (Lk. 6:46).

"Whoever does not bear his cross and come after Me cannot be My disciple. . . . Whoever of you does not forsake all that he has cannot be My disciple" (Lk. 14:27, 33).

ஒஒஒ

In the early days of His ministry, Jesus was surrounded by large numbers of sunshine disciples who were enamored with the novelty of His charisma and teaching, but had no intention of committing to real change in their personal lives. Jesus didn't need that kind of followers.

His message to these people, therefore, was a warning. "Bearing the cross" signifies, not discomfort or inconvenience, but real suffering. Is being a disciple of Jesus worth that kind of sacrifice? "Forsaking all" is high price to pay for allegiance. Am I really willing to go that far? Jesus' message was stern, because He deliberately intended to filter out the groupies from the true believers.

Today the situation has not changed much. Vast numbers of people claim to follow Jesus, but their discipleship is a flimsy knock-off of what Jesus wants from them.

People wrap themselves in the mantle of the gospel to support trendy social justice movements they believe will fix all the problems of modern society. But the emphasis in these movements is almost always on superficial, external behaviors, rather than the heart. Compelling people to "change" by exerting government power is not justice; it's tyranny, and the real underlying problems only get worse.

Others co-opt Jesus in promoting a Bible-infused pop psychology to address people's emotional problems. True, Jesus offers rest for our souls (Matt. 11:29); but His prescription for achieving that healing has been watered down into a shallow, feel-good approach to life that bypasses many of the hard decisions He demands of us.

Then there are the celebrities who wear their love for Jesus on their sleeve for all to see—but get drunk on weekends and have no intention of marrying their live-in girlfriends. Jesus is little more than a token in their lives, and His words carry little weight in their lifestyle choices.

Study carefully the teachings of Jesus, and it's obvious that He calls us to a high standard of moral conduct growing out of a transformed way of thinking about God, self, and others. To claim Jesus as our Lord is to adopt a radical outlook on all of life. In our self-centered, narcissistic culture, truly following Jesus is not just radical, it's dangerous. It challenges all our assumptions about "the good life," and rips the mask off our pretentious self-righteousness. Until we understand that, we cannot be His disciple.

It is good that we want to follow Jesus. But before we declare Him to be "Lord, Lord," we need to ask ourselves if we are really committed to doing what He says we should do. Until we are willing to surrender every detail of our soul, body, and life to Him, we are not ready to follow Him.

Say vs. Do

When trying convince others that we love God,
talk is cheap. The best evidence that we love God
is simply living our lives as He directs.

---

*"Why do you call Me 'Lord, Lord,' and do not do the
things which I say?" (Lk. 6:46).*

*Most men will proclaim each his own goodness, but who
can find a faithful man? (Prov. 20:6)*

*Show me your faith without your works, and I will show
you my faith by my works (Jas. 2:18).*

৩৽৶৩

Every preacher can tell stories of encountering folks who
try to ingratiate themselves with the man of God by profusive
expressions of religion. Oh, how they love Jesus! Their great-
uncle was a deacon in the church! The Lord healed their
bunion! On and on the stories go.

The reason preachers remember these stories is because
the lives of most of those who talk so loudly about their faith
are such a horrid mess. This experience is so common that I'll
give it a name: Dave's Law: "The volume with which people
talk about their faith is inversely proportional to the legitimacy of their faith." Expressed more simply, people who are
loudest in declaring their love for the Lord usually are doing
the poorest job of living it. Call me cynical, but when I encounter people who start carrying on about their love for
God, red flags go up in my mind. They're probably trying to
hide something.

I'm not the only one who is cynical. Solomon was
surrounded by sycophants who "proclaimed each his own

goodness," but ultimately proved untrustworthy. When Jesus walked upon this earth, He knew the frustration of hearing people call Him "Lord, Lord," yet ignore what He taught. This is not a modern phenomenon, but an endemic flaw of human nature. It's so much easier for people to talk about doing right, than to actually do it.

Even people of the world who make no pretense of religion recognize this empty language for the hypocrisy it is. Far from currying favor with God, it does enormous damage to His cause, linking God's name to a lot of ungodly behavior. Don't think for a moment that God is indifferent to His name being dragged through the mud in such a fashion.

To be sure, there is a time and place for declaring our faith with boldness and courage. But in everyday life, those occasions are few and far between (and trying to impress the preacher is not one of them). The far more effective display of our faith is seen in how we live. James summarized the issue perfectly: If we want to show others our faith, the only legitimate way we can do it is by our *works*. People who are actually living the life God wants them to live have no need of broadcasting it. Their lives provide a quiet but unmistakable testimony to what they believe.

Of course, that's not easy. Doing what God asks us to do in our lives requires a great deal of self-discipline, sacrifice, and hard work. Sadly, most people are not willing to invest that level of commitment. They prefer to just skate by on words alone, while doing pretty much whatever they please. In the end, they will find that the only ones they were fooling were themselves.

The real issue, as always, is what is in the heart. A heart that is humble in the presence of God has no desire, or even a need, for talking a big game. It knows that actions speak louder than words.

Understanding Authority

Understanding the will of God does not require a degree in theology. It requires a heart that is sensitive to the guidance of our Maker.

"I did not even think myself worthy to come to You. But say the word, and my servant will be healed. For I also am a man placed under authority, having soldiers under me. And I say to one, 'Go,' and he goes; and to another, 'Come,' and he comes; and to my servant, 'Do this,' and he does it." When Jesus heard these things, He marveled at him, and turned around and said to the crowd that followed Him, "I say to you, I have not found such great faith, not even in Israel!" (Lk. 7:7-9).

৽৽৽

In navigating our relationship with God, there is no greater topic we can explore than the concept of *authority*. If He is our King and we are His subjects, it is imperative that we learn how to respect His authority.

Recognizing that truth, brethren through the years have published a vast corpus of material on the subject of "How to Establish Bible Authority." Using charts, diagrams, and Biblical illustrations, these works provide a sort of decoder ring to help the serious Bible student master the task of knowing the will of God. Useful information can be gleaned from these sources, but there is a lot of obfuscation as well. Some of this material borders on human law-making ("The Law of Materiality," "The Law of Competence," "The Law of Limited Application," and so forth). In our quest to leave no stone unturned, this approach to authority veers dangerously close to the theology of the scribes and Pharisees, who "bind heavy burdens, hard to bear" on unsophisticated followers of God (Matt. 23:4). Just as the Pharisees turned God's Sabbath law into a maze of regulations that subverted the original intent of the Law, we tend to make the subject of authority more complicated than God intends it to be.

The centurion in this episode had a perspective on authority that cut through all the legalese and went straight to the heart of the matter: "I say to one man, 'go' and he goes; and to another, 'Come,' and he comes; and to my servant, 'Do this,' and he does it." In these few words, the centurion tells us everything we need to know about authority. In its most fundamental form, authority is simply *God telling us what to do*. Simple declarative statements define the boundaries; examples clarify and inform those boundaries; occasionally we may need to "connect the dots" from multiple pieces of evidence to draw an unavoidable inference. But at the end of the day, it's a fairly simple process of study and reasoning that even an uneducated farm laborer can perform. And he can do this without a six-month study in a workbook on authority.

But if we look at this story closely, we'll notice a deeper prerequisite to understanding God's authority. The centurion—a leader who knew how to give orders—admitted that "I did not even think myself worthy to come to You" (v. 7). This is *humility* in action, an awareness of one's inadequacy to chart his own path. In far too many cases, people over-complicate Biblical truth by their prideful insistence on doing things their own way. Their self-will is an impediment to understanding.

When Jesus heard the plea of this Roman soldier, He was amazed. "I have not found such great faith, not even in Israel." Jesus saw in this man's simple expression of trust a faith that exceeded all the learning of his religious superiors. That's what God is still looking for today: People who trust His word to shine a light on their path through life.

Jesus and Sin

How Jesus addressed the subject of sin provides some important lessons on how we should deal with the subject in our lives today.

Now when the Pharisee who had invited Him saw this, he spoke to himself, saying, "This man, if He were a prophet, would know who and what manner of woman this is who is touching Him, for she is a sinner." . . . Then [Jesus] said to her, "Your sins are forgiven" (Lk. 7:39, 48).

෴

The woman in this story had washed Jesus' feet, wiped them with her hair, and anointed them with precious oil. It was an act of honor that scandalized the Pharisees in the room, because she had a reputation as an immoral woman. No self-respecting Jew would allow such a woman to touch him. Yet Jesus not only allowed her to touch Him, He also forgave her sins.

Stories like this in the Gospels have led some to conclude that Jesus was not all that concerned about sin, preferring instead to promote a more positive message of love and tolerance. This is a misreading of the evidence.

Jesus was not indifferent to sin. He had strong convictions about right and wrong, and taught them. His famous Sermon on the Mount (Matt. 5–7), for example, is based on the premise that God's law is binding and must be honored (5:17-20). In that same Sermon, He urged His listeners to make whatever sacrifices necessary (plucking out eyes, cutting off hands) to avoid getting caught up in sin (5:29-30; see 18:8-9). Elsewhere, He described sin as a cruel master that enslaves those who practice it (Jn. 8:31-36), and warned against leading others into it (Matt. 18:6). At least twice He admonished those who received His forgiveness to "sin no more" (Jn. 5:14; 8:11). These are not the words of someone who has a careless "whatever" attitude toward sin.

At the same time, we must acknowledge that Jesus' approach to dealing with sin was profoundly different from that of the Pharisees, who often excoriated Him for being soft on violations of God's law. There was something about Jesus' treatment of human imperfection that they saw as loose, even dangerous. It is in His responses to these critics that we gain a deeper insight into how Jesus viewed sin.

The sins of the masses that so incensed the Pharisees were indeed character flaws that needed to be addressed, and Jesus addressed them. But Jesus saw another, more insidious sin at work among His critics. It was the sin of *pride*, a condescending self-importance that despised others as inferior and contemptible. In the very act of condemning the weaknesses of others, these critics were guilty of an altogether different sin that was just as deadly, just as despicable, as anything their inferiors were committing. Jesus' strongest rebukes were reserved for that sin.

What some in His day (and many today) interpreted as careless indifference to sin was not indifference at all. Rather, Jesus was restoring a sense of balance to the subject. Even when we think we are good people, we are likely guilty of the same error that doomed the Pharisees, and are no better than those whose sins we scorn.

Jesus hated sin and gave His life to overcome its disastrous impact on humanity. Whether sinful woman or proud Pharisee, our first response to His sacrifice should be to acknowledge the fact of sin in our own lives.

Good but Barren

One of the great dangers in a life of faith is
settling into a comfortable routine of niceness
that bears no fruit for God.

---

*"Now the ones that fell among thorns are those who,
when they have heard, go out and are choked with cares,
riches, and pleasures of life, and bring no fruit to maturity"*
(Lk. 8:14).

৽৽৽

In His parable of the sower, Jesus explained why the
gospel often does not accomplish its intended purpose. The
defect is not in the message, but in the hearts of those who
hear it. Some simply have no interest in spiritual matters, and
reject it outright. Others get excited about it for awhile, but
their ardor soon cools and they drift away.

Our attention here is drawn to a third category: Those
who embrace the gospel and at some level remain faithful to
it, but they never accomplish anything with it. They "bring no
fruit to maturity."

These disciples live a decent enough life, avoiding the
more notorious sins of the flesh, thereby contributing to a
civil society. They wear the "Christian" label proudly, confident of their connection with God. They even show up
regularly at church—at least when it's convenient.

But as far as kingdom priorities are concerned, they're
MIA. They are so busy with their careers, hobbies, investments, vacations, houses, entertainments, and so on, that they
have no time for the real work that the Master has called them
to do: Encouraging the weak, visiting the sick, helping the

poor, teaching the lost, comforting the hopeless, confronting evil. These are the duties that make a real difference in this world, yet when opportunities arise to pursue any of these tasks, these disciples are nowhere to be found. They are choked by the cares of this world, and can't be bothered.

Admittedly, there is no glamour in any of this work. It's not intended to be glamorous. It certainly wasn't glamorous for Jesus when He walked among us. But it's the very messiness of this work that makes it so essential. *Somebody* needs to do it, and God has prepared a people who are committed to doing it. But these sunshine disciples choose to take a pass. They have more important things to do with their time.

These disciples are not bad people. But they are practically useless in the great mission God has called them to perform. If we call ourselves "Christian," we need to take a long, hard look at our personal priorities. Perhaps we are good people—but are we *fruitful*?

Someday, God will judge us on that standard. Let us use our time accordingly.

Seed and Fruit

How people respond to the gospel message is determined by one consideration alone: What do they love in their hearts above all else?

"But the ones that fell on the good ground are those who, having heard the word with a noble and good heart, keep it and bear fruit with patience" (Lk. 8:15).

༄༅༅

In a half-century of teaching the Bible in classes, sermons, articles, home studies, personal counseling, and casual conversations, I have seen the wisdom of Jesus' parable of the sower displayed again and again. The details may vary, but people react to God's word in one of the four ways Jesus spells out in this parable.

For many people, the message of the Bible holds no interest whatsoever. Their hearts are so cold and indifferent to spiritual truth that the message cannot penetrate. No amount of pleading or arguing will ever move them to consider it, and we're wasting our time trying to force it upon them.

Others accept the gospel eagerly, even joyfully—but it doesn't stick. As soon as the initial excitement wears off and they have to confront the real world again, they lose interest and drift away. Their faith is shallow, so their commitment is shallow. These wanderers rarely return to the faith.

Then there are those who embrace the message and maintain some degree of allegiance to it throughout their lives. However, their affections are divided. They are so busy with their worldly pursuits that their religion becomes little more than a minor placeholder in their daily routine. Oh, they'll show up, but they cannot be depended upon to contribute anything useful to the Lord's cause.

Finally, there are those few for whom the gospel was designed. These people have "noble and good" hearts that see in this message a power to transform their lives. They receive the word gladly, grateful for the wisdom and guidance it provides. That commitment to truth bears fruit in a thousand little ways as they interact with the world around them. They give freely of themselves to lift up the weak, comfort the sick, and strengthen the discouraged. They are generous with their time, money, and encouragement. They are the first to pitch in and help, and the last to seek any credit for their labors. And they're not ashamed to share with others the message of grace that has had such an impact in their own lives. Those who populate this group bear this fruit "with patience." Whatever obstacles and disappointments they encounter, they never give up. Rather, the hardships seem to make them even stronger and more productive in their faith.

What is the determining factor in the disparate responses of these four groups? It is *the heart of the hearer*. Deep down inside, each one of us has something that we love above all else. For three of these groups, that object of affection is some form of selfishness. Only those in the fourth group have enthroned God as the chief object of love in their hearts.

Identify what you love more than anything else, and you'll know the group to which you belong.

What God Has Done

God has done great things for us, but He does not intend for us to keep them to ourselves. If they are great for us, they should be shared with others.

Now the man from whom the demons had departed begged Him that he might be with Him. But Jesus sent him away, saying, "Return to your own house, and tell what great things God has done for you." And he went his way and proclaimed throughout the whole city what great things Jesus had done for him (Lk. 8:38-39).

৵৵

To appreciate this story, we have to go back and look at the miracle that set up this exchange. This Gadarene demoniac was no garden variety case of demon possession. He called himself "Legion," because many demons possessed him (v. 30). The effect of this multiple demon possession was awful. He wore no clothes and lived in tombs (v. 27). When others tried to bring his madness under control using chains, he would break free and run into the wilderness (v. 29). This poor man's life was a living horror show.

But all that changed when Jesus came into his life. Jesus cast the demons into a nearby herd of swine, who were destroyed by their new masters. The pigs were lost, but the man was transformed, "clothed and in his right mind." The Lord had given this man a new life. The change was so dramatic, it frightened those who knew him in his previous state (v. 35).

It's no surprise, therefore, to read of this man begging to follow Jesus. The Lord had given him his life back; how much more could he learn from Jesus if he stayed close by

His side in the days and months to come?! But Jesus had other plans for His new disciple. Hanging around Jesus might have been personally satisfying, but he could be far more useful to the Lord's cause by returning to his people and sharing the story of what God had done for him. It was an effective strategy, for "the whole city" heard about this man's amazing story.

There are three lessons in this episode for God's people today.

First, our salvation is not just a personal gift from God, but also *an instrument through which God's grace is shared with others*. That's why God does not whisk us away to glory as soon as we come up out of the waters of baptism. Our own victory over sin may be accomplished, but God wants that experience to be shared with others, as a means of introducing them to the hope of a better life. The most effective evangelism is that which is spread person-to-person, by those who have already experienced God's grace.

Second, *there is a strong correlation between our level of appreciation for what God has done for us and our willingness to share that story with others*. If we're too embarrassed or indifferent to tell others about the changes that God has wrought in our own life, then what does that say about our level of gratitude for His gift? If, on the other hand, we see the salvation of the Lord as the greatest thing that ever happened in our life, then we can't help but share it with others.

Finally, *the message that God would have us share with others is not a complicated one.* We do not have to be Bible scholars to talk to others about the Lord. Like this man, all Jesus asks of us is to "tell what great things God has done for you." The simple story of how God has transformed your life can be a powerful incentive to others who are looking for improvement in their own lives.

Of course, all of this assumes the Lord has done "great things" for you. Has He?

Only Believe

Entering a relationship with Jesus is not done by faith alone. But there are other occasions when we have no other recourse but to "only believe."

While He was still speaking, someone came from the ruler of the synagogue's house, saying to him, "Your daughter is dead. Do not trouble the Teacher." But when Jesus heard it, He answered him, saying, "Do not be afraid; only believe, and she will be made well" (Lk. 8:49-50).

You see then that a man is justified by works, and not by faith only (Jas. 2:24).

ঙ৽৵

One of the most popular denominational errors—and one of our favorite targets—is the concept of salvation by faith only. All someone has to do to be saved, we are told, is to accept Jesus as their Savior in their heart, and they are saved. Nothing else is required. It is a false concept based on an incomplete understanding of the Bible, refuted by a host of passages that describe other actions as necessary for salvation (Ac. 2:38; 22:16; and others).

One of our favorite passages for responding to this teaching is James 2:24: "You see then that a man is justified by works, and *not by faith only.*" That's pretty clear, isn't it? This one verse should settle the matter once and for all. Faith alone is not adequate to save.

We are on solid ground when we make this argument. But we err when we go out on a limb and state confidently, "This is the only time that 'faith only' is found in the Bible." I've heard that statement from preachers all my life, and have used it dozens of times myself. But one day while reading the account of Jairus' daughter, I stumbled across our opening text. Right there in black and white was a phrase that I thought did not exist outside of James 2:24—"only believe." In fact, the older King James Version is even closer; it reads, "believe only." The same wording is found in the parallel account in Mk. 5:36. Our English translations use different words "faith" (James) and "believe" (Luke/Mark), but in the original Greek texts they are simply noun and verb forms of the same word, *pistos*.

So is our argument flawed? Not at all. Jesus was referring to the physical healing of a parent's little girl, not salvation. And we could argue that Jairus, the girl's father, had already demonstrated his faith by his efforts to track down Jesus and seek His help.

Even so, Jesus' use of the term "believe only" suggests that there may be times in our life when the only thing left to do is to quit trying to fix a problem on our own and just trust God to deal with it. When the Israelites were trapped between the Red Sea and Pharaoh's army, Moses ordered them to "stand still, and see the salvation of the Lord" (Ex. 14:13). A prophet gave the army of Jehoshaphat the same message when surrounded by their enemies (2 Chron. 20:17). In times of trouble, the Psalmist advises us to "be still, and know that I am God" (Psa. 46:10).

Faith in God requires that we act when so directed. But sometimes faith requires that we calmly stand aside and let God do the work. Indeed, sometimes the greatest test of faith of all can be our response to the Lord's command, "Do not be afraid; only believe."

The Long Sleep

The New Testament's frequent allusions to death as "sleep" should alter how we think of our own demise. We have a glorious morning awaiting us.

Now all wept and mourned for her; but He said, "Do not weep; she is not dead, but sleeping." And they ridiculed Him, knowing that she was dead (Lk. 8:52).

He said to them, "Our friend Lazarus sleeps, but I go that I may wake him up." . . . Jesus spoke of his death, but they thought that He was speaking about taking rest in sleep (Jn. 11:11, 13).

ഏൟ

The resurrections of Jairus' daughter and Lazarus were remarkable miracles in their own right. But the fact that in both cases Jesus spoke of the dead as "sleeping" suggests a deliberate lesson on the nature of death. This message is reinforced in the epistles of Paul, who also frequently uses sleep as a metaphor for death (1 Cor. 15:18, 20, 51; 1 Thess. 4:13-15; 5:10).

This euphemism teaches us two important truths about death that we fail to appreciate. Recalibrating our view of death to see it as nothing more than a long sleep can change how we prepare for our own demise.

First, just as sleep is a temporary state of unconsciousness that precedes a new day, *death is merely a transitory darkness on our journey toward a new life*. The Biblical doctrine of resurrection—confirmed by the resurrection of Jesus—should reassure us that we have something better to look forward to when that morning arrives. Death marks the end of our sojourn in this life, to be sure; but it does not eradicate our existence as a distinct personality. We shall rise again, and that new life is far beyond anything we can experience here (2 Cor. 5:1-8; Rev. 21:1-7).

It naturally follows, therefore, that *death is not to be feared.* We generally are not terrified about going to sleep at night, for we know it's a perfectly natural part of the cycle of life. If we embrace the hope of our resurrection in Christ, we should not fear going to sleep in death, either. It, too, is a perfectly natural part of the cycle of life that ends in eternal life. What is there to be afraid of?

Paul lived his life "having a desire to depart and be with Christ, which is far better" (Phil. 1:23). He looked forward to that day when he would lay his head down to rest for the last time, knowing that when he awakened on the other side, a glorious new life awaited him.

A long sleep awaits you, too. Are you ready for it?

Self-Knowledge

The greatest impediment to knowing Jesus is a failure to know ourselves. But only by knowing Him can we come to understand ourselves.

*And it happened, as they were parting from Him, that Peter said to Jesus, "Master, it is good for us to be here; and let us make three tabernacles: one for You, one for Moses, and one for Elijah"—**not knowing** what he said (Lk. 9:33).*

*"Let these words sink down into your ears, for the Son of Man is about to be delivered into the hands of men." But **they did not understand** this saying, and it was hidden from them so that they did not perceive it; and they were afraid to ask Him about this saying (Lk. 9:44-45).*

*And when His disciples James and John saw this, they said, "Lord, do You want us to command fire to come down from heaven and consume them, just as Elijah did?" But He turned and rebuked them, and said, "**You do not know** what manner of spirit you are of. For the Son of Man did not come to destroy men's lives but to save them" (Lk. 9:54-56, NKJV).*

৩০৵

Three times in this chapter, we are told that the apostles of Jesus "did not know" or "did not understand" something. More disturbing, two of those revelations concerned knowledge of themselves. Peter knew perfectly well the words that he spoke on the Mount of Transfiguration; but he didn't understand the implications of what he was saying. James and John thought they were defending the honor of their Master by calling down fire from heaven upon the Samaritans; but Jesus saw a more sinister motive at work, one that the brothers could not recognize in themselves. The intentions of these men were the best, but their imperfect knowledge of themselves left them vulnerable to errors of human pride.

If the apostles of Jesus had that much trouble understanding themselves, who am I to think that I have myself all figured out? The greatest battle any of us will ever have to fight is the one we fight with ourselves, as we try to untangle our innermost motives and ambitions. Jeremiah admitted, "The heart is deceitful above all things, and desperately wicked; who can know it?" (Jer. 17:9). Paul knew the frustration well: "For what I am doing, I do not understand" (Rom. 7:15). We are not nearly as perfect as we like to pretend we are; in fact, we are far more imperfect than we care to admit. That lack of self-awareness lies at the root of so many of the mistakes and blunders we commit.

So do we just shrug our shoulders and give up trying? Not at all! As Peter, James, John and the other apostles came to a better understanding of the selfless attitude that motivated Jesus's life, they began to see themselves in a different light as well. They became wiser men as their knowledge of Jesus grew, especially after His death and resurrection.

It's the same with us: Greater self-knowledge—and the reformed life that grows out of that knowledge—is the result of a more intimate relationship with Jesus. That change is not a one-time event, but an ongoing process that takes a lifetime to complete: "We all, with unveiled face, beholding as in a mirror the glory of the Lord, *are being transformed* into the same image from glory to glory" (2 Cor. 3:18; note the present tense).

Study to understand Jesus better, and you will come to understand yourself better.

Afraid to Ask

There is no shame in not understanding a subject or concept. The shame comes later, if we choose not to ask questions for fear of looking dumb.

"Listen carefully to what I am about to tell you: The Son of Man is going to be betrayed into the hands of men." But they did not understand what this meant. It was hidden from them, so that they did not grasp it, and they were afraid to ask Him about it (Lk. 9:44-45).

૭∾૭

This was the first time Jesus gave His apostles details about the fate that awaited Him. The announcement was so shocking, so out of touch with their pre-conceived notions of the Messiah's work, they couldn't comprehend what He was saying. How did the apostles respond to this puzzle? "They were afraid to ask Him about it." Jesus' words were bewildering, but rather than ask Him for clarification, they said nothing.

Why were the apostles afraid to question Jesus' statement? The simple answer is, they were afraid of looking ignorant and uninformed. We know the apostles at this stage were still struggling with a pride problem (see v. 46-56). Here, too, their pride forced them to keep their ignorance hidden; so instead of asking questions, they chose to remain silent, even though they had no clue what Jesus was talking about. Several months later, when Jesus' words were fulfilled, their ignorance left them unprepared, and they failed miserably. Their lack of curiosity about Jesus' words eventually hurt them badly.

The apostles' reticence to ask questions is a common human failing. Many of us, when faced with circumstances that don't make sense, prefer to "play cool" and pretend that we're up to speed. But inwardly, we have no idea what's going on; like the apostles, we're too proud to let our bewilderment show.

But the truth is, we *are* ignorant. None of us is born with innate knowledge about anything. Everything we know, we have learned—either from parents and teachers who pounded it into our heads, or from books and other media, or from mentors, counselors, friends, co-workers, or supervisors who took the time to share their knowledge. And no matter how much we have learned, our current level of knowledge is still limited. There will always be much that we don't know. That's not a failure, but a simple fact of life.

It's the person who can freely admit, "I don't understand, please explain," who is in the best position to learn. His questions do not brand him as ignorant, but as curious and desiring knowledge. People respect that. It was this respect for the curious mind that led Voltaire to say that we should "judge a man by his questions rather than by his answers." A lifetime spent asking questions will sharpen our skill at asking more, and learning more.

After all, asking questions is the quickest way to replace ignorance with knowledge. We should remember this when dealing with others who pepper us with honest questions. Instead of belittling them for their ignorance, we should reward their honesty with all the patient guidance we can provide them.

So the next time you encounter a situation or concept that appears inexplicable, don't try to preserve your dignity by pretending you know the answers. Just come out and state the truth: "I don't understand" . . . then start asking questions.

Eventually, others will start asking *you* the questions.

But First . . .

A major obstacle preventing us from being more productive is our failure to distinguish *good* things from *greater* things.

He said to another, "Follow Me." But he said, "Lord, let me first go and bury my father." Jesus said to him, "Let the dead bury their own dead, but you go and preach the kingdom of God." And another also said, "Lord, I will follow You, but let me first go and bid them farewell who are at my house." But Jesus said to him, "No one, having put his hand to the plow, and looking back, is fit for the kingdom of God" (Lk. 9:59-62).

❧

The men with whom Jesus had these exchanges were not His enemies. They did not mock or accuse Jesus, as His critics often did. They believed in Him, and if we can take their statements at face value, they really did want to follow Him. "But first" they had other priorities that required their attention, so they begged to be temporarily excused.

Which is another way of saying, Jesus was no better than second on their list of priorities.

The responses of Jesus to these men seem harsh, but He saw a serious problem underlying their excuses. If it was that easy for them to dodge the Master's call on this occasion, they would continue dodging it through the rest of their lives. Whatever service they offered Him would be squishy and inconsistent. Jesus was telling these men up front that He didn't need that kind of disciple. They had to be all in, or go elsewhere.

Jesus challenged these men because He understood human nature. He knew that once people start making excuses, the excuses never stop coming. One excuse is followed by another which is followed by another . . . and somehow we never get around to doing the very thing that we acknowledge is most important.

This story warns the rest of us of how easy it is to allow earthly concerns to interfere with our service to the Lord.

- I know I ought to go visit that elderly shut-in who is lonely . . . but first I need to clean house and do the laundry.
- I really do want to spend more quality time with the kids . . . but first I need to catch up on all the latest news on my electronic device.
- It would be great if somebody would do some door-knocking in the neighborhood to promote our upcoming gospel meeting . . . but please excuse me, I really need to clean out my garage that day.

Who are we kidding? The problem in all these scenarios is not that we are choosing evil over good; it's that we're choosing a *lesser* good over a *greater* good. The really important tasks are being neglected for the sake of more mundane obligations that could be postponed or re-arranged with a little effort. Whether we realize it or not, we are revealing the things that our heart considers to be of greater importance. The Lord and His work can wait; I have more important things to tend to.

The church today is filled with decent people who, in their own way, love the Lord and want to do the right thing; but their lives are too cluttered with trivial matters to be of much use in His kingdom. So the critical work never gets done. No wonder the church is not growing.

Jesus is still looking for followers today. But what He really needs are those few who are ready to put Him first in their lives. Are you game?

Lambs Among Wolves

Jesus bids us follow Him all the way—into a pack of wolves, if necessary. The prospect need not frighten us, if we recognize the final outcome.

"Go your way; behold, I send you out as lambs among wolves" (Lk. 10:3).

§∞∞§

If Jesus is the Good Shepherd (Jn. 10:11), then we must ask: What kind of shepherd would send his sheep into an environment crawling with predators like wolves? This doesn't sound like a very loving thing to do.

Of course, Jesus knew exactly what He was asking these seventy disciples to do. Sending these men forth was not a fool's errand, but an essential training exercise. These disciples (apparently distinct from the twelve apostles, v. 1) needed to learn lessons in courage, trust, and perseverance. The day would come when they would no longer have Jesus around to personally tutor them, so this short-term assignment, as difficult as it might be, would serve as a useful exercise to prepare them for the challenges they would face after His departure. The growth of the church amid persecution in the early chapters of Acts confirms the wisdom of Jesus' strategy.

We, too, are lambs among wolves. We do not become disciples of Jesus in order to find protection from hardship. On the contrary, the more likely outcome of that decision is ridicule and persecution. We are signing up for a life of struggle in a hostile world, a world that has no appreciation for who we follow or what we represent.

How could it be any other way? It is not our job to defeat the enemy in epic battle. We must never forget that we are *sheep*. It is our unfailing commitment to a lifestyle of unconditional love and forgiveness that will carry the day. The weapons of our warfare are spiritual, not carnal, and the forces of evil that oppose us have no idea how to counter an army of sheep.

Yes, some of the flock will be devoured by the wolves; that's a stark reality of life. They did the same thing to the Lamb of God—and how did that crime finally play out? This world needs *more* kindness, *more* tenderness, *more* meekness, *more* gentleness, *more* courage, not less. And it is our job to manifest those qualities in the face of unrelenting antagonism.

The love of God will someday conquer this wreck of a world, and this little flock of sheep, ironically, are His shock troops in the opening assault. Let us take on this assignment with courage and hope, looking to the Lion of Judah for the final deliverance that one day will be ours.

What Is Written

If we genuinely want to know the will of God, we must go to the primary source through which He has made it known: The Scriptures.

And behold, a certain lawyer stood up and tested Him, saying, "Teacher, what shall I do to inherit eternal life?" He said to him, "What is written in the law? What is your reading of it?" (Lk. 10:25-26).

Now these things, brethren, I have figuratively transferred to myself and Apollos for your sakes, that you may learn in us not to think beyond what is written, that none of you may be puffed up on behalf of one against the other (1 Cor. 4:6).

❧

When God brought Israel out of Egypt and forged them into a new nation, one of the first things He did was give them a written Law. From that time forward, God's preferred means of communicating His will to His people was through writing. Over the next millennium and a half, His prophets recorded numerous works of history, wisdom, rebuke, and encouragement, all as a means of providing a definitive source of guidance for His people.

The value of written revelation is not hard to understand. A written message provides a uniform standard that is accessible to a wide audience. It can be copied, distributed, and translated, then read by individuals or to a large group. And because it is written, there is a reduced risk of corruption compared to oral communication.

This written revelation can be inspiring (think of the courage of Job in the face of his trials), exciting (David taking on Goliath with his sling), and even entertaining (Haman's blundering efforts to destroy the Jews in the book of Esther). But above all, the Scriptures are intended to be *authoritative*. When the lawyer asked Jesus "What shall I do?" Jesus did not give him the answer; instead, He directed him to an existing body of instruction: "What is written in the law?" (To his credit, the lawyer was familiar with the source documents and gave a correct response, quoting Deut. 6:5 and Lev. 19:18).

In the same manner, Paul's approach to the problems plaguing the church at Corinth was to train them "not to exceed what was written" (NASB). God had already revealed and recorded the attitudes and behaviors that were necessary for His people to work together in harmony. The Corinthians had been ignoring that testimony, and were paying a terrible price for their ignorance.

Historically, that has always been the problem. "I have written for him the great things of My law," God once told an earlier generation, "but they were considered a strange thing" (Hos. 8:12). If people don't bother to read or listen to what God has revealed, they aren't going to be knowledgeable of what He wants them to do. And ignorance of what is written always leads to disaster.

When we face questions and issues today, either in our personal lives or as a body of believers, our response should always be that of Jesus to the lawyer: "What is written in the law?" It may take a lot of study and careful sifting and sorting of material to properly interpret the message, but there is no alternative. Relying on feelings, popular opinion, or human "experts" for quick answers will inevitably get us in trouble.

God has expended great effort to give us His word for our benefit. Our duty is to respect what He has written.

Who Is My Neighbor?

"Love your neighbor" is the second-greatest command. But we dilute that duty by our efforts to narrowly define "neighbor." Shame on us.

A certain lawyer stood up and tested Him, saying, "Teacher, what shall I do to inherit eternal life?" He said to him, "What is written in the law? What is your reading of it?" So he answered and said, "'You shall love the Lord your God with all your heart, with all your soul, with all your strength, and with all your mind,' and 'Your neighbor as yourself.'" And He said to him, "You have answered rightly; do this and you will live." But he, wanting to justify himself, said to Jesus, "And who is my neighbor?" (Lk. 10:25-29).

❧

To his credit, the lawyer who posed this question to Jesus rightly understood the foundation of God's law: love God and love my neighbor. But then the conversation took a strange turn; the lawyer wanted to parse the meaning of the second commandment: "And who is my neighbor?" It was a lawyerly way of probing the limits of that requirement. Surely, he thought, there must be some boundaries to the love we extend to others. Luke's commentary that this man was "wanting to justify himself" suggests that he was looking for a loophole, some exception that would minimize the scope of his obligation.

In His response, Jesus gave the beloved parable of the Good Samaritan, the story of a foreign businessman who, at great risk to himself, dropped everything to give aid to a stranger who was in dire circumstances. Even today, the label

"Good Samaritan" is used to describe those who go out of their way to render assistance to strangers.

But Jesus ended the parable with a curious question: "Who proved to be a neighbor to the one in need?" We usually read right over that question and fail to catch the subtle switch Jesus made. The lawyer wanted to know the identity of *the one being served*; but Jesus put the emphasis on the character of *the one doing the serving*.

That distinction makes all the difference in the world. Being a neighbor to others is more important than correctly cataloging everyone into "worthy" and "unworthy" buckets. When we approach our fellow human beings with jaundiced eyes, looking for excuses not be hospitable to them, we can usually find one. Our job is to be a neighbor to those who are in need, not to pre-qualify them for consideration. Certainly there are egregious cases where we must exercise good judgment (even Jesus refused to feed a multitude that was merely looking for a handout, Jn. 6:26-27). But our default position should be one of unconditional goodness toward those in need.

Our world is perishing for a lack of love. It is the duty of God's people to demonstrate that love by being neighbors to everyone.

What Made the
Samaritan "Good"?

Jesus did not call the Samaritan "good." But we do
because of his unusual kindness. What does the
behavior of this man say about *our* character?

*"But a certain Samaritan, as he journeyed, came where
he was. And when he saw him, he had compassion" (Lk.
10:33).*

ഔ

The parable of the Good Samaritan is one of the best
known of Jesus' parables. It's a simple story with a profound
message for anyone who is serious about going to heaven.

The parable was set up by a question posed to Jesus by a
lawyer: "What shall I do to inherit eternal life?" (v. 25). Jesus
prompted the scribe to give his own answer: love God with
all your heart, and your neighbor as yourself (v. 27). But the
lawyer sought a loophole in the second part of the command.
He asked Jesus, "And who is my neighbor?" (v. 29). The
parable of the Good Samaritan was Jesus' answer.

Jesus approached the lawyer's question indirectly. He set
up His story using the unfortunate circumstances of "a certain
man," implying that anyone who is in need is our neighbor.
But Jesus did not stop there. By describing in detail what the
Samaritan did for the poor man, Jesus made the central theme
in the parable not the definition of "neighbor," but of "love."

By making the hero of this story a Samaritan—a despised class in Jewish eyes—Jesus reinforced His message
that goodness is not a function of racial or ethnic identity, but
of behavior, a behavior that is available to everyone.

Consider what the Samaritan did for this man that displayed his love for him:

First, the fact that he even *"had compassion"* for the man when he first saw his bruised and battered body (v. 33) is an indication of his love. Many people are so jaded by the constant news of crime, poverty, brutality, and tragedy that they no longer feel anything for the misfortunes of others. This Samaritan still had a heart that could be touched.

Next, consider that the Samaritan *stopped to help the man*, despite the grave personal risk to himself. The same thieves who had beaten and robbed this man could have been lurking nearby. But he was willing to take that risk, in order to help a fellow human being who was obviously in dire need.

The good deed he did for this man *was not pleasant*. He no doubt had to deal with a lot of blood and filth to stabilize his condition (v. 34). But he looked past the ugliness to the value of the human life he was saving.

Finally, note that the Samaritan's good deed *cost him time and money*. Whatever business he was pursuing on this trip had to wait while he took care of this man. Paying for the man's care at the inn for several days cost him a couple days' wages (v. 35).

And remember: All this was done, not for a close relative or dear friend, but for a man whom he didn't know from Adam.

Just for good measure, Jesus contrasted the actions of the Samaritan with the behavior of a priest and Levite, who "passed by" the crime victim rather than soil their holy hands with the untidiness of active love (v. 31-32).

The Samaritan was "good," not because he was one of the chosen race, or because he was sound on all the current issues of the day, but because he showed love to a neighbor. Jesus' lesson is simple, but stern: If I desire a place in the kingdom of heaven, I must "go and do likewise" (v. 37).

Resolving Moral Quandaries

Many of our dilemmas that involve helping others are obfuscated by the demands involved in doing the right thing. But it's not that complicated.

"So which of these three do you think was neighbor to him who fell among the thieves?" And he said, "He who showed mercy on him." Then Jesus said to him, "Go and do likewise" (Lk. 10:36-37).

৩৽৵৻

The parable of the Good Samaritan was prompted by a lawyerly question about The Second Greatest Law, namely, the duty to "love your neighbor as yourself" (v. 27-29). The lawyer's question ("Who is my neighbor?") was not designed to identify the proper candidates for compassion, but to find a loophole that would limit the obligation.

In the end, of course, the lawyer understood perfectly well who his neighbor was. His own response to the parable ("He who showed mercy on him") revealed the simple truth behind the command: Our neighbor is anyone who needs the help that we are in a position to provide.

In the majority of cases, moral quandaries are not as problematic as we make them out to be, and knowing the right thing to do is really not that hard to figure out. The complication stems from the price we know we'll have pay to do it. Doing the right thing often involves sacrifice, inconvenience, or even social awkwardness. It certainly imposed a cost on the Samaritan in this parable.

But when faced with an opportunity to serve others in our own lives, we often allow these background considerations to twist our minds into knots. The priest and the Levite in this parable no doubt struggled with the moral dilemma of what to do about this man who obviously needed help. Whatever calculations they performed in making their decisions, they concluded that they had justifiable reasons for not getting involved in his plight. We often do the same thing: We deliberate, we waffle, we dither, we evaluate all the options . . . until the opportunity goes away, or we decide that the benefit is not worth the trouble. The priest and Levite would be so proud.

The genius of this parable is that it strips away all those extraneous deliberations and exposes the key issue in every humanitarian decision: *Will I step up and offer my services to help this person in need, or not?* We have no problem identifying the hero and villains in this story; so why do we struggle to see our own opportunities to do good in the same bright light?

"Go and do likewise" is Jesus' challenge to each one of us to practice our faith. When the Lord places a genuine humanitarian crisis in your path, don't agonize over the decision about what to do. Just do it. Someone will appreciate your kindness, and you'll feel a lot better for having stepped out of your comfort zone.

Go and Do

The religion of Jesus is a religion of action. But followers of Jesus have become quite good at replacing action with cheap imitations.

"So which of these three do you think was neighbor to him who fell among the thieves?" And he said, "He who showed mercy on him." Then Jesus said to him, "Go and do likewise" (Lk. 10:36-37).

❧

The lawyer with whom Jesus was speaking on this occasion correctly understood that loving one's neighbor was essential to obtaining eternal life (v. 25-28). But in typical lawyerly fashion, the man sought to analyze the requirement in terms of a legal distinction: "But who is my neighbor?" (v. 29).

Jesus responded with the parable of the Good Samaritan. At the end of the parable, even the lawyer got the message: my neighbor is anyone whom I have the opportunity to help. "Go and do likewise" is a call to imitate the unselfish kindness of the Samaritan in our own lives toward anyone and everyone.

The parable provides a wonderful lesson in applied Christianity, but there is a deeper lesson here that deserves attention. Boil down this exchange to its basic components, and a vital truth emerges: eternal life requires that I "go and do" something. Salvation, in other words, requires action on my part. Furthermore, it is not left up to me to define the nature of that action. The parable demands action that is personal, direct, and sacrificial.

243

Our problem today is not that we do nothing. It's that we replace the action with a variety of cheap imitations that fall short of what Jesus taught.

For example, some people "go and talk." They truly believe with all their heart everything Jesus ever taught, including the beautiful message in this parable. Really, they do—just ask them. They freely share that conviction in their conversations. But for all their talk, they never find the time or opportunity to translate the talk into meaningful deeds.

Others "go and preach." The world needs to hear the message of this parable, along with everything else Jesus taught, and they have committed their lives to declaring that message. Some of them can become quite eloquent in articulating the message—and can appeal to the original Greek to support their argument. But their academic erudition often becomes a stumbling block to personally performing what they are preaching. You see, their work is much too important to be bothered with such messy chores.

Still others "go and advocate." These are some of the busiest people you'll know. They work tirelessly to "raise awareness" of all the suffering and injustice in the world, and expose the privileged interests who shamelessly exploit the disadvantaged. Ironically, for all their lofty ideals, these agitators usually accomplish the least good for the objects of their organized compassion.

And then there are those who "go and pretend." They put on just enough of a facade of religion to give the appearance of charity. It's all a sham, of course, but as long as the charade holds and people are impressed, who cares?

Against all these substitutes, the call of Jesus remains a simple, "go and do." No shallow promises, no boasting, no fakery, no excuses—just go out into the world and live the life that God wants us to live. Whatever others might see or not see, God knows what we are doing, and that's all that matters.

Managing Priorities

Martha's decision showed a lack of judgment in managing priorities. We often make the same mistake in deciding how to use our time.

"Martha, Martha, you are worried and troubled about many things. But one thing is needed, and Mary has chosen that good part, which will not be taken away from her" (Lk. 10:41-42).

❧

When Jesus passed through their village and chose to stay at the home of Mary and Martha, the sisters were thrilled at the opportunity to have Jesus as their guest—but for entirely different reasons. Like most siblings, Mary and Martha had different personalities, and those personalities were manifested on this occasion. Mary saw it as a rare opportunity to sit at the feet of Jesus and feast on His words. Martha saw it as a rare opportunity to prepare a meal for the Messiah.

No one can criticize Martha for her hospitality and hard work. But by focusing exclusively on her hostess duties, she was passing up a much greater opportunity that lay right front of her, a chance to participate in a Bible study conducted by the Son of God Himself in her own home. The food she was preparing would soon be eaten and gone; but the spiritual feast Jesus was serving could change her life forever—if she took the time to listen.

Jesus' rebuke of Martha was gentle but firm. Her decision to focus so much attention on the meal was not an act of defiance or moral evil; rather, it was a mistake in priorities. Jesus reminded Martha of "that good part" (or "good portion," ESV) that she was ignoring. Martha had two starkly different options before her, and she prioritized them poorly. In making a good thing her top objective, she missed a chance to acquire a better thing. It was an unfortunate choice that, once made, she would regret forever.

Martha's mistake should be familiar to all of us. Life is a complex tangle of responsibilities, and we frequently have to weigh the merits of all the duties that press upon us and decide which should come first. Jobs, families, civic and social interactions, benevolent needs, spiritual development—all of these are important and deserve our attention. But in a well-rounded life, each can get only a part of our time. The trick is knowing which part deserves my full attention *right now*. Given a set of overlapping obligations, which one is "that good part" that I should move to the top of the list, while putting the others off to a later time? The ability to make those judgments is often the difference between doing something good and achieving something great.

So when we face a choice like this, how should we prioritize the options before us? There are several factors we could mention, but we will look at only two.

First, *what are the payoffs?* Weigh the potential short-term and long-term benefits among all the options. Which choice will accomplish the greatest overall good, as opposed to a temporary gain in the present moment?

Second, *which option holds the smallest window of opportunity?* Is one of these options so unique, so fleeting, that if I pass it up now, I won't see it again?

In Martha's case, both of these tests should have led her to skip the meal and listen to Jesus teach. But she missed the clues, and thus missed a far greater gift.

In rebuking Martha, Jesus was not insisting that we spend all our time in home Bible studies; nor was He condemning hospitality. Each has its rightful place and time. Rather, He was teaching us to discern, at any point in time, what is "that good part" that represents the best possible use of our time and resources.

The Higher Challenge

As disciples of Jesus, it's easy to get distracted by
peripheral issues that do not contribute to our
greater duty: to hear and keep God's word.

And it happened, as He spoke these things, that a certain
woman from the crowd raised her voice and said to Him,
"Blessed is the womb that bore You, and the breasts which
nursed You!" But He said, "More than that, blessed are those
who hear the word of God and keep it!" (Lk. 11:27-28).

૭∽૭

This incident in the life of Jesus speaks directly to those
today who venerate Mary as an object of worship. Jesus
specifically discouraged such worship, pointing people instead to something that should be of greater importance.

Our purpose here is not to bash those who engage in
Mariolatry, but to examine a larger principle implicit in Jesus'
words. In our efforts to follow Jesus, we could be guilty of the
same misguided affections as this woman.

First, ponder the reason why this woman felt compelled
to pronounce a blessing on Jesus' mother. There can be no
doubt that she had a great deal of respect for Jesus. But as a
woman, her mind had wandered beyond that loyalty to the
intense feelings that His mother must have experienced as the
bearer of the Messiah. Oh, to have a son like this! So gifted!
So perfect! So famous! To be the mother of such an extraordinary son must be the highest blessing God could bestow
upon a woman!

All true, yes . . . but all so utterly irrelevant. Whatever
respect (or envy, or empathy) this woman may have felt for

Jesus' mother meant absolutely nothing in defining her own relationship with God. That's why Jesus' rebuke went straight to the heart of the matter: The only blessing that counts is the one that comes from hearing and keeping God's word. This woman needed to get her head out of the clouds and focus on the task at hand: What does God want me to do with my life?

There is a broader lesson here for us today. In our enthusiasm for the cause of Jesus, how often do we get drawn away after topics that, although related to Jesus in some way, have no direct bearing on the central question of our lives, namely, how does God want me to live? We expend a good chunk of our time chasing after issues like the age of the earth, or the nature of the Trinity, or harmonizing details in the four Gospels—issues that, even if we could resolve them expertly, would have no appreciable impact on how we live.

Look carefully at the overall scope of Jesus' teaching (the Sermon on the Mount [Matt. 5–7] is a good place to start). The bulk of His teaching emphasized *development of personal character* as the highest obligation, starting with a profound love for God and a love for our fellow man. If we fail to make progress in that higher challenge, we are no better than Pharisees—very religious, but clueless about what it means to serve God.

To be sure, Mary was a blessed woman, and there was nothing wrong with saying so. Likewise, there is nothing wrong with probing all these other subjects that have a Biblical basis. But we must be careful that our pursuit of these things does not distract us from the more important obligation before us, namely, to "hear the word of God and keep it."

Of Lawyers and Burdens

Those who make a living teaching God's law have a duty to do it right. If we're not careful, we can make people's lives worse rather than better.

Then one of the lawyers answered and said to Him, "Teacher, by saying these things You reproach us also." And He said, "Woe to you also, lawyers! For you load men with burdens hard to bear, and you yourselves do not touch the burdens with one of your fingers" (Lk. 11:45-46).

৵৽৻

What do you get when you send the Godfather to law school? *An offer you can't understand.*

The Jewish people in Jesus' day were all too familiar with that kind of lawyer. And those who make a living studying and teaching God's law today would do well to ponder the occupational hazards associated with that work.

This lawyer was a man whose life was devoted to studying, interpreting, and teaching the Law of Moses in behalf of his fellow Jews. The Law was a civil code that touched every aspect of Jewish life, and the lawyer's job was to help people apply that Law in their lives. The lawyers were not the same as the scribes (note that this lawyer saw himself in a third category after the scribes and Pharisees, v. 44). The scribes likely were more involved in the physical transcription of the Law, while the lawyers were concerned with giving legal advice based on the contents of that Law. Whatever the details, the Jewish lawyers were not much different from modern day lawyers: essential to staying out of trouble with the legal system, but consumed by a spirit of censorious legalism.

Unfortunately, the way the lawyers handled the Law served not to help the people, but to increase their misery. Their convoluted interpretations of the Scriptures, derived from a deep background of rabbinical studies, laid upon the people "burdens hard to bear." The book that should have been a source of wisdom and encouragement to God's people was turned into a minefield of legalese that entangled even the most honest hearts in contrived transgression. People who were already struggling under a load of hardship and sin in their daily lives (Matt. 9:36) had an extra—and entirely unnecessary—weight of guilt pressed upon their shoulders.

The clever legal skills used by these lawyers not only become a bludgeon that crushed the faithful, they were also useful in extricating themselves from the very burdens they created for others. Just as lawyers today have a reputation for finding loopholes through which they can escape legal jeopardy, so these Jewish lawyers knew how to contort the details in such a way as to give themselves an "out." The common people suspected they were being scammed by all this legal mumbo-jumbo, but what could they do? The lawyers controlled all the levers of theological authority, and the ordinary citizen was powerless to push back or question it.

The spirit of these lawyers lives on today. There are preachers and editors who fancy themselves authorities on every issue or question that arises among brethren, and they are not bashful about issuing edicts to keep the faithful in line. Several generations of this theological hair-splitting have created a "burden hard to bear" for ordinary Christians trying to survive daily life.

One last lawyer joke: What's the difference between a good lawyer and a great lawyer? *A good lawyer knows the law, and a great lawyer knows the judge.* Before you laugh, recognize the nugget of truth hidden in that barb. The job of a conscientious law expert is not to lose people in a maze of legal complexity, but to help them stand before the Lawgiver and Judge with confidence. The gospel is "good news," and the teacher's message should be one of hope, not despair.

Sinner or Hypocrite?

All hypocrites are sinners, but not all sinners are hypocrites. We need to understand the difference between the two, if we're serious about heaven.

"Beware of the leaven of the Pharisees, which is hypocrisy. For there is nothing covered that will not be revealed, nor hidden that will not be known. Therefore whatever you have spoken in the dark will be heard in the light, and what you have spoken in the ear in inner rooms will be proclaimed on the housetops" (Lk. 12:1-3).

৵৽৽৶

There are *sinners*, then there are *hypocrites*, a particularly despicable breed of sinner. There's little shame in being called a sinner, because we're all imperfect. But to be called a hypocrite is a real insult. So what's the difference between the two? When does an ordinary sinner become a hypocrite?

First, *a sinner acknowledges his imperfections; a hypocrite hides them*. When we honestly admit our flaws, especially to ourselves, at least we are being truthful. When we pretend that these failings do not exist, or try to excuse or defend them, we are compounding our crime with deceit. This is well illustrated in the parable of the Pharisee and the tax collector, who both prayed to God (Lk. 18:9-14). The Pharisee sought to highlight all his good qualities, and conveniently passed over his faults. The tax collector, on the other hand, cut straight to the bottom line: "God, be merciful to me a sinner." There's something refreshing about a person who is honest about his shortcomings and doesn't try to fake perfection.

Because he acknowledges his imperfections, *a sinner makes progress toward improving his character and overcoming his weaknesses; a hypocrite, however, really has no intention of changing.* How can he? If he won't even acknowledge his shortcomings, he can hardly be expected to deal with them. As the sinner grows older, he becomes wiser, more mature, a truly better person. A lifetime of grappling with sin in your life will do that. The hypocrite just becomes more adept at practicing his fraud.

Finally, *a sinner is patient with other sinners; a hypocrite tends to be harsh and judgmental.* Because the sinner confronts his own sins, he is painfully aware of how difficult it is to fight temptation and overcome his faults. So he is sympathetic toward those who are fighting their own battles with sin. He does not excuse the sins of others—after all, sin is still a violation of God's law—but he understands the nature of the struggle, and is willing to extend mercy to those who are engaged in the fight. But in the fantasy world of the hypocrite, sin is easily overcome—after all, he has accomplished it—so he expects others to get with the program, too. Of course, by highlighting the failures of others, the hypocrite makes himself look better—another tactic in his campaign of self-deception.

The irony in this contrast is that the hypocrite—the one who goes to such great pains to hide his flaws—is usually recognized by others as the phony he is, and they despise him for it. But the person who admits his faults and is working to deal with them is respected as the genuine article.

How can I avoid being a hypocrite? Instead of arranging the externals trying to *look* righteous, I must train my heart to *be* righteous. When my heart wanders, I should seek God's forgiveness and press the battle harder. If I fix what's on the inside, the outside will naturally reflect this inner beauty.

There will be no hypocrites in heaven. I might as well get used to it here in this life.

Beware of Covetousness

We can see the problems others have with their money and possessions, but remain blind to our own greed. We must open our eyes to the danger.

Then one from the crowd said to Him, "Teacher, tell my brother to divide the inheritance with me." But He said to him, "Man, who made Me a judge or an arbitrator over you?" And He said to them, "Take heed and beware of covetousness, for one's life does not consist in the abundance of the things he possesses" (Lk. 12:13-15).

❦

We have no reason to believe that the man who came to Jesus with this inheritance dispute was misrepresenting his case against his brother. Perhaps he really was being cheated and deserved justice. Moreover, the fact that he appealed to Jesus for a ruling shows a great deal of respect for Jesus and His ability to render a wise judgment.

But it was precisely because Jesus was so wise that He refused to get involved in this personal affair. His mission in life was not to provide free legal aid service, but to help people prepare for a greater Judgment. So Jesus brushed aside the man's request, and homed in on a more serious problem that He saw lurking under the surface: a spirit of *covetousness*.

Regardless of the legitimacy of the man's complaint, his willingness to go to war with his own family over money was a symptom of a deeper problem. The dictionary defines covetousness as an "excessive desire for riches or money." There is nothing wrong with desiring to make a comfortable living. But when the desire for money or possessions becomes so powerful that it dominates everything else in our life—even our relationship with those closest to us—then we have a problem with covetousness.

Jesus reminds us that the quality of our life is not measured by the amount of goodies we possess. We will leave this world with exactly what we brought into it—nothing. So the time we spend in between birth and death should be devoted to something more important than hoarding stuff for ourselves.

In the next few verses, Jesus illustrated this truth with the parable of the rich fool (v. 16-21). This man devised a master plan to build bigger barns to hold all his possessions, not knowing that he had less than twenty-four hours to live. On the morrow, his possessions would mean nothing to him. So what was the point in allowing his life to be consumed by them today?

We have no problem seeing this principle in the life of the rich fool, but struggle to see it in our own lives. Surrounded by a culture of material wealth, we get caught up in the mad dash to accumulate more and more, never stopping to realize that our possessions are, in fact, possessing us. We seem never to have the time to help others who are in need, because we must spend all our time maintaining and protecting "our things." So we live out our days in pursuit of that which, in the end, will bring us the least satisfaction.

Don't let covetousness ruin your life. Live frugally, stay busy helping others, and focus on the treasures that await you in heaven.

The Measure of Our Success

Success in any endeavor requires that we measure our progress. But the metrics won't be worth much if they target the wrong outcome.

"One's life does not consist in the abundance of the things he possesses" (Lk. 12:15).

Then I looked on all the works that my hands had done and on the labor in which I had toiled; and indeed all was vanity and grasping for the wind. There was no profit under the sun (Eccl. 2:11).

৵৽৻

Our modern scientific age is dominated by metrics. Every detail of human life is governed by the mantra, "If you can measure it, you can control it." Most of us carry that same mentality into evaluating success in our personal lives. Consider some of the criteria by which people define success:

In prosperous Western societies, the most common metric for measuring one's value is *money*. People knock themselves out earning, saving, investing, and managing money. They closely monitor their holdings—and their moods track with the swings in the market.

Some are less interested in money than in *what money can buy*. Financially, they are not rich because whatever money they earn is quickly spent on houses, cars, clothes, gadgets, tools, toys, and other hot consumer fads. Their success is measured by their inventory of stuff.

Others define their success by the degree of *power* they have over others. Climbing the ladder of prestige and position gives their lives purpose.

Some people find the greatest meaning in their *life experiences*. They explore exotic locales and pursue adventures that other mere mortals can only read about in travel magazines. Their success is measured by the stories they can tell and the photographs they can share.

Finally, there are those whose success is measured by *what their ingenuity can create*: art, music, craftsmanship, scholarship, corporate empires. Their goal is to leave behind a legacy of work that will be remembered by future generations.

However, the problem with all these approaches to measuring success is that they are so shallow and temporary. Our money can be lost in an economic collapse. Our possessions can be stolen or destroyed. Our authority will be eclipsed by younger and sharper people moving up the ladder. Old age will diminish our ability to pursue the adventures or create the works that once gave our lives purpose. What then?

The author of Ecclesiastes learned that lesson the hard way. He had the privilege of chasing success in all these areas of life. After spending a lifetime building, accumulating, and learning, he arrived at the conclusion that none of it really mattered. It was all "vanity and grasping for the wind." The things that he once thought would define his success were only illusions. He reached the end drained and empty.

Jesus knew that these approaches to measuring our life's worth were a dead end: "One's life does not consist in the abundance of the things he possesses"; or as the NLT renders it, "Life is not measured by how much you own." Yet most of us never get that memo, and go on chasing success using faulty metrics.

By the standards of the world, Jesus' life was a dismal failure. But He was not measuring his life by those standards. Instead, He used His time and talents to serve humanity, sacrificing everything to that end. If we could learn to define success as He did, our lives would be quite different—but far more enriching.

It's All about Me . . . Right?

A life that is dedicated to satisfying selfish desires is ultimately unfulfilling, no matter how much we may accumulate or achieve.

Then He spoke a parable to them, saying: "The ground of a certain rich man yielded plentifully. And he thought within himself, saying, 'What shall I do, since I have no room to store my crops?' So he said, 'I will do this: I will pull down my barns and build greater, and there I will store all my crops and my goods. And I will say to my soul, "Soul, you have many goods laid up for many years; take your ease; eat, drink, and be merry."' But God said to him, 'Fool! This night your soul will be required of you; then whose will those things be which you have provided?' So is he who lays up treasure for himself, and is not rich toward God" (Lk. 12:16-21).

❧

In the deliberations of the rich fool in Jesus' parable, notice how often this man uses the words "I" and "my." God and others are completely outside the scope of his consideration. In this man's thinking, everything in life was about one person: "me."

This rich fool illustrates a disease that afflicts many people in our materialistic culture. We are conditioned from a very early age to want, get, buy, grab, accumulate, possess— all focused on gratification of selfish desires. This emphasis on material things in turn affects the more abstract elements of our life, such as our relationships with others and our sense of self-worth. Everything tends to be measured by what it does for me. If it does not stroke my ego, or satisfy my lust, or pamper my feelings, then it's not important.

There are two problems with this approach to life, neither of which is too hard to figure out—if we can turn away from the mirror long enough to think about them.

First, *this fixation on self tends to isolate us from the very things that can bring us the greatest happiness, namely, friends.* If the most important thing in my life is me, then by definition everybody else exists only to serve me. People don't like to be used, but that's precisely what I'm doing when I make myself the center of my little universe. Those around me quickly figure out that my friendship is shallow, self-centered, and untrustworthy. So my relationships tend to become barren and unfulfilling. It's a lonely life when I make myself the center of it.

Second, *investing all my energy on myself will, in the end, result in a life that is wasted.* As the rich fool learned too late, everything that I amass for myself, I must someday leave behind. I can't take a single penny, a single trinket, a single thimble of dirt, with me when I go. God asked the fool, "Whose will those things be which you have provided?" The answer is: It really doesn't matter anymore, does it? They are no longer his, so all his work, all his ambition, all his struggle to carve out a comfortable niche for himself, was ultimately wasted. Nothing of any real significance was left behind.

Jesus introduced the parable of the rich fool with a word of caution: "Take heed and beware of covetousness, for one's life does not consist in the abundance of the things he possesses" (v. 15). He concluded the parable with a practical piece of advice: "Do not worry about your life, what you will eat; nor about the body, what you will put on" (v. 22). Covetousness and worry are symptoms of a heart that has not yet learned the lesson of the rich fool.

No, life is not all about me. Jesus calls us to a life of self-denial and service to others. Once we understand that concept and practice it, life takes on a whole new meaning.

Christ the Divider

Christianity is plagued with division, but it doesn't have to be that way. The underlying cause should make all of us a little uncomfortable.

"Do you suppose that I came to give peace on earth? I tell you, not at all, but rather division. For from now on five in one house will be divided: three against two, and two against three. Father will be divided against son and son against father, mother against daughter and daughter against mother, mother-in-law against her daughter-in-law and daughter-in-law against her mother-in-law" (Lk. 12:51-53).

So there was a division among the people because of Him (Jn. 7:43).

৵৽৻

Jesus may be the "Prince of Peace" (Isa. 9:6), but you wouldn't know it reading the story of His life.

The gospel of John recounts several occasions where division followed in the wake of Jesus' teaching. Among the crowds at a Feast of Tabernacles there was widespread disagreement about Him. Some said, "He is good," while others insisted, "No, on the contrary, He deceives the people" (7:12). A few were convinced that "This is the Christ," while critics countered, "Will the Christ come out of Galilee?" (7:41). The net result was predictable: "There was a division among the people because of Him" (7:43).

Later, His healing of the blind man at the Pool of Siloam and the teaching that followed produced a similar outcome.

Many people said, "He has a demon and is mad. Why do you listen to Him?" Others said, "These are not the words of one who has a demon. Can a demon open the eyes of the blind?" (10:20-21). Once again, "there was a division among the Jews because of these sayings" (10:19).

Jesus "caused" division the same way a principled politician causes it: *He spoke the truth that people needed to hear.* Some folks appreciated that truth and accepted it; others rejected it and pushed back against it. Prejudice, stubbornness, partisanship, jealousy, fear, pride—these and a host of other faulty attitudes muddied the water and prevented many people from embracing His message. The result—division—was predetermined. The more intense the defiance, the more intense the discord.

The ministry of Jesus was deliberately designed to fracture humanity into two groups: those who yield to His guidance, and those who don't. His message challenges all of us to make uncomfortable changes in our thinking and behavior, and each one of us must make our own decision regarding who Jesus is and what role, if any, He will play in our life. Whatever decision we arrive at, somebody will disagree with it. We must be prepared to deal with the consequences of such a divide.

The irony, of course, is that among those who follow Jesus, the Great Divider is also the Great Uniter. In Christ, people from a wide variety of backgrounds and ethnic groups come together in harmony. They sacrifice much to become His disciples, but they gain so much more in the fellowship of brothers and sisters who have discovered in Jesus the answers to the big questions of life.

If the religion of Jesus is divisive, it is because human pride makes it so. Peace is possible, but people must first learn to open their hearts and minds to deal honestly with the truth Jesus taught, whatever it may be.

True Hospitality

Hospitality is a characteristic of God's people. But hospitality can easily become an expression of social conceit—the opposite of what it should be.

Then He also said to him who invited Him, "When you give a dinner or a supper, do not ask your friends, your brothers, your relatives, nor rich neighbors, lest they also invite you back, and you be repaid. But when you give a feast, invite the poor, the maimed, the lame, the blind. And you will be blessed, because they cannot repay you; for you shall be repaid at the resurrection of the just" (Lk. 14:12-14).

৽৽৽

One of the warmest acts of kindness that a person can extend to his neighbor is to invite him into his home to share a meal. Not only is the host supplying his guest's most basic necessity, he is also signaling that his companionship is desired. For that reason, hospitality is often mentioned in the Bible as a mark of genuine godliness (Deut. 10:18-19; Job 31:31-32; Rom. 12:13; Heb. 13:2; 1 Pet. 4:9).

But so much of what we call hospitality is a diminished version of the Biblical concept. This variant can be better defined as *cliquishness*, the mutual back-scratching of a tight little group of friends who have much in common already. Their gatherings are an expression of a special relationship that is not shared with others. Those who do not fit into that small circle have little chance of ever getting in.

If our guest list is permanently restricted to a select number of peers whom we consider worthy to have in our home, based on their economic position, social background, moral standing, or shared interests, then we really have not grasped the meaning of hospitality. Our close friends may appreciate the kindness we extend to them, but to the rest of the world, our behavior is really little more than an expression of social snobbery. As far as Jesus was concerned, that kind of hospitality proves little about a person's generosity. "If you do good to those who do good to you, what credit is that to you? For even sinners do the same" (Lk. 6:33).

True hospitality is sincere, impartial, and unaffected by selfish motives. It is freely offered to all, regardless of their usefulness or their ability to repay the favor. Who can question the inner goodness of a man who regularly entertains the poor, the crippled, and the socially inferior? His hospitality is clearly not motivated by mutual friendship or the desire for social advancement, but by the sheer joy of sharing his good things with fellow travelers on life's journey.

There is nothing wrong with having a circle of close friends with whom we can enjoy special occasions. Even Jesus had a unique relationship with the apostles and a few other companions that He did not share with the multitudes. He valued their friendship, and enjoyed their time together. But His closeness with this select group did not limit His kindness to others. He was a friend to all humanity, and His life of service reflected that friendship.

If we desire to be followers of the Master, we, too, must demonstrate the same impartiality in our love for all men. And the best way to express that impartial love is to open our homes to those outside our circle of close friends, especially to those who cannot repay our kindness. Whatever awkwardness may attend that act of generosity will be more than repaid in the resurrection.

On Making Excuses

For most of us, our lack of productivity is not due to limited abilities or resources, but limited desire. Our weak alibis hide a weak will.

"A certain man gave a great supper and invited many, and sent his servant at supper time to say to those who were invited, 'Come, for all things are now ready.' But they all with one accord began to make excuses . . ." (Lk. 14:16-18).

❧

And all their excuses were quite valid. One had just acquired some land and needed to evaluate his new holding. Another had just purchased five yoke of oxen and had to try them out on the farm. Another had just gotten married—what could possibly be more important than his honeymoon?

All these men had their reasons for not coming to the feast. But whatever their reasons, the end result was the same: "None of those men who were invited shall taste my supper" (v. 24). The land, the oxen, and even the new wife would still be around, no matter what. But the opportunity to enjoy their friend's hospitality had passed—and would likely never come again.

There are three lessons this parable teaches us about the human art of making excuses.

First, *every excuse seems valid to the one who offers it.* There will always be a host of reasons why we cannot do something that is unpleasant or troublesome. But those reasons do not measure up to the value of conquering the difficult task before us.

Second, *excuses are never insurmountable.* If the excuse-maker really wanted to overcome the obstacle, he could find a way to do it. In reality, every excuse is just another way of saying, I'd rather not bother trying.

Finally, *excuses always result in the same outcome: a lost opportunity to accomplish something good.* We avoid the hard work alright, but at the cost of a reward that we will likely never see again.

Most people live out their lives in obscurity without accomplishing much of anything that is meaningful. Behind every one of those wasted lives is a long history of making excuses. The problem is not that people can't accomplish great things; it's that they allow fear, timidity, self-doubt, or trivial pursuits to keep them from trying. So their lives are spent running away from challenges.

A few people, on the other hand, seem destined to greatness. They achieve amazing results, sometimes with the most unlikely resources. The rest of us marvel at their ability to accomplish so much. What is the secret to their success? In the majority of cases, they have disciplined themselves not to make excuses when faced with hard tasks.

They do not necessarily possess greater intellect or skill. Instead, they have learned to meet every challenge with a steady determination to overcome it, whatever the cost. *No excuses!*

When the path to their goal seems dark and foreboding, and others around them give up from the struggle, they lower their heads and press on. *No excuses!*

The next time you face a serious challenge in life, and a thousand reasons come to mind why you should turn around and walk away, think about this parable. What would happen if you looked the challenge straight in the eye, shouted "No excuses!" and charged in? You might be surprised what you could accomplish—and how easy it was to do it.

The Cost of Discipleship

Following Jesus is easy when it's fashionable. But what happens when it's no longer favored, and we must pay a price? Are we prepared for that?

Now great multitudes went with Him. And He turned and said to them, "If anyone comes to Me and does not hate his father and mother, wife and children, brothers and sisters, yes, and his own life also, he cannot be My disciple. And whoever does not bear his cross and come after Me cannot be My disciple. . . . So likewise, whoever of you does not forsake all that he has cannot be My disciple" (Lk. 14:25, 26, 33).

୧୨୬

This is the same Jesus who, a few months later, commissioned His apostles to go throughout the earth and "make disciples of all nations" (Matt. 28:19). He wants disciples, yes—the more the better. But He wants *real* disciples, not a fan club of fickle, half-hearted admirers.

Jesus was honest with His audiences. He warned them that the cost of discipleship was not cheap. If they committed to this task, it would demand everything they had—possibly even their lives. Jesus was not pushing people away; He was being honest with them.

That's why He spoke so brusquely to the crowds that thronged around Him. "Great multitudes went with Him"—but were they committed followers, or merely camp followers who were out for a little excitement and maybe some free goodies? "Disciples" who were just along for the ride were worse than worthless. Their inconsistent behavior would give Jesus' enemies plenty of ammunition to use against Him. And

265

when the going got tough and these fickle followers began bailing in large numbers, it would be a blow to the morale of those who were truly committed.

So Jesus served notice to the crowds: If they wanted to follow Him—really follow Him—they needed to seriously assess the impact of that decision on every aspect of their lives. Did they have families? Then Jesus must be more important than any of them. Were they people of means? Did they have houses, lands, silver and gold, fine clothes? Then they must be prepared to walk away from all that, and never look back. Like a doomed criminal forced to carry his own cross to the place of execution, they would have to accept whatever burden came with being a disciple of Jesus—public humiliation, poverty, maybe even death. Were they ready to sign up for this life?

In time, of course, most of the crowds proved to be just as shallow as Jesus feared. Almost to a person, they abandoned Him as His popularity declined and the legal threats began to mount. These people demonstrated that they were not ready to be His disciples. That picture changed following His resurrection, when people finally caught on to what His mission was all about. But it took a miracle to change their perspective.

The words of Jesus still challenge us today. If we are not willing to give up everything for Him, to commit our lives to following His teachings and example all the way, then He prefers that we not bother. If our involvement is half-hearted and inconsistent, He really doesn't need us.

Sadly, that message has been largely lost on modern Christianity. Far too many people today wear the label "Christian" with little or no appreciation for what that identification demands of them. And the result, as Jesus feared, is predictable: "Christianity," as the world knows it, is scorned as a motley collection of shallow, self-righteous hypocrites.

Can you be a disciple of Jesus? Before you say "yes," count the costs. Are you ready to pay that price?

Lost and Found

The grand narrative of the Bible is one of God seeking to rescue a humanity lost in a maze of its own making. We play a role in that narrative.

"Rejoice with me, for I have found my sheep which was lost! . . . Rejoice with me, for I have found the piece which I lost!" (Lk. 15:6, 9).

৵৽৻

Several years ago Melissa and I flew to Lake Tahoe for a long weekend getaway. After getting on the plane in Wichita, I realized that my cellphone was missing. It had apparently fallen out somewhere in the airport. There was nothing we could do until we returned. Upon arriving back in Wichita, our first stop was the lost-and-found desk at the airport. The lady opened a drawer to reveal a large pile of lost cell phones—with my phone sitting on top.

I was happy to get my phone back. But it's a scenario that is played out countless times throughout our lives with all kinds of things that we consider valuable. In Luke 15, Jesus uses several stories that play on this theme of something being lost then found: the parables of the lost sheep, the lost coin, and the lost son. A quick scan through these three parables reveals some important lessons for our edification.

In the first two parables, the lost objects are incapable of making their way back to their owners. The owners must take the initiative to mount a search to find them. In both cases, the lost items (a sheep and a coin) are considered too valuable to lose. The owners consider the time and trouble spent in looking for them to be worth it. Both parables highlight God's love for fallen humanity. He has gone to great trouble to seek and save the creatures He loves.

The third parable introduces a new wrinkle in the equation: human free will. In this parable, the "lost" item—a wayward son—knows where home is, but deliberately chooses to run away, against his father's wishes. The father does not forcibly drag him back. Though it breaks his heart, he honors his son's freedom to make his own decisions. So he patiently waits for his son to come to his senses and return of his own accord. Eventually his hope is rewarded. The son stumbles home, chastened and humbled, and a grand reunion takes place. This human version of the lost-and-found theme highlights the role that the lost individual plays in returning to God. God will not coerce anyone to come to Him without that individual's desire to do so. But once that decision is made, oh, what an outpouring of undeserved grace awaits him!

There are other details in these stories that we could dig into, but let's limit our attention to one overarching theme here: The story of humanity is an epic tale of creatures lost in their own arrogance, and the Creator's tireless quest to reclaim them. Every one of these fallen creatures—including me!—are precious in His sight, and He will expend every effort to restore the relationship that was destroyed, consistent with our free will. Ever since God called out to Adam in Eden, "Where are you?," He has pursued that agenda with grim determination. He will not force His love upon us; but if we acknowledge our fallenness and return to Him, He is quick to forgive and reconcile.

These little stories should force each one of us to wrestle with two questions: Who am I to dismiss anyone as unworthy of my time and attention? And how dare I dismiss myself as worthless in God's sight?

Give Me

Many of our problems are self-inflicted, rooted in a selfish heart that views all of the life as one big exercise in serving self. That goal never ends well.

*"A certain man had two sons, and the younger of them said to his father, 'Father, **give me** the portion of goods that falls to me.' So he divided to them his livelihood. And not many days after, the younger son gathered all together, journeyed to a far country, and there wasted his possessions with prodigal living. But when he had spent all, there arose a severe famine in that land, and he began to be in want. . . . And **no one gave him anything**" (Lk. 15:11-14, 16).*

৵৹৵

Jesus used the parable of the prodigal son to teach a lesson about God's love for fallen humanity. But in setting up the story, Jesus also provided a lesson on how humanity got in this mess in the first place.

The younger son in this parable was blessed to live in a well-to-do family, with a father who loved and cared for him. It was a life of privilege, but also one of responsibility; notice the reference to the older son coming in from the field (v. 25). Both sons were expected to pull their weight in running the family business. There were benefits living under his father's roof—food, clothing, shelter, familial love—but the younger son saw it as a life of drudgery and hardship. He chafed under the constraints imposed by his father. Rather than appreciate what he had, he fantasized about life out in the world. While others were traveling to exotic locations, playing, partying, and having fun with their friends, he was stuck on the farm. Clearly, life was just not fair.

So he did what every young person would love to do, but few have the opportunity to do: He demanded his share of his inheritance money, and left home. (We might question the father's wisdom in granting his son's request, but it's not as foolish as it appears. Sometimes parents have to let their children learn life's lessons the hard way.)

Notice the younger son's demand of his father: "Give me" (v. 12). In those two words, this young man summarized his entire philosophy of life. Everything around him, even his closest relationships, existed only as a means of gratifying his own selfish desires. Life was all about him. Nothing else mattered.

Eventually, of course, this young man learned that the world did *not* revolve around him. When he blew all his money, and his "friends" abandoned him, and the bad times hit, he ended up with nothing. It was only when he was reduced to slopping pigs on starvation wages that he experienced a brutal reality about life: "No one gave him anything" (v. 16).

Indeed, this world does not owe us a living. It does not owe us happiness, contentment, comfort, fun, or any of the other things that we expect to find in it. Whatever good things we gain in this life are the result of self-discipline, hard work, and a generous portion of undeserved divine grace.

Our world is filled with prodigal children who have yet to learn this lesson. They wake up every morning thinking, "What will life give me today?" They never stop to think that maybe their lives have an entirely different purpose, that genuine satisfaction is defined not by what life gives us, but by what we give to others.

What hardship will it take for them to learn that lesson? And are they willing to accept it?

Coming to Our Senses

The transition from a life of sin to a life of faith
usually begins with a flash of mental clarity, when
we suddenly recognize our foolish choices.

---

*"But when he came to himself, he said, 'How many of my
father's hired servants have bread enough and to spare, and
I perish with hunger!'" (Lk. 15:17).*

*And a servant of the Lord must not quarrel but be gentle
to all, able to teach, patient, in humility correcting those who
are in opposition, if God perhaps will grant them repentance,
so that they may know the truth, and that they may come to
their senses and escape the snare of the devil (2 Tim. 2:24-
26).*

৩০৫

Placing these two passages alongside each other reveals
a curious parallel. Notice Jesus' description of the prodigal
son's restoration, starting with "he came to himself." Compare that to Paul's comment that the role of preachers is to
help people "come to their senses." The original words in the
two passages are not identical (the former means to return to
a sensible frame of mind; the latter means, literally, to re-
cover from a state of drunkenness, to become sober again).
Nevertheless, the idea in both passages is remarkably similar:
Conversion is triggered by a process of suddenly awakening
to a state of mental acuity that was previously missing in our
life of sin.

This comparison offers several vital lessons about sin
and conversion.

First, we learn that *when we're entangled in a life of sin, we are not ourselves.* Our minds are caught in "the snare of the devil," and it distorts everything we touch. Our warped view of reality in turn leads us to make poor choices—and to blame others for the chaos that surely follows. Our lives are messed up because we're not thinking straight, and the mess cannot be cleaned up until we take the blinders off and finally see the world for what it really is.

It follows, therefore, that *the transition from a life of sin requires a kind of mental wake-up call*, a moment of sharp clarity when we confront ourselves with the question, "What am I doing?" What triggers this sudden shock of self-awareness? A clue can be seen in the Timothy passage. People come to their senses, Paul says, when they "know the truth." This is much more than just encountering a Bible verse. When we are hit full in the face with the reality of our circumstances, we are motivated to re-examine how and why we got there. Sometimes that new knowledge can be imparted by words of wisdom delivered by a concerned friend. In other cases, we must learn the truth as the prodigal son learned it—by reaping the painful consequences of a series of foolish decisions. However we come to that knowledge, it opens the door to a realization that life doesn't have to be that way, that there is an alternative to the sorry existence we have been living. This realization is the first giant step in the direction of *repentance*.

Finally, this concept speaks to the broader topic of *evangelism*. We should teach the gospel to any and all as we have opportunity; but our best chance of success lies with people who are living their own version of the prodigal son story. They may appear to be beyond the reach of God—and might even smell bad—but they are, ironically, the very ones who are most likely to listen to the gospel message. At least they know that their lives are a mess, and need help. Our job is to help them "come to their senses" and turn to God.

What the Prodigal Did Not Say

A fresh look at this parable reveals insights into the nature of true repentance—and how we can sabotage that process before it even begins.

"But when he came to himself, he said, 'How many of my father's hired servants have bread enough and to spare, and I perish with hunger! I will arise and go to my father, and will say to him, "Father, I have sinned against heaven and before you, and I am no longer worthy to be called your son. Make me like one of your hired servants"'" (Lk. 15:17-19).

৩০৫২

The parable of the prodigal son is a beautiful story of rebellion, repentance, and redemption. The progression of the young man from arrogant rebel to chastened son has been the basis of countless sermons highlighting the mercy of God and the role of repentance in finding it.

The key to the young man's turn-around is seen in his self-reflection while sitting in the pig pen. "He came to himself" marks the eureka moment when all his past mistakes came into sharp focus and he finally realized why his life was such a disaster. More importantly, he also came to understand what he needed to do to make things right with those he had wronged. "I will get up and go" was the first big step toward reconciliation, without which his life would never improve.

The lecture this young man gave himself—and the resolution that grew out of it—is a model for all of us who have struggled with sin in our lives. But it is also helpful to consider what the prodigal son did *not* say as he evaluated his circumstances.

For example, he did not say, *"I'm a victim! Everyone is out to get me!"* He could have blamed his father ("He's never done anything for me!"), his older brother ("I wouldn't be here if it wasn't for that intolerable Pharisee!"), his employer ("The working conditions here are pure slavery!"), or his party friends ("I thought they cared about me."). All such blame-shifting, of course, would have been a disingenuous attempt to avoid the truth of what happened: He made a series of stupid decisions that landed him in this predicament. He had no one to blame but himself.

The ultimate in blame-shifting would have been for him to *charge God with wrong*: "Why did God allow this to happen to me?" It is amazing how often people will live their lives with reckless abandon, then when the bill comes due, turn on God in righteous fury for letting their lives go to ruin. This young man had the honesty of heart to recognize that it was his own rebellion against God, not God's indifference, that led to his troubles.

Finally, the young man did not scream, *"Somebody's gonna pay for this!"* When we respond to adversity with anger and bitterness, lashing out against anybody and everybody who gets in our way, we only make things worse for ourselves—and drag down a lot of other people with us. Even if some external mistreatment has contributed to our pain, taking out our frustrations on the world only pours gasoline on the flames. It intensifies the suffering, not heals it.

The fact that this young man did not resort to any of these strategies speaks to the authenticity of his repentance. He took full responsibility for his condition and for the changes he needed to make to get his life back on track.

There was one thing, however, that the prodigal son could not foresee: The unqualified love his father showered upon him when he returned. Heart-felt repentance is essential, but it is meaningless without a God who is eager to take us back into His embrace.

The Path to a Changed Life

If we don't like the direction our life is going, we have the option of changing it. But that change requires some serious internal adjustments first.

"But when he came to himself, he said, 'How many of my father's hired servants have bread enough and to spare, and I perish with hunger! I will arise and go to my father, and will say to him, "Father, I have sinned against heaven and before you, and I am no longer worthy to be called your son. Make me like one of your hired servants."' And he arose and came to his father" (Lk. 15:17-20).

❦

It's one thing to recognize that our life is a wreck and needs to change. But it's quite another to actually make that change a reality. The story of the prodigal son provides an excellent "how to" guide for those who want to make a serious course correction in their lives.

First, notice that this young man's determination to change was formed while groveling in a pig pen, destitute and hungry. Every resolution begins with *the conviction that one's life is not as it should be.* Whether we're dealing with a little excess flab or a serious character flaw, the motivation to change comes from a dissatisfaction with some aspect of our life. If we're only moderately irritated with the way things are, there's no compelling incentive to change it. One reason we have a problem keeping our new year's resolutions, for example, is that our dissatisfaction with our current condition is not all that deep. Are we *really* displeased with the direction our life is going, or just mildly annoyed? Do we *really* want to change, or do we just have a casual wish for improvement? Until the discontent becomes a deep-seated anger at our self-imposed circumstances, nothing will change.

Second, notice that this young man *translated his desire for a changed life into a specific goal:* He would become a hired servant in his father's house. It was an humble position compared to what he once enjoyed, but it was preferable to his current condition. More importantly, it was achievable, given the resources he had to work with. Meaningful resolutions are not vague fantasies about a better life. They are specific, targeted goals for improving one's life. If you really want to change, then spell out exactly what it is you want to accomplish.

Third, notice that once the young man made the determination to improve his lot, *he formulated a plan for making it happen.* He did not daydream about how great life would be in his father's house. He devised concrete steps for getting there. He detailed what he would do and even what he would say. Our resolutions, too, must be fleshed out with details if we are to have any hope of realizing them. Break your long-term goal down into achievable short-term milestones, and devise a strategy for reaching each milestone. Even if you stumble on one or two, you will make much more progress than if you strike out blindly for a vague faraway objective.

Finally, the young man's ambition and plans meant nothing until *he followed through on them.* He determined to "arise . . . go . . . say"; so he "arose . . . came . . . said." It took a lot of humility and courage, but he executed his plan, intent on reaching his goal. To his surprise, his father did not accept his offer of hiring him; instead, he embraced him again as his son, and restored him to a place of honor that he had no hope of ever seeing again. The young man achieved more than he dreamed possible.

We, too, can achieve more than we imagine, if we set clear goals, plan to reach them, and work hard to execute our plans.

Treasure in Heaven

Material possessions can be a threat to our faith, or a means of accomplishing great things for God. It all depends on how we view them.

"Make friends for yourselves by unrighteousness mammon, that when you fail, they may receive you into an everlasting home" (Lk. 16:9).

"But God said to him, 'Fool! This night your soul will be required of you; then whose will those things be which you have provided?' So is he who lays up treasure for himself, and is not rich toward God" (Lk. 12:20-21).

જ્જ

These verses, separated by several chapters, mark the conclusions of two parables dealing with the same subject: material possessions. A close look at the two parables makes an interesting study.

The parable of the rich fool illustrates Jesus' warning to "beware of covetousness." This rich man's land was so productive that he struggled to manage all his abundance. His plan was to expand his warehouses so he could store his belongings "for many years." The rich man's language as he reviewed his plans ("I," "me," "my") betrayed a heart consumed with selfishness. He viewed his wealth solely in terms of how it served his own interests. But all his plans came to naught with his untimely death, and the possessions in which he had placed all his hope became worthless to him.

From this parable it would be easy to conclude that the wise course of action is to avoid accumulating possessions altogether. If we took a vow of poverty, there would be no way for possessions to gain control of our heart.

But that conclusion would be premature. The parable of the unjust steward invites us to look at riches in a different, even unorthodox, light. The main character in this story is a steward who mismanaged his master's investments, and was terminated with a very small window of time to wrap up his affairs. He used that brief opportunity to position himself favorably with his master's creditors, using the master's money. The master took a financial beating from these cut-rate deals, but as the steward headed for the door, he was prepared for life after termination. Despite his losses, even the master was amazed at the steward's shrewdness in preparing for his exit.

To the casual reader, it seems like Jesus is endorsing embezzlement here. But that misses the point. What Jesus is emphasizing is the temporary access we have to our possessions in this life, *and the importance of using them wisely to secure a happy future in eternity.*

Together, these two parables present a balanced view of wealth. The unjust steward was shrewd, not because he defrauded his master, but because he saw the wealth at his disposal as a tool that could be leveraged for his long-term benefit. The rich fool was a fool, not because he was rich, but because he used his riches only for himself, giving no thought to the day he would have to leave it all behind.

The lesson for us in this study is simple: It's okay to accumulate wealth, but only if we will use it in view of eternity. We do that by being generous with our goods in the service of others. Paul, for example, urged the rich "to be ready to give, willing to share, storing up for themselves a good foundation for the time to come" (1 Tim. 5:17-19).

From an earthly perspective, such open-ended charity seems wasteful. But from a heavenly perspective, it's just smart.

Faithful in Little Things

Success in life is a product of how we use the little opportunities that God sends our way every day, rather than waiting for big ones that never come.

"He who is faithful in what is least is faithful also in much; and he who is unjust in what is least is unjust also in much" (Lk. 16:10).

೪∾ళ

Jesus is addressing here a common fallacy in our thinking that prevents most of us from achieving our potential in life. We convince ourselves that we cannot accomplish great things because we lack adequate resources, so we do nothing. In the meantime, we ignore countless little opportunities that God sends our way to achieve the very goals we say we want to achieve. By neglecting the little things in life, we lose the big ones as well.

The secret to accomplishing great things in life is found in how we use the small opportunities God gives us. Take, for example, our use of *time*. Many of us never get around to completing the important goals we set for ourselves because we "don't have enough time." In reality, we have plenty of time; it's just spread out in small chunks over a long period. But instead of using those small chunks wisely, we fritter them away chasing more trivial interests. After spending a whole lifetime in that manner, we have little to show for it. So a whole life is wasted because we were not faithful in our use of the minutes that comprised that life.

This principle also applies in our use of *money*. One of the greatest hindrances to people using their money wisely is the excuse, "If I were rich, I would . . . ." Of course, we don't consider ourselves rich, so the rest of the scenario is left unfinished. In the meantime, a lot of money slips through our fingers, squandered on trinkets and pleasures, money that could have gone toward more worthwhile goals, had we made better decisions along the way.

Finally, consider the application of this principle to our *character*. It's usually not the big sins that trip us up and hurt us. It's the small character flaws that make us small people: gossip, petty jealousies, careless thoughts and words, bad work habits, neglected opportunities to do little acts of kindness. These are the behaviors that we pay no attention to, because they seem so insignificant. Yet they combine together to create a character that is weak and pathetic. Only by focusing on the little decisions we make along the way can we build the kind of character that will have a positive influence in this world. Our life's portrait is painted by such small brush strokes.

If we want our life to count for something, we must train ourselves to see the little things in our life as building blocks for something bigger. We must seize every minute of every day as an opportunity to do something meaningful. We must use our money carefully, not only to have it grow for ourselves, but to share with others in need. We must watch every thought, every word, every deed, as matters of great importance. Because they are.

Being faithful in the little things of life is a habit that must be carefully cultivated. It does not come easily. But if we will train ourselves to think in terms of the little things in our life, we will some day come to realize the value of that investment. We will be counted as "faithful in much"—because we were faithful in what was least.

The Esteem of Men

We waste our lives trying to gain the approval of others based on external characteristics. Jesus points us to a different measure of self-worth.

"You are those who justify yourselves before men, but God knows your hearts. For what is highly esteemed among men is an abomination in the sight of God" (Lk. 16:15).

తిఖ

Of all the traits that define our humanity, perhaps the greatest is our intense desire for the approval of others. In one form or another, we crave assurance that people around us not only accept us but like us. And we will pay almost any price to get that affirmation.

We see this desire for acceptance among the rich, the famous, and the powerful. Politicians plaster their names and pictures all over the news. (Their accomplishments are for the Little Guy, you know.) Celebrities pose for the cameras at their congratulatory awards ceremonies. Journalists knock themselves out—even to the point of fudging facts—for a Pulitzer or a Peabody. Academicians strut their profundities to much applause at their high-brow conferences. The ultra-wealthy carouse together at their posh European resorts. The common thread that ties all these groups together is a deep desire for the adulation of their peers. They are seeking to "justify themselves before men."

Jesus saw plenty of this kind of self-promotion during His time on earth, and much of His teaching exposed the foolishness of this mindset. The standards by which men seek approval from one another are almost always superficial and shallow: wealth, good looks, social connections, intellect, athletic prowess. None of these things define who we really are, yet people knock themselves out chasing them.

Of course, this phenomenon is not limited to the high and mighty. The rest of us display the same trait in more modest ways. How often do we make decisions in our everyday life in hope that "now they will like me"? That's called "peer pressure," and it's not limited to teenagers.

That's not all. Jesus taught that even moral virtue can become a tool of vain self-promotion. When we wear our piety as a badge of superiority, as the Pharisees did, what are we doing but seeking the applause of others? How are we any different from the glitterati who bask in the praise of their cronies?

The common element in all these standards is the desire to establish our self-worth on the basis of our *performance*— to convince those around us that we are better, smarter, stronger, more connected, more praiseworthy, or holier than our contemporaries. We want people to like us because of how we perform in our life.

But Jesus swept all these pretensions aside with a stark declaration: These external metrics are not what God looks at. We are *all*—every last one of us—sinners with serious flaws, and we're kidding ourselves if we think our outward achievements will earn us a ticket to heaven. No, God judges all of us on the basis of what is in our hearts. On that standard, the proud person occupies a very precarious position, regardless of what he owns or achieves or knows—or what other people think of him.

The things that men esteem highly are worthless in the sight of God. Once we understand that fundamental fact, we can quit with all the posturing that dominates our outward lives, and focus on what really matters: cultivating a heart of unselfish love that produces the fruit of true righteousness.

Marriage and Hypocrisy

The state of our marriage impacts more than just our personal happiness. It also broadcasts to the world the quality of our core faith commitment.

"It is easier for heaven and earth to pass away than for one tittle of the law to fail. Whoever divorces his wife and marries another commits adultery; and whoever marries her who is divorced from her husband commits adultery" (Lk. 16:17-18).

❧

Jesus' teaching on marriage and divorce in verse 18 aligns with what He taught elsewhere on the subject (Matt. 5:31-32; Matt. 19:9; Mk. 10:11-12). However, its presence in this context seems to be out of place. Some commentators treat verse 18 as a stand-alone fragment having no connection with what precedes or follows. Given Luke's penchant for careful presentation of the Jesus story, that seems unlikely. Why did Jesus insert His pronouncement on divorce at this point in His monologue?

Other expositors discern (correctly, I believe) a logical flow of thought in the context that lends a special significance to His comments on marriage and divorce.

Read the entire chapter, and it's clear that the Pharisees were the target to whom Jesus was directing His criticism. The Pharisees had ridiculed His parable of the unjust steward (v. 1-14), but Jesus turned the tables, charging them with being more concerned about trying to look good before others. "God knows your hearts," He reminded them (v. 15), and what He saw in their hearts was ugly. While everyone (including the Pharisees) were clamoring to get into the kingdom on their own terms (v. 16), God's Law remained unchanged: Not one tiny detail of the Law would fail (v. 17).

With that lead-in, Jesus then illustrated the darkness that corrupted their hearts with this commentary on marriage and divorce (v. 18). The Pharisees claimed to be champions of the Law, but their mistreatment of their wives exposed them as ruthless hypocrites. Jesus was not using this occasion to trot out a new law on marriage and divorce. Rather, He was summarizing God's standard for what marriage ought to be, a standard that began in the Garden of Eden and extended right down to Jesus' day. By tossing aside their wives in divorce, the Pharisees were routinely violating that standard. The parable of the rich man and Lazarus that immediately followed (v. 19-31) was a stark warning of the fate that awaited the Pharisees in their sanctimonious condition.

So, returning to verse 18, what is Jesus' message for our marriages today? Simply this, that *marriage is the single most significant demonstration of the legitimacy of our faith*. If we are not devoted to our spouse in a lifetime commitment of love and fidelity, any claims of devotion to God are just like those of the Pharisees: shallow and insincere.

Husbands and wives, think about it. The state of your marriage is displaying to the world the state of your faith. Even if your spouse is falling short in his/her commitment, *your response* to that shortfall is still a reflection of your devotion to a higher calling.

Christian, what message is *your* marriage broadcasting to the world?

Why People Go to Hell

The concept of hell bothers folks. But Jesus explained it in a way that is not only logical, but strikes close to home for each one of us.

"So it was that the beggar died, and was carried by the angels to Abraham's bosom. The rich man also died and was buried. And being in torments in Hades, he lifted up his eyes and saw Abraham afar off, and Lazarus in his bosom" (Lk. 16:22-23).

§

People do not go to hell for the soft tropical breezes or the majestic views. This parable identifies the key reason as *selfishness*.

Look at the evidence in this parable. In his earthly life, the rich man cared only for himself and his comfort. He "received his good things" (v. 25), while his poor neighbor did without—and he didn't care. Only on the other side did he finally realize how distorted his priorities had been.

Notice that the rich man's selfishness did not end at death. His plea to father Abraham was not to get *out* of hell, but to have Lazarus come serve him *in* hell. "Have mercy on *me* . . . cool *my* tongue" (v. 24). Even in hell, it was still all about him. Others existed only to serve his needs.

That's not all. Consider his follow-up request to have Lazarus return from the dead to warn his brothers of this awful place. When Abraham reminded him that they already had Moses and the prophets, he protested, that's not enough: "No, father Abraham; but if one goes to them from the dead, they will repent" (v. 30)—the implication being that he ended up in hell because he had not been given enough information. Poor, pitiful rich man; so mistreated!

This man's self-centeredness in this life followed him into the next. It was so deeply ingrained in his character, he couldn't escape it—even in hell.

People who object to the idea of God sending people to hell have not spent much time studying human nature. God does not "send" people to hell; they create their own hell by their life of careless narcissism. Everything this man complained about in his new environment was fabricated by his selfish life on earth. In this life, he could not be bothered by the concerns of others; in the next, there would be no "others" to be concerned about. He would have all eternity to marinate in the vast loneliness of Self.

Before we shake our heads at the rich man's self-importance, we should take a long, hard look at ourselves. How much of our own decision-making is influenced by the same kind of selfish considerations that got this man in trouble? How much of our time and energy is spent looking out for our own interests rather than the interests of others? The answers to those questions tell us everything we need to know about the current trajectory of our lives.

And that trajectory will take us either to heaven . . . or to hell.

Remember

Memories of lost opportunities in the past are painful, but the greatest pain awaits those who will spend all eternity remembering a wasted life.

"Then he cried and said, 'Father Abraham, have mercy on me, and send Lazarus that he may dip the tip of his finger in water and cool my tongue; for I am tormented in this flame.' But Abraham said, 'Son, remember that in your lifetime you received your good things, and likewise Lazarus evil things; but now he is comforted and you are tormented'" (Lk. 16:24-25).

৩৯৩

The story of the rich man and Lazarus is often used as a prooftext to explain what happens after death. Details like Abraham's bosom, Hades, the great gulf, torment in flames, and so on, paint a vivid word picture that captures our attention. Preachers have often used elaborate diagrams based on this story to illustrate the bifurcation that awaits all humanity in the afterlife.

While I don't question the fact of a final judgment and the different fates of the righteous and the wicked after death, I'm not so sure that our use of this text is legitimate. If our existence between death and resurrection is a bodiless state (as indicated in 2 Cor. 5:3-4 and Rev. 6:9-11), then why are there so many references to *body parts* in this story (eyes, bosom, finger, tongue)? There is something else going on here that should occupy our attention.

Recall that this story was directed at the Pharisees, "who were lovers of money" (v. 14). Their aim in life was prestige, status, acclaim, recognition. Like the rich man in the parable, they "fared sumptuously every day." And like the beggar at the gate, the sinners "out there" were of no concern to these men. The good life they lived was all the evidence they needed of God's approval.

In the story of Lazarus and the rich man, Jesus was using the Pharisees' own theology of the afterlife to puncture their smugness. Material prosperity in this life has no correlation to God's judgment in the next. In fact, it is often an *impediment* to godliness. The rich man found out too late that he had squandered his life on earth by directing all his resources on himself. There would be no do-over, no second chance, no opportunity to fix his mistake.

Instead, he would have the rest of eternity to do only one thing: *remember*. He would remember the poor beggar sitting at his gate, whom he could have helped but chose to ignore. He would remember the words of Moses and the prophets about loving one's neighbor and showing mercy to the poor, words that were easy to explain away at the time. He would remember the vanity of chasing after wealth and status, while more pressing needs went unanswered.

Like the rich man on this side of the grave, we, too, have opportunities to glorify God by using our time and resources to make a difference in the lives of others around us. If we fail to get our priorities straight in this life, we too will wake up some day on the far side of a great gulf, begging for another chance that will never come. We will have the rest of eternity to do only one thing . . .

Remember.

Unpersuaded

In most cases, people fail to accept God's truth not because the evidence is so thin, but because their own hearts are so thick.

"Then he said, 'I beg you therefore, father, that you would send him to my father's house, for I have five brothers, that he may testify to them, lest they also come to this place of torment.' Abraham said to him, 'They have Moses and the prophets; let them hear them.' And he said, 'No, father Abraham; but if one goes to them from the dead, they will repent.' But he said to him, 'If they do not hear Moses and the prophets, neither will they be persuaded though one rise from the dead'" (Lk. 16:27-31).

৽৽৽

The rich man in this story eventually realized how he had squandered his life, but the revelation came too late to do him any good. If he could send a message to his brothers back on earth, at least he could spare them from sharing his fate. Or so he thought.

His plea to Abraham was earnest and sincere: Send Lazarus back to warn them of this terrible place, and to encourage them to change their selfish ways! But Abraham's response was terse: Why bother? They have access to Moses and the prophets. Those sources of instruction should be sufficient to provide all the warning and encouragement they need.

But the rich man knew that was not enough. During his time on earth, he had access to that revelation, too, but had been too busy or disinterested to pay it any attention. Surely if someone came back from the dead, that would awaken his brothers from their spiritual lethargy!

But human hearts don't work that way. "If they do not hear Moses and the prophets"—messages from God confirmed by extraordinary miracles—"neither will they be persuaded though one rise from the dead." One more miracle will not change people whose hearts are hardened by sin and worldly pleasure.

This parable, of course, was a precursor to what happened a short time later. Jesus Himself was raised from the dead, and the majority of the Jewish people still refused to accept Him as their Messiah. Human free will can be astonishingly irrational when corrupted by stubbornness.

This story explains in graphic fashion why people fail to understand the Bible as they should, or why there is so much disagreement about what the Bible teaches on a variety of topics. Some subjects are hard to understand, that's true; but others are more *challenging* than obscure. The Bible insists on changes in beliefs, attitudes, or behaviors that people are not willing to accept. So rather than change their lives, they simply ignore the evidence, and no amount of pleading or special effects will shake them from their position.

That's why the first and most important criteria for understanding the Bible is a good heart: "On this one I will look: On him who is poor and of a contrite spirit, and who trembles at My word" (Isa. 66:2). Until we see ourselves as weak and lost, and God as infinitely greater and wiser than ourselves, we will never be disposed to take His word seriously. Oh, we might accept the pieces and parts that are convenient, but deep inside, it's still all about what *I* want, not what *God* wants. That's what got the rich man and his brothers in trouble. Someday we'll join him in his regrets.

Of course, there is another option: We could humble our pride, open our hearts to God's wisdom, and make the changes *now* that we know we need to make.

The Art of Confronting

In a broken world, the need for confronting others about their faults is an unfortunate necessity. But there is a right and wrong way to go about it.

"Take heed to yourselves. If your brother sins against you, rebuke him; and if he repents, forgive him" (Lk. 17:3).

"If your brother sins against you, go and tell him his fault between you and him alone. If he hears you, you have gained your brother" (Matt. 18:15).

Brethren, if a man is overtaken in any trespass, you who are spiritual restore such a one in a spirit of gentleness, considering yourself lest you also be tempted (Gal. 6:1).

৵৵

The Bible enjoins on us the duty to confront others about their sins. The language of Jesus and Paul in these verses ("rebuke him," "tell him his fault," "restore such a one") leaves no room for evading this responsibility.

Some people take this injunction as a license to be professional critics, haranguing others about the tiniest mistakes. Others of a quieter nature dread these uncomfortable discussions, and will go out of their way to avoid addressing a problem, even to the point of allowing others to walk over them. Neither of these approaches is healthy.

Confronting others about their faults is an art form that requires much thought, practice, and patience. These verses provide some important guidelines that can point us in the right direction in mastering this skill.

First, notice Paul's qualifier in the Galatians passage: "considering yourself lest you also be tempted." Some interpret this to mean, don't allow yourself to be drawn into the sinner's sin. That may be a risk in some cases, but it hardly seems applicable as a general rule. The more likely danger is that the confrontation turns into an opportunity to flaunt our superiority. Am I trying to help a brother, or am I showing off my own purity? The sinner can spot the difference and will respond accordingly. Before we challenge a friend about his wrong, we need to evaluate our own motive in the affair. Pride has no place in this task.

The first requirement sets up the second, namely, that we administer the rebuke "between you and him alone." That is, we keep it as private as possible. Broadcasting another's sin will deepen the sinner's sense of humiliation and create a barrier to resolving the matter. Of course, some sins are so flagrantly public that this may not be an option. But as much as possible, we should seek to protect the sinner's privacy.

Third, the confrontation must be conducted "in a spirit of gentleness." To be effective, our words of rebuke must be firm, direct, and pointed—but they must also be gentle. Those are hard attributes to balance; how can we say something that will pierce the sinner's heart, yet in a tone that conveys the love behind the rebuke? We can learn much by studying the rebukes of Jesus and Paul, but real skill here can only come with a lot of practice.

Finally, thought must be given to the aftermath. What if the sinner accepts the rebuke and repents? Jesus says, "forgive him." No exceptions, no qualifications, no probations, no grudges. The matter is done, buried, and behind us. "You have gained your brother," Jesus adds. So treat him like one.

Throughout our lives, we will frequently encounter the need to confront others: spouses, children, co-workers, friends, brothers in the Lord. We must not shy away from these occasions, but neither should we thoughtlessly charge into them unprepared. Learn how to confront wisely, and you will be respected by all—especially by those who have benefited from your corrective counsel.

Doing Our Duty

In our role as servants of God, our purpose is not to accrue bragging rights, but to press on with the work God has assigned us.

"And which of you, having a servant plowing or tending sheep, will say to him when he has come in from the field, 'Come at once and sit down to eat'? But will he not rather say to him, 'Prepare something for my supper, and gird yourself and serve me till I have eaten and drunk, and afterward you will eat and drink'? Does he thank that servant because he did the things that were commanded him? I think not. So likewise you, when you have done all those things which you are commanded, say, 'We are unprofitable servants. We have done what was our duty to do'" (Lk. 17:7-10).

ॐ

This odd little parable follows immediately Jesus' teaching concerning forgiveness and—in view of the difficulty of meeting that obligation—the apostles' request to Jesus to "increase our faith" (v. 1-6). If only we had the faith to forgive those who sin against us, how noble our service to God would be!

Not so fast, Jesus warns us. The master-servant relationship upon which Jesus builds this parable may seem harsh to modern American sensibilities, but to His original audience the story made perfect sense. To be a servant in a master's house was a stable life that was far preferable to living as a beggar in the streets. Still, the role of the servant consisted of only one obligation: to serve the master. If the servant came into the house after a long day in the field and the master or-

293

dered him to prepare his evening meal, the servant had no choice but to comply. Only when the master's needs were fully met could the servant tend to his own affairs. Even then, the master did not owe his servant so much as a "thank you." It was just another day in the life of a servant—doing his duty.

That spirit of humble service, Jesus tells us, is how we ought to view our service to God. At no point in our life of faith can we call God's attention to our hard work and sacrifices and demand, "Look at me! Aren't I doing a great job?!" Instead, we should see our lives as perpetually unfinished business, always ready to do more, learn more, serve more. Until the Lord calls us home, we are only unprofitable servants, forever in debt to a gift we can never repay.

Jesus is not portraying God as a heartless master who treats our service with disdain. In an earlier parable, He spoke of the master (God) welcoming his servants to a feast, where he will "gird himself and have them sit down to eat, and will come and serve them" (Lk. 12:37). In that parable, the emphasis is on the Master's generosity; here, it's on the servants' duty. Jesus is pushing a single lesson: When we lose sight of our life of service and develop a sense of entitlement, we lose our effectiveness in the kingdom.

Recall the forgiveness-and-faith issue that prompted this parable: Suppose that forgiving others is a challenge for us, yet somehow we overcome that obstacle and learn how to forgive even the worst offenses. That's great! But remember, that's only a tiny part of everything God wants us to do. There will be another challenge—then another, and another, and another. Instead of boasting of past victories won, we need to keep our eyes fixed on the journey ahead, and keep on humbly responding to the tasks that God places before us.

Someday there will be a time for resting and reflecting on what we've accomplished. Until then, our attention must be set on doing the duty that lies before us.

Where Are the Nine?

Faith and obedience are essential in our relationship with God, but they mean little in the absence of one more critical requirement.

"Were there not ten cleansed? But where are the nine? Were there not any found who returned to give glory to God except this foreigner?" (Lk. 17:17-18).

❧

As Jesus passed through a village on the border of Samaria and Galilee, ten lepers appealed to Him for healing. Jesus granted their request, but in a most unusual manner. Instead of healing them outright, He ordered them to go to the local priest, who had the responsibility of examining and certifying those who had been healed of skin disorders. Somewhere along their way to see the priest, the ten lepers were miraculously healed.

One of the lepers, a Samaritan, was so overcome with joy at his new health that he returned to express his gratitude to Jesus. Jesus was surprised that only one came back to thank Him—and a foreigner at that.

Like many of the recorded incidents in the life of Christ, this story has a deeper message for us today. Let's examine some of the details in this story and draw a parallel with our own spiritual experience.

First, we should give credit to all ten lepers for having faith in Jesus. All ten cried out to Jesus for healing—they believed He had the power to heal them (v. 13). When the one leper returned to give thanks, Jesus noted that "your faith has made you well" (v. 19). There is no reason to limit this explanation to the one. The other nine evidently had faith to be made well also. All had faith; all were cleansed.

Second, all ten of these lepers were obedient to the Lord. Their response to the order to go the priest for their cleansing, when as yet they had no indication of being healed, is the very essence of unqualified obedience. Like Abraham offering up his son of promise, these lepers were willing to do whatever the Master said, even when it didn't make any sense.

What distinguished the Samaritan from the others—and what disappointed Jesus about the other nine—was that he was the only one who took the trouble to thank Jesus for the gift he had received. He was faithful, and he was obedient; but he was also profoundly grateful for what Jesus had done for him. The others were faithful and obedient; but they took their divine gift for granted.

This story should cause each one of us to pause and consider how often we express our thanks to God for what He has done for us. There is no question that we believe in Him; and we may be the most obedient servants in all of Christendom. But if we do not frequently, fervently, and with passion let God know how much we appreciate His gift of salvation, along with all the other blessings He showers upon us, we are no better than the ungrateful lepers who took Jesus' gift of healing and walked away without a word of thanks.

Like the lepers, our obedient faith does not earn our salvation. Salvation is a blessing that God bestows on us from the goodness of His heart. Let us never cease thanking Him for that precious gift.

The Kingdom Within

Jesus' view of the kingdom was a stumbling block
to many of His contemporaries. Today many
continue to struggle with that concept.

*Now when He was asked by the Pharisees when the king-
dom of God would come, He answered them and said, "The
kingdom of God does not come with observation; nor will
they say, 'See here!' or 'See there!' For indeed, the kingdom
of God is within you" (Lk. 17:20-21).*

☙❧

Belief in a coming Kingdom ran deep in the Jewish psyche in Jesus' day. Through all their hardships, the Jews clung
tightly to their hope of a day when God would pierce the
dome of heaven and directly intervene in the affairs of men.
They believed that when that day came, God's Messiah
would conquer their enemies and establish peace and justice
over the earth, ruling from His throne in Jerusalem.

So when John the Baptist and Jesus began proclaiming
that the kingdom of God was at hand, it didn't take long for
the excitement to reach fever pitch. This question posed to
Jesus regarding the timing of the kingdom reflected that excitement. The kingdom is coming! When?! Where?!

But Jesus' response poured cold water on these expectations. "The kingdom of God is within you" reframed the
subject in a manner that took His audience by surprise. Other
translations read: "is among you" or "is in your midst." In
other words, the kingdom of God was available right in front
of them, if they would open their eyes to see it. But blinded

by their preconceived ideas, it was difficult for these people to recognize it for what it really was.

What Jesus taught in correcting the popular "kingdom" misconceptions of His day provides us an important lesson concerning the nature of the kingdom.

Unlike the kingdoms of men, the kingdom of God is not a political institution or a geographical region. It knows no borders, cannot be defended by armies or natural barriers, and cannot be evaluated by any of the usual criteria (GDP, per capita wealth, military strength, and so forth). Rather, the kingdom of God is *the rule of God in the heart of each individual.* It is a mindset, a heart so captive to the love of God that it motivates every detail of how we live our lives.

The kingdom of heaven belongs to the poor in spirit (Matt. 5:3), not to those who can wield the power to seize and hold it. Citizenship in this kingdom supersedes every distinction known to humanity. Race, gender, ethnicity, socio-economic status, intelligence, academic credentials—none of these serve as a barrier to the kingdom within. Whoever is willing to humble his heart before God is a fit subject for God's rule.

Those today who obsess over obscure prophecies to determine when and where Jesus will come the second time make the same mistake as the Pharisees of old: They are conflating God's kingdom with an earthly power structure. Likewise, those who use political tactics to manipulate and coerce people into conformity (always in the name of "truth," of course) are missing the spiritual nature of the kingdom.

God's kingdom consists of all people everywhere whose hearts are wholly devoted to serving Him. Once we grasp that fundamental fact, it will alter how we live, and how we teach the gospel to others.

Trusting in Ourselves

A holy life is a good thing, but not if it spawns
contempt for others. Humility requires a deeper
recognition of our own standing before God.

*He spoke this parable to some who trusted in themselves
that they were righteous, and despised others (Lk. 18:9).*

୨୭

What follows is the parable of the Pharisee and the
tax collector, two men who approached God with entirely
different attitudes and very different prayers (v. 10-14). The
parable is powerful in its own right, but Luke's introduction
leaves no room for missing the main lesson.

Jesus' target audience were those who "trusted in themselves that they were righteous, and despised others." Let's
examine the details of this character profile.

The one who "trusts in himself" is not necessarily someone who defies God's authority in favor of finding his own
way. The Pharisee in this parable saw himself as God's cham-
pion. He acknowledged God's role in his life by the prayer he
prayed. Furthermore, unlike many of his contemporaries, this
Pharisee was not a hypocrite. There is nothing in this text to
indicate that he was altering the facts of his performance. The
type of person of whom Jesus is speaking can be a paragon of
moral strength ("I am not an extortioner, unjust, adulterer"),
self-discipline ("I fast twice a week"), and generosity ("I give
tithes of all I possess"). Here is a man who is seemingly everything God wants him to be. So what's the problem?

The problem is the attitude of self-congratulation this
virtuous life can create. Jesus is condemning the delusion that

we can become so good at understanding and applying God's law that we earn the right to pat ourselves on the back for our brilliance. We have everything figured out, and our ticket to heaven is punched.

Not only are we proud of what we have accomplished, but our sterling character grants us a license to "despise others" who have not achieved our superior level of performance. The Pharisee was thankful to God, to be sure—but more for his superiority over his neighbor (v. 11), rather than for God's mercy in dealing with his own imperfections.

In this parable Jesus was not condemning the Pharisee's goodness. He was condemning the self-righteous pride that grew out of that goodness.

Instead of trusting in ourselves, our trust should be in Jesus and His sacrifice. Paul was one of the best men who ever lived, yet his desire was to be found in Christ, "not having my own righteousness, which is from the law, but that which is through faith in Christ, the righteousness which is from God by faith" (Phil. 3:9). Despite all his goodness, he still saw himself as the chief of sinners (1 Tim. 1:15), forever in need of the grace of God.

That is why I am a little uneasy with the style of preaching that offers a steady diet of "We're right and they're wrong." Certainly truth must be taught and error must be exposed. But if we are not careful, we can lull ourselves into a self-righteous stupor that leaves little incentive for self-improvement—and little compassion for others.

Whatever degree of righteousness we may achieve in this life, our attitude should always be that of the tax collector: "God, be merciful to me a sinner!" (v. 13). It is the man who trusts God for righteousness rather than himself who will be justified.

Me, a Sinner

Of all the defects that can derail our relationship with God and others, a lack of humility is the most damaging. We need to reassess who we really are.

"God, be merciful to me a sinner!" (Lk. 18:13).

ॐ

Jesus addressed the parable of the Pharisee and the tax collector to those "who trusted in themselves that they were righteous, and despised others" (Lk. 18:9). These people had a fundamental attitude problem that poisoned their view both of themselves (too inflated) and of others (too harsh). The cure to this attitude problem is summed up in the simple prayer of the tax collector, "God, be merciful to me a sinner!" Of the two prayers offered that day, this was the only one to which God listened. That fact should compel us to do some serious introspection.

I am a sinner. I am a flawed, fallen creature who does not measure up to the ideal that God wants me to be. Whether through ignorance or stubbornness, I say and do things that I shouldn't, or fail to do things that I should. Because I am a sinner, I stand in constant need of the grace of God. If I am saved at all, it will be because God was merciful to me, not because I earned it.

The fact that I am a sinner, therefore, should help me develop two important qualities.

First, my imperfections should *teach me humility*. I am not as good as I pretend to be, nor as righteous as others tell me I am. I struggle with bad habits and long-standing character flaws that keep me from reaching my potential. Hopefully

I've made some progress dealing with these shortcomings thus far in my life. But I'm still a long way from perfect. Therefore, I can't brag about what I've accomplished, or parade my knowledge before others. For every good deed I have done, God can remind me of a dozen bad ones—and opportunities for other good deeds that I failed to pursue. Rather than looking with pride to past achievements, I should look forward to the challenges I have not yet conquered. I still have so much to learn.

Second, my imperfections should *teach me patience with others*. My own struggle with sin is not unique. Everyone around me in this world is fighting the same kind of battle with themselves. The details may be different, but the basic story is the same. Some may be winning that battle, others may have given up trying; but they are all sinners, just like me. Consequently, I can't look down my self-righteous nose at them as unworthy of my association. If I want God to be patient with my faults, I must be patient with theirs. My efforts to help others improve their lives must be tempered with gentleness and kindness, remembering my own struggles with temptation. I cannot despise in others what I have yet to master in myself.

The fact that none of us is perfect does not mean that we adopt a policy of "I'm okay, you're okay," and let everyone do their own thing without judgment or censure. God still has a high standard to which He has called us, and we must all strive to reach that standard. But let us do so with humility and patience, knowing that none of us have yet reached that goal.

Why They Hated Jesus

The murderous rage with which Jesus' enemies pursued Him is hard to fathom—until we realize how His work impacted their social status.

And He was teaching daily in the temple. But the chief priests, the scribes, and the leaders of the people sought to destroy Him, and were unable to do anything; for all the people were very attentive to hear Him (Lk. 19:47-48).

৩৯৶

Throughout His career, Jesus lived under the constant threat of death. From almost the very beginning of His ministry, in His hometown of Nazareth (Lk. 4:28-30), until the final Passover in which His enemies finally succeeded, Jesus faced a level of hate that was off the chart. His critics were not content merely to debate Him; they were determined to destroy Him. It was only a matter of time before they finally found a way to make it happen.

But why did His enemies have such a furious rage against Jesus? What did He do to arouse such hostility against Himself?

We could understand this reaction if Jesus was kidnapping and abusing little kids, or if He was leading a band of thieves on a rampage through the villages of Galilee, or if He was stirring up insurrection against the government. People can get pretty upset when their social order is disrupted.

But Jesus was doing none of those things. Everything He did can be summarized in two activities: He taught people how to live so as to find true happiness, and He performed acts of kindness on those who were hurting. Jesus' life was devoted to helping people, and He accomplished that to a degree that no other man had ever done. So why did some people find this work so offensive? Why did they seek to kill Him?

There were two factors in Jesus' work that led to this murderous response.

First, the success of Jesus' work among the common people *exposed the deficiencies of the current leadership*. When the Jewish rulers brought Jesus before Pilate to have Him executed, the governor knew instantly the real motivation that drove their demand: *envy* (Matt. 27:18). The message of Jesus resonated with the daily lives of the people, unlike the tired, obtuse pronouncements of the theological gatekeepers who dominated Judaism.

The second factor is related to the first. Jesus did not merely offer an alternative to the empty teaching of the Jewish rulers, *He also challenged it*. Jesus spoke directly to the hypocrisy, faulty logic, and bad attitudes that lay at the foundation of the prevailing religious structure of His day. And the leaders understood His meaning perfectly. Either they had to acknowledge their mistakes and change, or Jesus had to be silenced. The second option was much easier. So they killed Him.

If we choose to throw our lot in with Jesus, we can expect the same treatment. Jesus warns us, "If the world hates you, you know that it hated Me before it hated you" (Jn. 15:18). Those whose lives are challenged by our teaching and example will "think it strange that you do not run with them in the same flood of dissipation, speaking evil of you" (1 Pet. 4:4). We do not have enemies because we harm them; we have enemies because we are showing a better way—and they know it. They hate us for the same reasons they hated Jesus.

Our duty, like Jesus, is to stay true to the Father's will until the end, trusting Him to handle the fallout.

Giving Everything

Giving to God is a ubiquitous part of our religion.
But a simple story reveals that our giving habits
may be blinding us to a greater obligation.

---

*And He looked up and saw the rich putting their gifts
into the treasury, and He saw also a certain poor widow
putting in two mites. So He said, "Truly I say to you that this
poor widow has put in more than all; for all these out of their
abundance have put in offerings for God, but she out of her
poverty put in all the livelihood that she had" (Lk. 21:1-4).*

৯৽৹

The principle of giving something of value to God lies at
the core of the Bible message. Even pagans grasp the importance of sacrifice as an essential ingredient in serving their
gods. But the story of the widow's mites reveals an angle on
this principle that we rarely think about.

Let's start by addressing a simple question: How do we
measure value? The most obvious way is by assessing pur-
chasing power; that is, how many goods or services can I buy
with what I possess? Typically we define that value in terms
of a dollar amount. So a million dollars is more valuable than
one dollar. That's a simple calculation.

But there is another way of measuring value that takes
into account a different factor: *What is available for use?* A
bottle of water that normally sells for a dollar can fetch ten
times that amount in an emergency (that's why price gouging
is so common in natural disasters). The less there is of something, the more valuable it is to the one who possesses it (or
wants it).

Which brings us back to the story of the widow in the temple. The rich men were donating gifts to the treasury that far surpassed in dollar value what the widow gave. But as Jesus noted, their donations came "out of their abundance." There was plenty more where that came from, and their lifestyle was not impacted by their gifts.

The widow, on the other hand, though the monetary value of her gift was negligible (a "mite" was a small copper coin worth a few pennies), it was all she had to live on. The gifts of the rich donors were a trifle compared to all they possessed; but the widow's gift represented "all the livelihood that she had." Their sacrifice was trivial; hers was total. That's why Jesus honored her gift above theirs.

We need to keep this principle in mind when making decisions on how to use our money and possessions. Jesus told the rich young ruler to "sell what you have and give to the poor" (Matt. 19:21), not because that is a universal requirement, but because He knew this young man's real loyalty was to his riches, not God. Jesus' command was a test to help him see where his true affections lay. Like his rich brethren in the temple, he was happy to give to God out of his abundance, but when the call came to give his entire livelihood, he couldn't do it. The poor widow out-performed him.

The lesson here involves more than just money. Whether we're talking about our money, our abilities, our talents, our skills, or our opportunities, the Lord judges us not in comparison to what others have, but by what He has given us—what is available to us for use in His service. Until we can see *everything* we possess as belonging to Him, and are willing to use it all in His service, we are no better than rich guys tossing their chump change in the treasury.

And a widow's two mites puts us to shame.

People Power

Masses of people can exert influence on their
leaders for good, or be manipulated for evil.
We each play a role in how "our" crowd behaves.

---

*The chief priests and the scribes sought how they might
kill Him, for they feared the people (Lk. 22:2).*

*But the chief priests and elders persuaded the multitudes
that they should ask for Barabbas and destroy Jesus (Matt.
27:20).*

৩৩

These two verses, both relating to events surrounding the
final Passover during which Jesus was put to death, illustrate
a curious paradox of human nature. Popular opinion (summarized here as "the people" or "the multitudes") is at the
same time both powerful and weak, capable of standing up to
the strongest tyrant, while being easily manipulated by the
same.

The Bible offers numerous examples of leaders modifying their conduct because of pressure from the people. While
Moses was on Mt. Sinai receiving the Law, the people prevailed upon Aaron to make a golden calf to worship. Moses
later chastised Aaron, "What did this people do to you that
you have brought so great a sin upon them?" (Ex. 32:21). In
like manner, King Saul disobeyed God and did not utterly destroy the Amalekites "because I feared the people and obeyed
their voice" (1 Sam. 15:24).

In these two cases, the people pressured their leaders to
do wrong. But sometimes the people can push a leader to
do the right thing. For example, during a battle with the

Philistines, King Saul had foolishly decreed that no one was to eat anything throughout the course of the day-long engagement. When his own son, Jonathan, was found enjoying a little snack of honey, Saul felt honor-bound to kill him. But the people objected that Jonathan's heroic conduct had won the battle for Israel that day. "So the people rescued Jonathan, and he did not die" (1 Sam. 14:45). Likewise, Herod Antipas imprisoned John the Baptist, and wanted to kill him, but he could not because "he feared the multitude, because they counted him as a prophet" (Matt. 14:5).

The power of the people for good or bad can shift drastically, due to the smallest of influences. The behavior of the crowds during Jesus' last Passover provide the best illustration of the fickleness of groupthink. The same crowd that one day welcomed Jesus as the Messiah with palm branches and praise, a few days later jeered "Crucify Him! Crucify Him!" A crowd can be easily manipulated by shrewd men who know how to pull their strings.

There are two important lessons that we should draw from this study.

First, each one of us who belong to this collective called "the people" need to recognize *the power that we have to influence our leaders*. Ordinary people who hold no position of leadership can still wield enormous influence for good (or evil), if they have strong convictions and are not afraid to express them.

Second, there is a lesson here for those who lead: *There is a fine line between serving the public and becoming a lapdog of public opinion*. True leadership must be sensitive to the needs of those being led, but it also requires the courage to take positions that may be unpopular. "The people" are not always right.

Like individuals, crowds have great potential for good or ill. Whatever crowd to which we belong, we should take seriously our role in it.

When Satan Takes Over

Satan cannot force his way into our lives.
But sometimes we make his job easier by the
careless way we respond to his trickery.

Then Satan entered Judas, surnamed Iscariot, who was numbered among the twelve. So he went his way and conferred with the chief priests and captains, how he might betray Him to them (Lk. 22:3-4).

And having dipped the bread, He gave it to Judas Iscariot, the son of Simon. Now after the piece of bread, Satan entered him (Jn. 13:26-27).

❧

The Bible attributes the treachery of Judas to Satan having "entered" him. This intrusion not only resulted in the execution of Jesus but culminated in the suicide of Judas himself a short time later. For Satan, it was a twofer.

This is not the only time we read of Satan sneaking into someone's inner life to create mayhem. Satan "filled the heart" of Ananias, leading him to lie to God (Ac. 5:3). Satan likewise "moved David" to conduct a census of Israel, contrary to God's law (1 Chron. 21:1).

This is scary stuff! Can Satan really take over people's hearts against their will? Can he take over my thinking? Could I wake up one morning as a pawn of Satan, with a sudden urge to go out and commit some random act of evil?

This sounds ominous, but there's more to the picture than these simple descriptions suggest. Satan influences humans through *agents*, and never against their will. (Demon possession is a topic for another occasion.) Consider the story of Eve in the garden of Eden. Satan approached Eve through the agency of a serpent. He did not twist Eve's arm to get her to eat the forbidden fruit; rather, he deceived her by telling a convincing lie. Satan "entered" Eve's heart, not through a forced takeover, but by a gradual breakdown of her spiritual defenses. Satan achieved his aim, but Eve was a willing participant in the rebellion.

Satan weasels his way into the hearts of all of us via the same strategy. We are surrounded by countless evil influences that chip away at our allegiance to God. If we relax our guard just a little, the day will come when we no longer care, and Satan will have us in his grip. We can do the unthinkable, not because Satan seized control of the steering wheel, but because we meekly let him have it. It was by this process that David, "a man after God's own heart," came to commit adultery and murder. It's how Judas reached a point where he was willing to betray his Master for thirty pieces of silver. These collapses take a while, but Satan is a patient manipulator.

Ironically, Satan can even gain access to our hearts through a misguided sense of loyalty to God. When Simon Peter tried to correct Jesus' prediction of His coming death, Jesus responded with a harsh rebuke: "Get behind me Satan!" (Matt. 16:22-23). Peter's devotion to the Master was strong but uninformed, and his ignorance unwittingly played into Satan's desire to discourage Jesus. Some of Satan's greatest victories are won with the help of over-zealous disciples who lack the wisdom to know how to do the Lord's work with prudence.

How can we prevent Satan from getting a toehold in our hearts? James lays out the strategy for us: "Resist the devil and he will flee from you. Draw near to God and He will draw near to you" (Jas. 4:7-8). There must be a conscious commitment to resist Satan and draw near to God. When that intent guides all our thinking and conduct, Satan cannot take over our lives. He may throw us a curveball now and then, but we can survive that. What we cannot survive is a weak, sloppy faith that doesn't care.

Servant Leadership

In a world where naked power gets all the prizes,
it's hard to see any other path to greatness.
But Jesus not only taught that path, He lived it.

---

*Now there was also a dispute among them, as to which
of them should be considered the greatest. And He said to
them, "The kings of the Gentiles exercise lordship over them,
and those who exercise authority over them are called 'bene-
factors.' But not so among you; on the contrary, he who is
greatest among you, let him be as the younger, and he who
governs as he who serves. For who is greater, he who sits at
the table, or he who serves? Is it not he who sits at the table?
Yet I am among you as the One who serves" (Lk. 22:24-27).*

౨౿

Jesus' time on earth was nearing the end, and His work
with His apostles was almost finished. But there was one
more lesson they needed to learn. And, boy, did they need to
learn it.

The first Lord's Supper had barely ended, when the apostles begin to argue among themselves over who was the
greatest among them. It was a childish display of rivalry that
undermined everything Jesus had been trying to teach them
for the past three years.

So once again, Jesus had to spell it out for them: Greatness in His kingdom is not an exercise in naked power. Quite
the opposite, it is a work of service, a humble labor in behalf
of those under our care. Unlike the tyrants of this world, leaders in God's kingdom are, first and foremost, servants.

In John's account, Jesus underscored this lesson in dramatic fashion by then washing the feet of the apostles, a task customarily assigned to the lowest servant in the household (Jn. 13:3-17). If they really aspired to greatness, that spirit of serving others is how they would achieve it. "I have given you an example, that you should do as I have done to you" (v. 15).

Two thousand years later, His example of humility still challenges our assumptions about success. The Lord's people achieve greatness, not by amassing positions and titles and privileges, but by expending their talents in behalf of others. "Servant leadership" is not an oxymoron; it is the only leadership style that inspires the best in its followers. Even in organizations that rely heavily on strict lines of command, such as the military, the best leaders are those who lead from the front, making sacrifices for those who follow.

Unfortunately, many of us are still struggling to learn that lesson. In a variety of ways, some subtle, some not so subtle, we still behave like the apostles—disputing, fighting, quarreling, forever trying to gain an advantage over one another. We are no different from everyone else in this broken, chaotic world.

Humanity yearns for servant leaders. Jesus showed us how to do it. Do we have the courage to follow His example?

The Sifting of Peter

Satan is a cunning adversary who knows how to turn our weaknesses to his advantage. The fall of Peter is a masterclass in how he works.

And the Lord said, "Simon, Simon! Indeed, Satan has asked for you, that he may sift you as wheat. But I have prayed for you, that your faith should not fail; and when you have returned to Me, strengthen your brethren." But he said to Him, "Lord, I am ready to go with You, both to prison and to death." Then He said, "I tell you, Peter, the rooster shall not crow this day before you will deny three times that you know Me" (Lk. 22:31-34).

ശ്ലേ

Only a few hours after this exchange, the sifting of Simon Peter began.

Peter was still rubbing the sleep from his eyes, embarrassed that he couldn't stay awake while his Master prayed, when the soldiers came. This was no theological debate with Pharisees. These men had come in the middle of the night clearly for the purpose of taking Jesus into custody. Perhaps Peter was still too groggy to think about the consequences of his actions; or maybe his fierce loyalty overwhelmed his better judgment. Whatever the motive, his sword flashed quickly, wounding one of the party. But before the soldiers could react, Jesus stepped in and ordered Peter to put his sword away. Jesus had undoubtedly saved his life; but the rebuke confused Peter. Why would Jesus not allow his most loyal disciple to defend Him? The other disciples took off running. Now Peter didn't know what to do; so he ran also.

But he didn't run far. As the troops took Jesus to the house of the high priest, Peter followed at a distance, determined to see what would happen. None of this made any sense. Jesus was the Son of God, the Messiah, the King of Israel. Yet they were hauling Him off like a common criminal. And worse, Jesus was meekly submitting to this humiliation. He had the power to turn these thugs into dust; why did He not resist?

Given an opportunity to come into the courtyard of the house, Peter took it, and sought warmth around a fire, alongside some of the soldiers and others. While Jesus was being interrogated inside the house, Peter was undergoing his own interrogation outside. One by one, three individuals thought they recognized Peter in the dim light, and quizzed him about his association with Jesus. There was no point in playing the hero role; he had already tried that, and been slapped down for it. Surrounded by enemies, confused by the surreal scene unfolding in the house nearby, and with no clue what to do next, Peter fell back on man's most primitive instinct: self-preservation. He denied that he even knew Jesus.

The moment he heard the rooster crow, he knew instantly what he had done. His head jerked toward the house, and there, through the window, he saw Jesus staring back at him. All his proud boasts were only ashes now. He had failed his Friend in His most desperate hour. "So Peter went out and wept bitterly." The sifting of Simon was complete.

Peter eventually recovered from this horrible ordeal, and became a better man for it. But that outcome was never guaranteed. Satan found Peter's weakness and exploited it, and the experience nearly destroyed him.

Satan will find our weaknesses, too, and sift us as he did Peter. That's why we must always remain vigilant and alert, clinging closely to Jesus for strength. After all, would any of this have happened to Peter, if instead of sleeping in the garden, he had been praying with Jesus?

Only One Angel

As death drew near, Jesus was comforted by an old friend from a familiar realm. In our suffering, too, God will provide the strength we need.

He knelt down and prayed, saying, "Father, if it is Your will, take this cup away from Me, nevertheless not my will, but Yours, be done." Then an angel appeared to Him from Heaven, strengthening Him. And being in agony, He prayed more earnestly. Then His sweat became like great drops of blood falling down to the ground (Lk. 22:41-44).

৩৯৫৩

Like any condemned man, Jesus spent the night before His death wrestling with anticipation of His execution. But thoughts about death were not what made this night so difficult for Him. Unlike other condemned men, Jesus had an escape hatch. At any time during this ordeal, Jesus could simply say, "I quit!," and twelve legions of angels would swoop down and rescue Him from His enemies. (Matt. 26:53). It was a temptation that had dogged Him all His life, and now at the end, it pressed upon Him with intense fury. He desperately wanted a way out of this fate, but He had to force Himself to stick with the original plan: "Not My will, but Yours, be done." It was this fierce internal battle with such a strong Satanic urge that made the Gethsemane experience so difficult.

Of course, Jesus won the battle, choosing to complete His mission and pay the cost for our sins. But He did not win the battle alone. He had help from an old friend from heaven. Even though He did not get an army of angels, Jesus got one angel—just one—to strengthen Him in His darkest hour. This one angel could have easily protected Jesus from the soldiers who came to arrest Him. After all, if one angel could wipe out an entire Assyrian army to save Jerusalem (2 Kgs. 19:35), this assignment would have been child's play. But that was not this angel's assignment.

Instead, this angel came to strengthen Jesus. I have often wondered what this exchange looked like. Perhaps the angel spoke words of comfort to Him, or gently wiped the sweat from His brow. Maybe he put an understanding arm around Him to reassure Him that everything would turn out okay. What words could an angel offer to encourage the Son of God? Whatever the details, spending a few minutes with this heavenly companion gave Jesus the strength He needed to finish His task.

The sufferings we endure in this life may not be on the same scale as those of Jesus, but they are just as real. Why does God allow us to suffer so? Why doesn't He strike down our tormentors, and line our path with roses? We can offer answers to such questions—all speculations—but the fact remains that we "suffer according to the will of God" (1 Pet. 4:19); that is, God has His own reasons for delaying justice. Suffering is a fact of life that we cannot avoid.

God will not rescue us with legions of angels, and it is foolish to expect Him to do so. He will, however, provide us with the strength we need to deal with the suffering. For Jesus, it came in the form of a solitary angel. For us it may come in the form of an encouraging word from a friend, or an isolated passage of Scripture that speaks directly to our circumstances, or some providential stroke of good fortune to rekindle fading hopes.

Whatever form this encouragement takes, we must, like Jesus, provide the willing heart that can profit from such divine aid, and press on to the goal that lies before us.

Your Will Be Done

Our indulgent culture exalts happiness as the highest ideal. But the story of Jesus reminds us that there is a greater purpose for our lives.

"Father, if it is Your will, take this cup away from Me; nevertheless not My will, but Yours, be done" (Lk. 22:42).

୨ෟ

Jesus sought solitude in the Garden of Gethsemane because He knew what awaited Him in the morning. His prayer to His Father was emphatic: "Take this cup away from Me." He didn't want to go through with this experience anymore than we would. If there was any possibility of a Plan B, please, Father, let's go that route.

But the Father did not grant His request (which reminds us that prayer is not a vending machine dispensing goodies on demand). Instead, Jesus had to go through an excruciating torture and death. Deep in His heart, He knew there was no other way. That's why He ended His prayer, "Nevertheless not My will, but Yours, be done." He steeled His soul for the task, and saw it through to the bitter end.

Up to this point, doing God's will had not been all that hard for Jesus. The adulation of the crowds, the tears of joy on the faces of the people He healed, the worship of good-hearted disciples who saw Him as their Messiah—all of this had been bearable, perhaps even pleasant. There were enemies who ridiculed and mocked Him, of course, but He could deal with that.

But here at the end, there was nothing pleasant or fulfilling about doing God's will. In fact, it was pure hell. "Take this cup away from Me" is not the prayer of a fearless warrior going out to meet his foe; it is the cry of a condemned man facing a horrible execution.

Yet for all His human fear of what was coming, Jesus did not flinch: "Not my will, but Yours be done." He grimly held to His Father's plan, went to the cross, and purchased our glory.

Remember that the next time you are faced with a divine mandate that vexes your soul. God is not in the business of making you happy. He has a much bigger design in view, and sometimes that design requires that you, like your Master, make a painful sacrifice. You may not see the value in it now, but someday it will all make sense.

"Not my will, but Yours be done." Make these words of Jesus your own, and you will find the strength to endure whatever life throws at you.

The Judas Complex

Judas' motivation in betraying Jesus speaks to a temptation that confronts all of us. We can easily betray our Master for same reason Judas did.

And while He was still speaking, behold, a multitude; and he who was called Judas, one of the twelve, went before them and drew near to Jesus to kiss Him. But Jesus said to him, "Judas, are you betraying the Son of Man with a kiss?" (Lk. 22:47-48).

❧

One of the perplexing mysteries of New Testament study is trying to unlock the motivation behind Judas' betrayal of Jesus. Here was a man personally chosen by Jesus, who saw the miracles, listened to the teachings, and experienced life with the Master Himself—yet was willing to betray Him into the hands of His enemies for a handful of coins. For his eleven fellow apostles, the three years living with Jesus changed their lives; but for Judas, it was a descent into perdition. What happened that caused one so privileged to come to such a miserable end?

Trying to understand Judas is like trying to go back and reconstruct what was in the mind of a criminal two thousand years ago. The evidence is meager, but sufficient to provide some clues to what he was thinking.

- We know that Judas was the treasurer for the group (Jn. 13:29), and that he sometimes used his position to pilfer from the money bag (Jn. 12:6).
- When Mary of Bethany anointed the feet of Jesus with "a pound of very costly oil of spikenard," it was Judas

who complained about the waste of such a valuable commodity (Jn. 12:4-5). The noble intent behind Mary's sacrifice was completely lost on him.

- When Judas approached the rulers with an offer to deliver Jesus to them, his objective was simple: "What will you give me?" (Matt. 26:15). He was motivated not by principle or a desire for power, but only for money. To Judas, Jesus was not a Savior but an opportunity to pick up some quick coin.

The evidence is compelling that Judas had a problem with *money*. Every decision he made was based on a financial calculation. He kept up his charade as an apostle of Jesus right up to the end, when he betrayed Him with a kiss; but his real ambition in life was enriching himself.

Judas is the classic example of what happens when our hearts are consumed by greed. We can keep up appearances as loyal disciples of the Lord, while our real love is the profit motive. Oh, we can be philanthropic alright—but always with an angle: "What will you give me?" We have no scruples about taking advantage even of our brethren if the price is right. The mercenary spirit drives everything.

"The love of money is a root of all kinds of evil" (1 Tim. 6:10), and the story of Judas is a tragic testimony to the truth of that principle. Money is a necessary tool in a world of commerce, but we must take care to keep its tentacles far away from our heart, lest we, too, become seduced by its power to corrupt.

Do Not Weep for Me

Even in the face of death, Jesus thought of others, not Himself. How He saw the world—and His life—exposes the smallness of our own thinking.

And a great multitude of the people followed Him, and women who also mourned and lamented Him. But Jesus, turning to them, said, "Daughters of Jerusalem, do not weep for Me, but weep for yourselves and for your children. For indeed the days are coming in which they will say, 'Blessed are the barren wombs that never bore and breasts which never nursed!' Then they will begin to say to the mountains, 'Fall on us!' and to the hills, 'Cover us!' For if they do these things in the green wood, what will be done in the dry?" (Lk. 23:27-31).

ৎৄৄ৶

As Jesus spoke these words, He had only a few hours to live. He had already been flogged and humiliated by the soldiers, and would shortly be nailed to a cross, the most painful manner of execution available to Roman justice.

But in this darkest hour, Jesus was not preoccupied with His own death. Instead, He saw in His circumstances a far greater tragedy. He knew that in the future, the people of Jerusalem would suffer unspeakable horrors at the hands of a vengeful Roman army. He could see with sharp clarity the awful suffering that would be inflicted that day upon many of these same women and their children. It was they who had cause to weep, not Him.

Jesus was not indifferent to His own pain; His anguish in the Garden of Gethsemane a few hours earlier showed that.

But He viewed His own experience in the context of the wider scope of history. His life and death were merely instruments in a divine plan that began long before He was born into this world, and would extend far into the future. His duty was to fulfill His role during His brief time here, and trust God to handle the aftermath.

And what was His role? To seek and save the lost (Lk. 19:10)—including these women who wept for Him. They were unaware of the threat that loomed before them, and with this warning Jesus was trying to open their eyes. This was typical Jesus, always thinking of others, even in the shadow of the cross.

Ponder this story for a moment: If you or I had been in His place, would we have paid any attention to the threat facing these bystanders? Probably not. Overwhelmed with terror at the prospect of our own impending death, we would likely give no thought to these people and their troubles. We would be weeping for ourselves, and expecting others to weep for us—the very opposite of Jesus.

Which is why we still have so much to learn from the example of our Savior. Until we can consistently—even in the face of death—see others with eyes of compassion, our lives will remain small and petty, preoccupied with our own selfish interests.

The issue here is not who gets all the attention when the drama starts. Rather, it's a failure to see our life as Jesus saw His—as a tool to be used by God for a purpose far more important than our own puny affairs. From beginning to end, Jesus' life was one of sacrifice, always giving, always sharing, always helping others, desiring no pity from others. If we wish to be disciples of Jesus, we must, like Him, seek no sympathy from others, devoting ourselves instead to their well-being.

They Do Not Know

There are many corrupt attitudes that get us in trouble, but underneath all those defects is one flaw that explains everything else.

Then Jesus said, "Father, forgive them, for they do not know what they do" (Lk. 23:34).

I was formerly a blasphemer, a persecutor, and an insolent man; but I obtained mercy because I did it ignorantly in unbelief (1 Tim. 1:13).

৩৵৵

Compassion was Jesus' trademark, but this request of Jesus on the cross beggars belief. After all the abuse He had suffered in the hours leading up to this moment, how could He possibly entertain thoughts of forgiveness for His tormentors? The raw hatred and maliciousness that drove these men was criminal to the extreme. There can be no forgiveness for this degree of villainy, right?

Yet Jesus could peer deep into the souls of these people and see something we cannot see: "They do not know what they do." At some level, they were acting out of *ignorance*; they genuinely had no idea what they were doing.

Many years later, as Paul reflected on the path his life had taken, he looked back on his early career as an enemy of Christianity and admitted, "I did it ignorantly in unbelief." In his case, it took a direct revelation from the Lord Himself to open his eyes to his mistake.

There are many reasons why people in great numbers reject God's truth: hardness of heart, love of pleasure, blind tradition, prejudice, false teaching, and so on. But if we could dig down deep beneath all these superficial impediments, we would find one universal, underlying problem: People are ignorant of Who they are dealing with and what is at stake. If they knew . . . if they *really* understood . . . they would instantly drop to their knees in adoration and worship.

How can we be so sure of that? Because a day is coming, says the Lord, when "*every* knee shall bow to Me, and *every* tongue shall confess to God" (Rom. 14:11). On that day, there will be no atheists, no defiant rebels, no haughty hypocrites. Instead, the reality will become crystal clear for all to see. The key question is: Do they gain that knowledge *now*, when they can act upon it? Or do they gain it *later*, when it will be too late to act upon it?

One final sobering thought: Do I fully understand everything *I* am doing right now?

The High Cost of Ignorance

"Ignorance is bliss" may work for kids too young
to understand, but for the rest of us it's a disaster.
Expanding our knowledge must be a high priority.

---

*"Father, forgive them, for they do not know what they
do" (Lk. 23:34).*

*The way of the wicked is like darkness; they do not know
what makes them stumble (Prov. 4:19).*

*For they being ignorant of God's righteousness, and
seeking to establish their own righteousness, have not sub-
mitted to the righteousness of God (Rom. 10:3).*

❧

Postmodernism has convinced our society that there is
no such thing as objective truth, that each one of us creates
our own "truth" based on our personal experiences, perspectives, and biases. Consequently, millions of people do not
recognize any external reality "out there" in the world around
them. They build their lives upon this fluid foundation, confident that they can pick and choose whatever beliefs and
behaviors they want and discard the rest. Their creed is, "I am
the master of my soul."

This philosophy ignores the presence of an external truth
that doesn't care about our proclivities. Both in the physical
realm and in the moral, these laws of nature operate indepen-
dently of our personal preferences. When we violate those
laws, they push back with relentless certitude. One of the
great challenges of life, therefore, is to recognize how these
principles work, and learn how to conform our lives to their
iron grip. The role of parents, mentors, educators, and sages

325

from past generations is to train us to recognize these eternal truths and build our lives around them.

That education process is long and laborious, tempting us to exchange it for the easy cultural *zeitgeist* of our day. But as comedy writer Robert Orben once said, "If you think education is expensive, try ignorance." We are free to ignore the wisdom of the ages, but that ignorance will inflict a terrible toll on our quality of life. Like someone trying to grope through a dark forest at midnight, "they do not know what makes them stumble." That's not an arbitrary punishment inflicted by God, but a natural outcome of not knowing how the world operates.

In our youth, ignorance usually comes from an honest lack of knowledge. We've not yet been exposed to all the cause-and-effect details of how life works, so we will make a fair number of mistakes. If we're smart, we'll learn from those mistakes and gain wisdom as we grow older.

But if we're *not* smart, we will deliberately reject the truth and its consequences, and charge full steam ahead into whatever make-believe "truth" we have invented for ourselves. The Bible calls this "willful ignorance" (2 Pet. 3:5, CSB). It was willful ignorance that sent ancient Israel spiraling into a vortex of violence and corruption (Hos. 4:1-6). Willful ignorance led the Jewish people to destroy Jesus rather than embrace Him as their Messiah. When people choose to ignore the bedrock truth this world is built on, they set themselves up for a terrible fall.

How can we escape the clutches of ignorance? First, we must pursue knowledge with all the passion of a treasure hunter. We should seek God's counsel by reading His word, and reach out to older mentors who have demonstrated their ability to navigate life's difficult journey. Listen and learn!

Finally, we must grow a heart of humility. When we make dumb mistakes, we should acknowledge our errors, learn from those mistakes, and take the necessary steps to correct them. Ignorance is destructive, but *pride* is the chain that keeps us locked in its deadly grip.

When Should I Forgive?

Love has no more noble expression than in unconditional forgiveness. But we cannot pick and choose when and to whom we offer forgiveness.

"Father, forgive them, for they do not know what they do" (Lk. 23:34).

". . . bearing with one another, and forgiving one another, if anyone has a complaint against another; even as Christ forgave you, so you also must do" (Col. 3:13).

৽৵৻

On October 2, 2006, Charlie Roberts walked into the West Nickel Mines school in Lancaster County, Pennsylvania, and shot ten Amish girls, killing five and maiming the others, before turning his gun on himself. The families of those little girls were forced to face an evil of unimaginable magnitude. Where was their God when their daughters were being slaughtered by this monster?

Almost two thousand years earlier, Jesus the Galilean was condemned in a rigged trial and executed on a Roman cross. He, too, was forced to bear the pain of a monstrous crime. He, too, felt the anguish of knowing that God was letting this injustice happen.

Yet even as he was dying, He forgave those who were killing Him. He prayed for His executioners, "Father, forgive them for they do not know what they do."

Jesus forgave His executioners, not out of some superhuman power, but from a love that could see past the irrational behavior to the inherent value of the perpetrators. That same love motivated Stephen to utter a similar prayer as his life was being beaten out of him (Ac. 7:60), and Paul to express the same sentiment just before he was executed (2 Tim. 4:16).

We laud the forgiveness extended by Jesus, Stephen, and Paul as fine examples of how to face persecution. How virtuous! How inspiring! If I am ever threatened with death for my faith, I hope I can have that same nobility of spirit!

Of course, it's easy to say that, because we know we're unlikely to ever face it. Here's a better test: How do I respond when someone spreads a malicious lie about me? Or when a co-worker stabs me in the back? Or when my spouse betrays our wedding vows? We live in a world that is in the grip of sin, deceit, and hatred, and we often encounter the symptoms of these evils. Do we forgive them? *Can* we forgive them?

The example of Jesus can be viewed as a blueprint for how to face martyrdom, but that's not its real purpose. It was intended as a model for how we ought to face all the frustrations and injustices that we encounter throughout the normal course of life. Whatever the abuses that are inflicted upon us, we are to forgive the abusers, "even as Christ forgave you."

That spirit starts with the minor wrongs that others inflict upon us. Both the transgression and the forgiveness may be insignificant, but the challenge is real. The greater test comes when a knife is plunged deep into our soul, and the pain is more than we can bear. Can we forgive our transgressor then? Or do we allow bitterness to take seed in our heart?

Instead of fantasizing about what we would do if faced with martyrdom for our faith, we need to re-evaluate how we react to the lesser offenses we encounter in our lives every day. This is where a forgiving heart will be manifested.

The Amish parents of those murdered little girls knew this lesson well. Even as they bore the burden of their own grief, they went out of their way to show kindness to the family of the murderer, who were living through their own nightmare. The forgiveness the Amish displayed in the aftermath of that tragedy touched a nation and showed us that genuine forgiveness can overcome even the most awful act of evil. We should do likewise.

328

How God Opens Hearts

If God's Spirit guides believers into understanding truth, then why are believers so hopelessly divided? Maybe the starting premise is flawed.

And beginning at Moses and all the Prophets, He expounded to them in all the Scriptures the things concerning Himself (Lk. 24:27).

And they said to one another, "Did not our heart burn within us while He talked with us on the road, and while He opened the Scriptures to us?" (Lk. 24:32).

And He opened their understanding, that they might comprehend the Scriptures (Lk. 24:45).

❧

In Calvinist theology, the unregenerate sinner is incapable of understanding, much less obeying, God's word. Only when God chooses to execute a direct operation of the Holy Spirit upon his heart ("irresistible grace"—the "I" in Calvinism's TULIP), is the sinner's heart opened to understand and obey the Word.

Is this a scriptural concept? The third verse in our trio of opening texts seems to support the idea. The apostles could not comprehend what the Scriptures taught about Christ until their hearts were "opened" to receive it. Looks simple, right?

But there are a number of problems with this view of the verse. First, these are not unregenerate sinners, but Jesus' own apostles, men who long ago had pledged their hearts and lives to Him, and had even performed miracles by the power of the Holy Spirit. If they had already received the saving grace of the Spirit, then how do we explain their deficiency on this occasion?

If God was providing these men some kind of miraculous insight into truth (that was heretofore miraculously hidden from them), then upon what basis does God decide when, where, and who gets this divine gift? There are plenty of passages in God's word that I would dearly love to have this kind of assistance in understanding. If He does not provide it to everyone, is He not then a respecter of persons?

Finally, if God gives people special access to understanding truth, then why is Christianity still plagued with so many disagreements? And these divisions exist among people who claim to have the Holy Spirit guiding their understanding of the Scriptures.

Clearly, God and the Holy Spirit are not responsible for the divisions among believers. Faulty interpretations among Bible students (and the divisions that follow) are the result of faulty knowledge and/or faulty attitudes in the readers, nothing more. Claiming special Holy Spirit guidance in our Bible study sets us up for self-reinforcing deception.

Look carefully at the earlier verses in this chapter describing the same phenomenon at work in the two travelers to Emmaus. They, too, claimed that Jesus "opened the Scriptures to us" (v. 32); but He did so by "expounding to them in all the Scriptures the things concerning Himself" (v. 27). Get it? Their minds were opened to understanding the Scriptures *by those Scriptures being explained to them.* There was nothing miraculous here. Just old-fashioned study, discussion, and thinking among people who had a deep love for truth in their hearts.

That's how God opens our hearts today. The gospel—an intelligent message communicated in Scripture—is still God's power to save among those who are disposed to listen and learn (Rom. 1:16).

Hearts on Fire

Unless our hearts blaze with excitement when we are exposed to Biblical truth, our religion is little more than a cold, academic exercise.

Then their eyes were opened and they knew Him; and He vanished from their sight. And they said to one another, "Did not our hearts burn within us while He talked with us on the road, and while He opened the Scriptures to us?" (Lk. 24:32).

ക

These words were spoken by two disciples a few days after the crucifixion of Jesus. They had been conversing with a stranger on the road to Emmaus, who explained many of the Old Testament passages dealing with the Messiah. As this fellow spoke, all the inexplicable events of the last few days started to make sense: the betrayal, the crucifixion, the rumors of the missing body. These events were not the collapse of an impostor's deluded scheme, but elements in God's master plan that had been foretold by the old prophets all along. This "stranger" had laid it all out for them, when suddenly, in a flash of recognition, they realized who they were talking to: It was Jesus Himself, returned from the dead!

We are interested here in the disciples' description of the intellectual clarity that Jesus brought to their minds as He explained the Scriptures to them: "Did not our hearts burn within us?" As Jesus stitched together these odd bits and pieces of Scripture, so difficult to understand, into a pattern that exposed a logical plan, these disciples became excited. As the broad outline began to emerge, no doubt they could start plugging in other Scriptures that Jesus had not mentioned. Their faith, which had been shattered a few days before, now had a solid foundation to rest upon.

There is no thrill quite like the "eureka moment" of finally unraveling a hidden truth in God's word. People often complain about the Bible being such a difficult book to understand, and it can be—sometimes frustratingly so. But it is not meaningless gibberish. It has a plan, a plot, along with a host of major and minor themes, all designed to address the deepest needs of the human condition. Understanding the Bible is not always easy, but with persistent study and thought, it will yield its secrets to the one who is determined to find them.

But that's the trick, isn't it? How badly do we really want to understand it? These disciples had been fervent followers of Jesus, hanging upon His every word. Even after He was killed, they couldn't stop talking about Him, trying to figure out what had happened. When Jesus came into their midst and began talking to them about the Scriptures, He was dealing with men whose minds were prepared to be enlightened. Their hearts burned with excitement at what they were learning—because they were mentally prepared to receive it.

If our hearts do not burn when the Scriptures are opened up to us, perhaps we need to re-examine our spiritual condition. How much time do we devote to reading and thinking about the Scriptures? How often do we talk about the Bible with other believers? How curious are we about those portions of the Bible that are still locked from our understanding?

Our hearts can burn, too, but only if we prepare them to be ignited when the right spark comes along.

Love Gives

Everyone agrees that love is essential in human relations, but few grasp what it is. The concept is simple, but requires much more than we realize.

---

*"For God so **loved** the world that He **gave** His only begotten Son, that whoever believes in Him should not perish but have everlasting life" (Jn. 3:16).*

*I have been crucified with Christ; it is no longer I who live, but Christ lives in me; and the life which I now live in the flesh I live by faith in the Son of God, who **loved** me and **gave** Himself for me (Gal. 2:20).*

*Husbands, love your wives, just as Christ also **loved** the church and **gave** Himself for her (Eph. 5:25).*

ॐ

Notice a common theme in these verses? All three describe the love of God or Christ in providing for our salvation. But our attention should be drawn to the close connection between the words "love" and "gave." God "loved . . . gave"; Christ "loved . . . and gave"; Christ "loved . . . and gave." Who needs a lot of thick Bible word study books, when you have such a direct commentary embedded right in the divine text itself?

Love gives. In an age that is dominated by selfish consumerism, this simple definition is revolutionary in its implications. It sweeps away all the phony imitations of true love, and reduces the concept to a single word—or rather, a single *behavior*. Love is not a feeling or an emotion. It is not a pit that you "fall" into. There are other words that are more suitable to describe those experiences. Rather, love is a commitment to reach out and do good to the object of its affection. The gift is not predicated on the worthiness of the recipient. No consideration is given to any selfish benefit in return. Instead, love is *the giving of oneself to benefit another.* It's that simple.

The meaning may be simple, but the implications are staggering. Take marriage, for example. Why do a man and woman get married? Because they love each other, of course. But in too many cases, this "love" is really "lust" or "romance" or "fun" or some other shallow imitation based on what the two individuals "get" from the relationship. These ephemeral qualities eventually fade away—and then what? When either party no longer feels the same excitement they once felt, the marriage is over. And no wonder. The marriage was not based on love ("giving"), but on "getting."

Suppose, however, that these two people enter this relationship with a deeper motivation. Each is committed first and foremost to pleasing his or her mate. Each makes a conscious effort to really understand the likes and dislikes of the other, and works hard to adapt to the needs of the partner. This will require sacrifices—in some cases, a lot of sacrifices. As both parties continue to pour themselves into this enterprise, a remarkable thing will begin to happen: They will start to genuinely like each other. Why? Because they have learned the secret to a happy marriage: *love gives.*

What works in marriage works in every other relationship in life. If we measure our relationships by what we get out of them, we will always end up disappointed, embroiled in never-ending drama and trouble. But if we train ourselves to think in terms of what we can give, with no thought of return, we will find a much deeper level of satisfaction—one that is rooted in love.

Conditional Salvation

The controversy over whether man must "do"
something to receive salvation ignores what
someone else had to "do" to make it possible.

---

*"For God so loved the world that He gave His only be-
gotten Son, that whoever believes in Him should not perish
but have everlasting life" (Jn. 3:16).*

৽৽৽

In the endless debates with our denominational friends
over what a person must do to be saved, we tend to focus all
our attention on man's side of the equation: What, if anything, must *we* do to receive salvation? But perhaps we're
approaching this subject from the wrong starting point. If we
first establish the conditional nature of *God's* role in our salvation, it will be much easier to understand our role in the
matter.

Most everyone will agree that we are "saved by grace";
that is, by God's unmerited mercy (Eph. 2:8; Rom. 3:24; Tit.
2:5). We can agree that this grace is the empowering element
in salvation; it is a gift so enormous in value that no amount
of human effort could ever replace it. Furthermore, we can
agree that God is the initiating party in bestowing this gift.
We did not ask for His mercy. He willingly offered it to us
while we were still enemies.

With this foundation of shared belief, consider this question: *Did God have to do anything for His grace to become
effective?* Was the mere fact that God loved us sufficient to
secure our salvation? Or did He have to express that love in
some fashion in order for it to do us any good? Worded an-

other way, could God's grace *alone*—a mere emotion, a feeling, a desire—be adequate to save man?

Though we customarily do not think of it in these terms, virtually everyone will agree that God's grace really wasn't efficacious until it was demonstrated in the sacrifice of His Son. "God so loved . . . that He gave," expresses eloquently the conditional nature of God's grace. He loved us, yes; but that love meant nothing until it was displayed on the cross.

If people can understand the conditional nature of *God's* role in salvation, why is it so difficult to understand the conditional nature of *man's* role in salvation? Just like God, man's role begins with an attitude in the heart (faith). But just like God, that attitude doesn't mean much until it is demonstrated in an outward act, in this case, an act of obedience (baptism). Baptism as a condition to salvation is taught just as clearly as is the death of Christ (Mk. 16:16; Ac. 2:38; Ac. 22:16; 1 Pet. 3:21). Why accept one condition (God's) and reject the other (man's)?

The fact that God has attached a human condition to His gift of grace does not in any way lessen the value of the gift; nor does it rob God of His glory in making it available to us. Rather, it acknowledges our status as free moral agents with the power to choose whether or not we will accept God's gift. By meeting His simple condition, we show the world what is in our hearts—just as God showed what was in His.

I Must Decrease

Unlike the world's definition, real success comes when we can see our lives as tools to be used in behalf of a purpose greater than ourselves.

"He who has the bride is the bridegroom; but the friend of the bridegroom, who stands and hears him, rejoices greatly because of the bridegroom's voice. Therefore this joy of mine is fulfilled. He must increase, but I must decrease" (Jn. 3:29-30).

৵৽৶

The disciples of John the Baptist were bothered over the rising popularity of Jesus. "All are coming to Him!" they complained (v. 26), and in their minds that encroachment posed a threat to John's work. How could he retain the affection of the people in the face of Jesus' growing influence?

John's response to this complaint reflected the wisdom of his position. Just as the best man is not in the business of competing with the bridegroom, so John felt no threat from Jesus' growing popularity. In fact, this shift in public affection was an intentional development in a larger plan. John played a supporting role in a production that featured Jesus as the star attraction, and he found his joy in seeing Jesus fulfill His destiny. The sequence of events was playing out exactly as the script called for. "He must increase, but I must decrease," and John was fine with that. John even may have had a premonition that his decrease would lead to an ignominious end. Shortly after this, he was thrown in prison and executed by a spineless tyrant. Not exactly a career highlight.

John's response to Jesus' rising popularity provides an important lesson in the nature of *humility*. Whatever great things John had accomplished in his career up to this point, he knew they were incidental to the larger mission that God was executing. His own fame or advancement was incidental to God's ultimate purpose, and he knew that. If God's plan called for him to fade into obscurity and die a shameful death, he could deal with it. "I must decrease" was not a cry of bitter resignation, but a cheerful acceptance of his place in God's master narrative.

It's a lesson that is so difficult for most of us to learn. We seethe with envy when others move ahead—especially if it's at our expense. We scratch and claw and fight to get "our fair share" of the credit for accomplishments achieved in a team setting. We get offended if no one acknowledges, or even notices, a contribution we make to the general good. The common thread in all these scenarios is a heart that is driven by the creed, "I must increase." As long as that is our objective, we will always be finding ourselves in situations that make us miserable and unhappy. A life devoted to self-promotion will never satisfy its owner.

"I must decrease" is not an easy mindset to develop, but it is essential to fulfilling our purpose in life. When we can accept that we are not the center of our world, that our happiness is not the ultimate goal in life, and that it's perfectly legitimate for others to have a calling that exceeds our own, only then we will be free to realize the purpose for which God has placed us here. When we are willing to sacrifice ourselves and our pride for God's greater purpose, we will find the true joy of a life well lived.

John accomplished what God sent him to do, and Jesus benefited from his sacrifice. Are we using our lives in a similar fashion?

In Spirit and in Truth

The elements of authentic religion have never changed throughout the ages. We should measure our own religion by this simple standard.

"But the hour is coming, and now is, when the true worshipers will worship the Father in spirit and truth; for the Father is seeking such to worship Him. God is Spirit, and those who worship Him must worship in spirit and truth" *(Jn. 4:23-24).*

୨୦ଓ

The topic of discussion in this context was the correct place of worship: Jerusalem in Judea or Mt. Gerazim in Samaria (v. 20). The Samaritan woman at the well argued for the latter, and expected Jesus to defend the former. But rather than take sides on this one issue, Jesus took the discussion to a higher plane, addressing a much more important question: *What defines a true worshiper of God?* The geographic location of worship was a legitimate topic of discussion in that day, but until this greater question was resolved, this lesser issue was of no consequence.

Jesus identified two factors that define the true worshiper: "spirit" and "truth." To worship God "in spirit" means to do it with a fervent heart, to invest one's whole soul in the matter. Our worship is not an empty ritual performed out of habit. Nor is it done to please men, but as an expression of our genuine love for God. To worship God "in truth" means to respect what God has revealed in His word. It is a commitment to align with the "true" standard that God has given to guide our behavior.

339

Of these two factors, one (spirit) is subjective, inward, involving attitudes, while the other (truth) is objective, outward, involving behaviors. Together, they define the "true worshiper" whom God seeks. Those who worship God in spirit (with the heart) but ignore His truth are libertines; those who worship in truth (careful to keep the details) but ignore the attitudes are legalists. Minimizing either element renders one's service to God unacceptable.

What Jesus taught here was not a new concept. Centuries before, Joshua taught the Israelites the same principle using almost exactly the same wording: "Now therefore, fear the Lord, serve Him in *sincerity* and in *truth*" (Josh. 24:14).

Actually, what Jesus and Joshua taught in these two passages is a formula that is repeated often throughout the Bible, using a variety of expressions: "Let us hear the conclusion of the whole matter: *Fear God* and *keep His commandments*, for this is man's all" (Eccl. 12:13). "In every nation whoever *fears Him* and *works righteousness* is accepted by Him" (Ac. 10:35). Sometimes the order might be reversed: "Blessed are those who *keep His testimonies*, who *seek Him with the whole heart*" (Psa. 119:2).

One could argue, in fact, that God's plan of salvation has never really changed throughout the entire span of human history. From the very beginning, all God has ever required of humanity is that we give Him our hearts completely, and honor what He tells us to do. What else is there?

The Samaritan woman saw religion as the offering of sacrifices on a holy mountain. Jesus challenged her to see religion not as a ritual confined to a holy place, but as a way of life that dominates how we think and how we act, everywhere and every day. Until we can see our own religion in that same light, we are just playing games with God.

What Do You Want?

The first step toward improving our lives is acknowledging we have a problem. For many people, that first step is the most difficult.

Now a certain man was there who had an infirmity thirty-eight years. When Jesus saw him lying there, and knew that he already had been in that condition a long time, He said to him, "Do you want to be made well?" (Jn. 5:5-6).

∽∾

This man's infirmity probably involved some disability in his legs, since he described others going ahead of him to the pool of Bethesda when the healing waters stirred (v. 7). Whatever the illness, one wonders why Jesus would ask such a pointless question. *Of course* the man wanted to be made well; who in his condition would not?

But Jesus was justified in challenging this man's intentions. I know that, because I've encountered quite a few people in my life who, I'm convinced, did *not* want to be made well. These are people who complain about their infirmities—and seem to enjoy the complaining. They milk their problems for all the sympathy they can get, and revel in the attention they attract. They relish their victim status, and play it to the hilt. To be healed of their affliction would rob them of one of their main sources of significance in life.

This phenomenon extends beyond physical illnesses. Some people are engaged in behaviors that even they will admit are self-destructive—but they will not let them go. They may not like the consequences of their bad habits, and will even bemoan the condition they've gotten themselves into;

but they love the habits too much to give them up. They prefer to live with their disordered life rather than address the problem that caused it.

The story of this lame man illustrates a similar scenario in the lives of those damaged by sin. Jesus can perform amazing transformations in the lives of such people; but it can happen only to those who honestly seek a different direction. That's why the first question Jesus asks of every sinner who comes to Him is, "Do you want to be made well?"

It is a legitimate question, because sadly, the response of many people is often, "No, thanks."

They reject Jesus' offer because they do not recognize the destructive role sin plays in their lives. They have a vague sense that something is amiss, but cannot identify the source of the problem. They blame others for the various debacles in their life, or convince themselves that a little more money or a few more thrills will buy them the satisfaction they seek. Of course, they never quite find what they are looking for, because the invisible hand of sin keeps pushing them down. These people can never be made well, because they won't admit they have an illness that needs to be healed. Genuine repentance is off the table.

The first step toward improving our lives is admitting we have a problem. That problem is *sin*, a violation of God's purpose for our lives. Once we admit that we don't know it all, and that our own bad attitudes and behaviors are the chief culprit, we can finally gain access to the healing that will allow us to grow into a richer, more satisfying life. That healing, of course, is the forgiveness that God offers us through His Son, Jesus Christ. The awareness that God is willing to accept us despite our failures is a powerful motivation to do better.

"Do you want to be made well?" Until we can answer that question affirmatively, we will never experience the growth we're looking for.

Why People Do Not Believe

Evidence for the key tenets of Christianity is not
that hard to assess. The real obstacle is the
integrity of the heart that is considering it.

*"You are not willing to come to Me that you may have
life" (Jn. 5:40).*

*"If anyone wills to do His will, he shall know concerning
the doctrine, whether it is from God or whether I speak on My
own authority" (Jn. 7:17).*

ঙ৹৶

Although separated by two chapters, these two verses
reference the same event in Jesus' career. An understanding
of this historical connection brings into sharper focus the lesson that Jesus is teaching in both passages.

In John 5, Jesus went to Jerusalem for "a feast of the
Jews" (v. 1). Scholars are divided as to whether this was the
Passover, Purim, or some other feast. (Westcott makes a
strong case for the New Year's feast, also known as the Feast
of Trumpets, held every year in early October—Lev. 23:23-
26; Num. 29:1-6; Neh. 8:1-12.) During this feast, on a Sabbath day, Jesus healed a lame man at the Pool of Bethesda.
Jesus had performed many miracles before, but mostly in
Galilee, far away from Jerusalem. This was apparently the
first time He had performed such a dramatic miracle right under the noses of the Jewish rulers. The healing created quite
a stir among the people; some even sought to kill Him (5:16-
18). This incident sparked a spirited debate between Jesus
and His critics (5:16-47). It was during this exchange that He

accused His critics of being "not willing" to come to Him (v. 40).

Scroll forward at least a year. A Passover feast comes and goes (6:4), then the Feast of Tabernacles, in late October of that next year (7:2). During this intervening year, if Jesus went to Jerusalem at all, He kept a low profile (7:1). But at this Feast of Tabernacles, Jesus went to Jerusalem again, and this time He openly taught in the temple (7:14). Although it had been at least a year since the lame man was healed, as far as Jesus and His critics were concerned, it was like it had happened only yesterday. The debate resumed right where it had left off. "I did one work," Jesus challenged them, "and you all marvel" (v. 21). They knew exactly which work He was talking about—and they still sought to kill Him for it (v. 19, 25, 44).

But notice the topic with which Jesus re-opened this debate: "If anyone wills to do His will, he shall know concerning the doctrine, whether it is from God or whether I speak on My own authority" (7:17). It was the same accusation He had made during the first exchange a year earlier: The Jews refused to believe Him, not because of a lack of evidence, but because *they didn't want to believe.* Their minds were shut to any possibility of accepting His claims.

Jesus' assessment of His critics' mindset explains much of the hostility that we see toward Christianity today. People hate the truth, not because the evidence is so flimsy, or because its fruit is so bitter, but because their hearts are so closed. They have made up their minds what they want to believe, and no amount of logic or evidence will dislodge them from their position.

The truth is not hard to figure out—once a person opens his heart to consider it. The real challenge is pushing past years of accumulated prejudice to give one's mind a chance to see it.

A Carnal Religion

The social reform efforts that occupy so many
churches today are well-intentioned, but ignore a
work that should receive far more attention.

---

*"Most assuredly, I say to you, you seek Me, not because
you saw the signs, but because you ate of the loaves and were
filled" (Jn. 6:26).*

ೞೞ

Following the feeding of the five thousand, the crowd
tried to forcibly install Jesus as their king, a move that would
have been seen as a direct challenge to Roman rule (v. 15).
Jesus refused to accept the honor. But the crowd continued to
follow Him anyway—until they realized there would be no
more free meals (v. 26-27). Instead of more food, Jesus gave
them only a sermon. Then they turned away and followed
Him no more (v. 66). A savior who could not provide them
with political freedom or basic physical needs held no appeal
to them.

On another occasion, a man approached Jesus with a request to sort out an inheritance dispute with his brother (Lk.
12:13). Jesus refused to get involved in the matter (v. 14), and
used the occasion instead as an opportunity to teach a lesson
on the dangers of covetousness (v. 15f). This man came to
Jesus looking for justice, but like the five thousand, all he got
was a sermon.

Look carefully at the range of issues Jesus refused to
tackle in these stories: political reform, eradication of world
hunger, social justice. Sound familiar? They should, because

they are the same issues that churches today have elevated as their primary mission in the world.

Jesus' response in these two episodes raises a disturbing question: If our Savior refused even to touch these pressing issues of His day, how can churches today justify making them such a core part of their mission? Are not these churches heading in a different direction than the One they claim to follow?

The religion of Christ is not a carnal religion. It is a religion dedicated to addressing the spiritual and moral needs of humanity. The physical necessities of life were never intended to be its primary concern.

To be sure, as people get their spiritual and moral issues sorted out, the physical aspects of their lives will likely improve as well. The self-control, the unselfish love for others, the commitment to integrity and fairness, and all the other attributes that are developed in following the teachings of Jesus will usually pay dividends in all areas of people's lives. And as larger numbers of people come to embrace this way of life, society as a whole will be transformed and elevated. But that transformation is a *by-product* of Christianity, not its *primary objective*.

History demonstrates that when churches move political and social issues to the top of their agenda, spiritual and moral education almost always gets lost in the bureaucratic fog. The result is a carnal religion that seeks to impose artificial solutions to the problems of humanity, but ends up only masking a deeper spiritual rot that continues to eat away at the foundations of society. Ironically, these churches end up exacerbating the very problems they're trying to solve.

The religion of Christ is primarily an *educational* enterprise. Its mission is to teach people how to live, not to step in and solve their problems for them. Only by equipping individuals with the basic skills to live their lives successfully will churches have any real impact on the social issues of humanity.

Drawn by God

Our salvation is initiated by God. Of that, there can be no doubt. But how we choose to respond to that influence is entirely on us.

"No one can come to Me unless the Father who sent Me ***draws*** *him; and I will raise him up at the last day. It is written in the prophets, 'And they shall all be taught by God.' Therefore everyone who has heard and learned from the Father comes to Me" (Jn. 6:44-45).*

"Now is the judgment of this world; now the ruler of this world will be cast out. And I, if I am lifted up from the earth, will ***draw*** *all peoples to Myself." This He said, signifying by what death He would die (Jn. 12:31-33).*

❧

The theological system known as Calvinism—named after the French reformer John Calvin (1509-1564)—holds that salvation is entirely the work of God, and that man is entirely passive in the matter. One Calvinist apologist summarizes the doctrine this way: "God sends His Holy Spirit to work in the lives of people so that they will definitely and certainly be changed from evil to good people. It means that the Holy Spirit will certainly—without any ands, ifs and buts—cause everyone whom God has chosen from eternity and for whom Christ died to believe on Jesus" (Edwin Palmer, *The Five Points of Calvinism*, 1972, p. 58). He then offers Jn. 6:44-45 as his first scriptural proof.

Is it true that God does everything and we do nothing in the matter of our eternal salvation? And how does God "draw" individuals to Himself?

The Greek word for "draw" in these verses (*elko*) describes a strong force pulling on an object, such as a magnet *pulling* a piece of iron (Oepke, *Theological Dictionary of the NT*), or a ship *towing* a smaller craft (Moulton & Milligan, *Vocabulary of the Greek NT*), or a fisherman *dragging* a net full of fish to shore (Jn. 21:11). Jeremiah used the same word to describe this divine action of God drawing people to Himself: "I have loved you with an everlasting love; therefore with lovingkindness I have *drawn* you" (Jer. 31:3, LXX). Despite Judah's rebellious spirit, God still loved His people, and worked to secure their affection.

There can be no dispute that God takes the initiative in salvation. It is God who draws (entices, attracts, pulls out) men to come to Christ. The key question here does not concern God's role in salvation, but the *means* by which He draws them. Jesus answers that question by quoting Isa. 54:13: "'They shall all be taught by God.' Therefore everyone who has heard and learned from the Father comes to Me." God's drawing power is not some mysterious heart surgery by the Holy Spirit, but *a rational message that appeals to the intellect and emotion of the listener*. As people hear and understand that message, they are drawn to Christ.

The heart of this drawing power is Christ being "lifted up from the earth." When people finally grasp the meaning of the death of Christ—the voluntary sacrifice of the Son of God for them, despite their imperfections—a powerful force deep in the human psyche is awakened, transforming their wills and their lives. It is not irresistible; some yield to its drawing power, others reject it. But it is God's way of drawing people to Himself. No bribes, no coffee and donuts, no fun and games, no lashes on the back—just a simple message of love and forgiveness for me, the sinner.

After his Damascus road experience, Paul no longer saw Jesus as an impostor, but as the one who "loved me and gave Himself for me" (Gal. 2:20). That new perspective radically changed his life. Our own thinking and teaching should rest on that same foundation.

To Whom Shall We Go?

The temptation to quit the life of faith can be strong. But before we bail, we should remember that every alternative has its own drawbacks.

From that time many of His disciples went back and walked with Him no more. Then Jesus said to the twelve, "Do you also want to go away?" But Simon Peter answered Him, "Lord, to whom shall we go? You have the words of eternal life. Also we have come to believe and know that You are the Christ, the Son of the living God" (Jn. 6:66-69).

৩৯৫

This exchange between Jesus and His apostles occurred following the feeding of the five thousand. The crowd continued to follow Jesus for a short while, expecting more free food. But instead of food, Jesus gave them a strange sermon about seeking more permanent sustenance, something about eating His flesh and drinking His blood. The multitude was not interested in all this metaphysical stuff, so they left.

It must have been a bitter disappointment to the apostles to see all their hard work of the past several months melt away to nothing—especially considering that it was this bizarre sermon of Jesus that drove them away. No doubt, the apostles also were probably scratching their heads trying to figure out what Jesus was talking about. Judging from His question to them, perhaps Jesus had some concern that even they would quit. But the apostles did not quit. Peter's response to Jesus' question reveals the heart of a true disciple of Christ: "To whom shall we go? You have the words of eternal life."

This was not the first time the apostles did not understand something Jesus taught, nor would it be the last. They frequently did not "get it," and Jesus had to repeat some concepts over and over. Some lessons they never did fully grasp until after His resurrection. But regardless of their limited understanding, they continued to cling to Him, convinced that He was their best hope of making sense of a crazy world.

"To whom shall we go?" is a question that still confronts followers of Jesus today, especially when His religion appears difficult or inadequate. People struggle to understand the deeper teachings of the Bible. They become disenchanted with the strife and hypocrisy among fellow believers. Or they grow tired of a faith that has become stale and boring.

Eventually the temptation looms to do what the multitude did: just walk away. Some go to Buddhism, some to Islam, some to atheism, and some to a vague "spirituality" that feels good, but makes few demands on lifestyle. There are plenty of options out there to satisfy everyone's desire for something different. Many simply reject spirituality altogether, choosing a life of crass materialism that lives for the present and refuses even to think about spiritual matters.

But as they eventually learn, all these alternatives have their own shortcomings, too. Futility, hypocrisy, and bewilderment is not limited to the religion of Christ. So their search for meaning in life goes off in yet another direction.

All of which brings us back to Peter's original question: *To whom shall we go?* Whatever difficulties a Christian encounters in his faith, the foundation of that faith is a bedrock that no alternative can match: Jesus is the Son of God, demonstrated by His death and resurrection, and He alone has words of eternal life. Even if we struggle to understand and apply those words, He is better than anything else out there.

Keep on studying, learning, and growing, clinging to Him in stubborn faith. Someday it will all make sense.

Who Is Jesus?

The contradictory opinions regarding the identity of Jesus of Nazareth are not due to a lack of evidence, but the lack of intellectual honesty.

There was much complaining among the people concerning Him. Some said, "He is good"; others said, "No, on the contrary, He deceives the people" (Jn. 7:12).

Some of the Pharisees said, "This Man is not from God, because He does not keep the Sabbath." Others said, "How can a man who is a sinner do such signs?" And there was a division among them (Jn. 9:16).

ഏൟ

In the gospel accounts it's obvious that even in His own day, people had a hard time figuring out who Jesus was. This confusion is especially noticeable in the gospel of John, who seems to go out of his way to highlight the diverse opinions about the Galilean that circulated throughout the land of Palestine. In all of history since then, no people have ever had a greater opportunity to study Jesus up close and personal. Yet with Jesus right in front of them, these people still couldn't agree on who He was.

It should not surprise us, therefore, to find that opinions about Jesus of Nazareth today, two thousand years later, are all over the map.

- Some think He was the Son of God, the Savior of the world.
- Others believe He was just an itinerant philosopher who had a pretty good understanding of human nature and the ability to lecture about it—but nothing more. His disci-

ples got a little carried away with the whole "Messiah" thing, but Jesus Himself had no such ambitions.

- Still others (Muslims) think He was indeed a prophet sent from God, but only one in a long list of such godly servants. (They also deny that He was crucified. They insist that it was someone else who hung on that cross.)
- Finally, there are those who deny that Jesus ever existed at all. He was a mythical character invented by delusional Jewish fanatics later in the first and second centuries.

So take your pick—which version of Jesus do *you* accept? And how can you make a rational choice, so far removed from the original events?

Unlike most characters from the ancient past, we have four independent documents—two written by His personal disciples, and two written by close associates of the apostles—that provide an account of the life, death, and resurrection of Jesus. Two of His physical brothers, James and Jude, and several other early disciples left behind their own corroborating testimony. The writings of Paul, who came on the scene shortly after Jesus lived and was personally acquainted with the original witnesses, augment this body of information.

In short, there is no other character in ancient history for whom we have such a wealth of first-hand documentation.

The resources for knowing who Jesus was and what He taught are abundant and compelling. That's not the issue. The real question is: *Are we willing to examine this evidence with an open mind?* The intellectual honesty (or lack thereof) among the listeners explains much of the confusion that existed then, and much of the confusion today.

Come to Jesus with an honest heart, and you'll learn soon enough who He really is.

Judging by Appearance

Much of the violence that has darkened human history is the result of judging others by group identity. Why are we returning to that madness?

"Do not judge according to appearance, but judge with righteous judgment" (Jn. 7:24).

૭∾⋞

"Righteous" judgment has long been a challenge for humanity. We are given to writing off others based on superficial traits such as race, ethnicity, tribal identity, socio-economic class, political affiliation, and so forth. In the first century, for example, the Jew/Gentile divide was exacerbated by attitudes on both sides of the fence, embodied in comments like, "All Jews are _____," or "All Gentiles are _____." (Fill in the blanks for your favorite libel.) Groups have long used these kinds of artificial distinctions as justification for waging war on other groups, resulting in horrible body counts.

That prejudicial impulse has played a major role in the history of our own nation. For a long time, the dominant race (whites) subjugated a minority race (blacks) as sub-human, subjecting them first to slavery, then to second-class citizenship. After a bloody civil war and a painful civil rights movement, we've finally moved beyond that dark period in our history. During the civil rights movement in the 1960s, Martin Luther King, Jr., longed for the day when children would be judged by the content of their character, not the color of their skin. We have even witnessed the election of a black man as President. That's progress.

Yet at the very moment when we are on the verge of achieving that goal, powerful institutions in our society are now pushing all of us back into the old paradigm of judging others solely on the basis of group identity. Under the guise of Critical Race Theory, our children are being judged explicitly, not by the content of their character, but by the color of their skin. We've replaced the old prejudice, "All black people are_____," with a new prejudice, "All white people are_____." The colors are reversed, but the net effect is the same: more injustice, conflict, resentment, envy, revenge. And this prejudice not limited to race:

"All men are_____."

"All women are_____."

"All cops are_____."

"All teenagers are _____."

"All Democrats/Republicans are _____."

On and on it goes. The irony here is striking. For a long time, the "judge not" statement of Jesus (Matt. 7:1) was used as a cudgel to shut down any and all criticism of others. Suddenly the script has been flipped, and judging people on the most frivolous grounds is not only acceptable, but compulsory. We are reverting back to a mode of thought and conduct that will exacerbate our divisions, not heal them. The aura of academic respectability that adorns this philosophy will not excuse the barbarism it is unleashing on our nation.

The antidote to every false religion—for that's what this is, a false religion—is the gospel of Christ. Jesus taught a message of loving our enemies, of extending unconditional forgiveness to those who wrong us, of living lives of humility, service, mercy, and compassion toward all, regardless of external peculiarities. Those who learn how to implement this teaching in their lives, and actively promote it among others, will have the greatest success in countering this destructive ideology.

Brethren, let's get busy living our faith. A drowning world needs what we have to offer.

Righteous Judgment

Our opinions of others are often formed on the basis of flimsy information. Charity requires that we be more careful when forming judgments.

"Do not judge according to appearance, but judge with righteous judgment" (Jn. 7:24).

৽৽৽

The spirit of our age is one of tolerance. It is considered impolite to offer any criticism or render any judgment regarding the behavior of others. The end result is a society that has lost the ability to blush. All manner of deviant behavior is excused on the premise that we do not have the right to criticize or condemn others. After all, who are we to judge?

Predictably, people can find Scripture to justify this spirit of unlimited openness. Their favorite passage is the saying of Jesus, "Judge not, that you be not judged" (Matt. 7:1).

But the same Jesus who said "judge not" also said "judge with righteous judgment." He did not forbid all judgments; rather, He warned against the kind of harsh, hyper-critical fault-finding that blows up relationships. On other occasions, judgment is not only allowed, it may be necessary, if administered properly. Jesus calls that "righteous judgment."

So how can we know when to criticize and when to keep silent? How can we discern between destructive judging and righteous judging? The Bible offers several guidelines.

First, *don't listen to gossip.* "He who goes about as a tale-bearer reveals secrets; therefore do not associate with one who flatters with his lips" (Prov. 20:19). Gossip is nothing more than one-sided testimony designed to make its victim look bad. By its very nature, it is unfair and partisan. When you encounter defamatory details about someone, don't accept it as gospel truth. As a counter-balance, seek out the subject's positive virtues offered by his friends; or better yet, let your own experiences with the individual inform your opinion. Blindly accepting derogatory information passed along in whispers is dangerously careless.

Second, *give your opponent a fair hearing.* The Jews of Berea were more noble than those of Thessalonica because of their willingness to listen patiently to what Paul was teaching, even though it differed from what they already believed (Ac. 17:11). A refusal even to listen puts us in the same category with those who physically covered their ears before stoning Stephen (Ac. 7:57). There is no honor in that kind of close-mindedness—and certainly no personal growth.

Finally, *remember your own flaws.* Even if a negative story proves to be true, does that reveal the full measure of the man? Every one of us has our own character blemishes. We have all made our share of dumb mistakes. Do we want others to judge us on the basis of those isolated faults? If not, then fairness requires that we extend charity to the mistakes of others. "Judgment is without mercy to the one who has shown no mercy. Mercy triumphs over judgment" (Jas. 2:13).

Jesus was murdered by people who were too blinded by prejudice and hostility to see the truth of the One with whom they were dealing. They judged Him to be a reprobate worthy of death, because they would not deal fairly with the facts before them. We are capable of making that same mistake, if we are not fair and honest when dealing with others.

Deceived

The greatest victims of deception are those whose superior learning has convinced them they are better than everyone else.

The officers answered, "No man ever spoke like this Man!" Then the Pharisees answered them, "Are you also deceived? Have any of the rulers or the Pharisees believed in Him? But this crowd that does not know the law is accursed" (Jn. 7:46-49).

৵৽৵

The Pharisees had a problem.

The young rabbi from Galilee was attracting large numbers of the common people. Even the officers who had been sent to arrest Jesus were awe-struck, and returned empty handed. It made no sense; this pretender was a carpenter, a nobody from the sticks who had no specialized training, no credentials, nothing to qualify Him as a great teacher. Yet His followers far outnumbered their own. How was that possible?

The evidence was so obvious, wasn't it? Who among the ruling class had embraced His movement? He was attracting the riff-raff of society—fishermen and tax-collectors, low-lifes who knew nothing of the Law. There was no chance that this movement would ever amount to anything.

Yet here He was, speaking boldly in the temple (v. 28), attracting more and more followers from among the rabble (v. 31). Even their own officers were falling under His spell. How could so many people be so deceived?

The Pharisees had a problem alright: *They* were the ones being deceived. Their culture of elitism had blinded them to the simple message Jesus was teaching. Their sophistication rendered them so smart, they couldn't see the truth right in front of their eyes. And what was the strongest evidence for the validity of their position? *That none of their own number believed in Him*—a classic example of the logical fallacy known as "begging the question."

Even today, anyone who sets out to master God's word is susceptible to this same kind of self-reinforcing delusion. Our learning can become so deep, so elegant, that only the few like-minded companions who have achieved our level of erudition are worthy of our fellowship. We can begin to look down our noses at those who have not achieved our mastery of the Book as unworthy of our company. As we descend further down that path, we begin to distance ourselves from the very people Jesus came to save. Our pride of learning turns us into insufferable snobs. Worse, we are distancing ourselves from God.

The solution to this problem is not to stop studying, but to give precedence in our study to the weightier matters of the law: justice, mercy, and faithfulness (Matt. 23:23)—a distinction that can be appreciated only through an abundance of humility. No matter how much we know, there remains so much we don't know. In God's eyes, we are no better than the proles we so despise.

To pretend otherwise is to deceive ourselves—and that is the greatest deception of all.

On Casting Stones

Distinguishing the sinner from the sin requires a depth of wisdom to perform properly. Jesus was a master at making that distinction.

Then the scribes and Pharisees brought to Him a woman caught in adultery. And when they had set her in the midst, they said to Him, "Teacher, this woman was caught in adultery, in the very act. Now Moses, in the law, commanded us that such should be stoned. But what do You say?" . . . So when they continued asking Him, He raised Himself up and said to them, "He who is without sin among you, let him throw a stone at her first" . . . And Jesus said to her, "Neither do I condemn you; go and sin no more" (Jn. 8:3-5, 7, 11).

ৎﾟঙ

This story has been adopted as the poster child for our non-judgmental culture. None of us is perfect; thus, none of us has any right to criticize others for their behavior. We must be willing to tolerate whatever others choose to do; after all, who are we to judge? The result, of course, is an amoral society that not only tolerates but openly embraces the most vile behavior as perfectly normal.

Is this what Jesus had in mind when He challenged his accusers to cast the first stone? To answer this question, let's take a closer look at the story.

First, consider the motives of Jesus' critics. These men were not concerned about public morality, or even the fate of the poor woman whose error was being put on public display. As John comments, "This they said, testing Him, that they might have something of which to accuse Him" (v. 6). The whole episode was an elaborately staged setup, designed to entrap Jesus in a no-win predicament. (Some commentators suggest that these critics may even have been complicit in setting up the adulterous affair.) Whatever His response, Jesus would either be in violation of Moses' law, or get in trouble with their Roman overlords. It was a perfect trap.

Of course, Jesus deftly dodged the trap by daring his critics to meet their own challenge: "He who is without sin among you, let him throw a stone at her first" (v. 7). It's easy to talk tough when we excuse ourselves from our own standards. The accusers got the message. In their hearts, they knew that, at least on some level, they were guilty of the same sin they were condemning in another.

In His challenge to these men, Jesus was exposing their hypocrisy, not prohibiting judgment. His critics were interested only in scoring points; He was interested in the welfare of this poor soul who was being publicly humiliated.

Those who love to quote Jesus' words on judging fail to read the rest of the story. After disarming His critics, Jesus then addressed the woman: "Neither do I condemn you; *go and sin no more*" (v. 11). Jesus indeed forgave the woman, but He also admonished her to change her behavior. What she had done was (gasp!) a *sin*. Not comfortable with that term? Then let's try another: It was wrong, evil, bad, it transgressed God's law. Whatever you choose to call it, Jesus judged her behavior as unacceptable, and insisted that she stop it.

When studied as a whole, the story of the woman taken in adultery provides a perfect illustration of how the gospel works. It emphasizes all the key elements of the gospel: *forgiveness* ("neither do I condemn you"), *repentance* ("go and sin no more"), and *charity* ("he who is without sin among you, let him throw a stone at her first"). We must be careful and kind when criticizing others; but we must also acknowledge the high standard of conduct to which all of us are accountable.

Relativism's Fatal Flaw

Our culture's embrace of relativism is a devil's bargain, inflicting enormous destruction. We must be prepared to explain why truth matters.

"You shall know the truth, and the truth shall make you free" (Jn. 8:32).

"Your word is truth" (Jn. 17:17).

"This is a nation that does not obey the voice of the Lord their God nor receive correction. Truth has perished and has been cut off from their mouth" (Jer. 7:28).

֍

In the introduction to his 1987 book, *The Closing of the American Mind*, Allan Bloom noted that "almost every student entering the university believes, or says he believes, that truth is relative." In the decades since Bloom made that observation, the idea that truth is relative has thoroughly saturated American culture. We hear it all the time in statements such as, "that may be true for you, but it is not true for me"; or "there is no such thing as absolute truth"; or "truth is a product of how you were raised."

The idea that there is no objective truth that applies to everyone all the time has enormous implications in everyday life. Once people are convinced that all moral judgments are mere opinions, moral reasoning is replaced by fluid emotions. When an entire society is dominated by relativism, it will be paralyzed when faced with an existential threat. After all, "who are we to judge" when enemies attack?

Long before Jesus commented on the subject, the Greek philosopher Aristotle offered a definition of truth that has served as a foundation of civilization for over two thousand years: "To say of what **is** that it **is not**, or of what **is not** that it **is**, is false, while to say of what **is** that it **is**, and of what **is not** that it **is not**, is true" (*Metaphysics* 1011b25). In simplified language, truth is whatever aligns with reality—what *is*. What we happen to believe or feel about that reality doesn't change the fact—the truth—about it. Truth is "out there," external to our opinions or feelings.

But we do not need a PhD in Aristotelian logic to see relativism's fatal flaw. Let's start by considering the claim, "all truth is relative." There are two, and only two, ways of processing that statement. First, we can take it as an absolute truth claim—all truth is relative, with no exceptions. But if that is *absolutely* true, then we have established that there is at least one truth that is absolute, not relative. The statement contradicts itself and cannot be valid.

Second, we can avoid that contradiction by insisting that the statement itself is relative. That is, the speaker speaks only for himself, not for others. But if the statement "all truth is relative" is limited to the speaker's perspective, then it *cannot* speak for all truth. Some other truth claims may, in fact, be absolute. The statement therefore is useless in establishing the nature of truth.

So those who insist that "all truth is relative" are stuck on the horns of a dilemma: Their relativism is either self-contradictory or irrelevant. It is a flawed approach to dealing with the real world.

This simple exercise does not address the question of what the truth is on any given subject. That requires a good deal of observation and study of evidence. But the search for truth is doomed from the outset if we insist that it doesn't exist as an external reality. *Objective truth exists*, and for our own welfare, we'd better believe it.

Slavery

Sin is more than an occasional mistake. It is a cruel taskmaster that drives us into bad habits that can destroy us. How can we escape its tyrannical grip?

"Whoever commits sin is a slave of sin" (Jn. 8:34).

While they promise them liberty, they themselves are slaves of corruption; for by whom a person is overcome, by him also he is brought into bondage (2 Pet. 2:19).

၅ၜ

According to a recent report by the International Labour Organization (2017), there are an estimated forty million people living in some form of slavery in the world today. This figure includes forced labor, sex trafficking, and forced marriages, with women and children disproportionately affected. These numbers are staggering, debunking the common belief that slavery is a relic of ancient times. Those of us who live in modern societies shaped by a Judeo-Christian worldview may not realize it, but throughout the rest of the world the barbaric practices of the past are still very much with us.

As awful as these numbers may be, Jesus and Peter both point to a far more pernicious form of slavery, inflicting far more misery on humanity: the bondage of *sin.*

Slavery is the involuntary binding of someone to a role that is detrimental to their well-being. A slave has no freedom to make his or her own decisions about their future, and no opportunity to leave that oppressive life. Sin, on the other hand, is the result of a conscious choice I make on my own.

But, someone might object, can't I just decide to get out? How is sin a form of slavery, if I can choose to leave it?

The tense of the Greek verb in Jesus' statement carries a meaning that is lost in our English translations. To "commit sin" is not a single mistake or stumble, but a persistent pattern of behavior. It describes someone "who is constantly doing sin . . . who lives in sin" (Hendrickson). This is the language of *addiction*. While it's true that sin is a conscious decision we make, that single decision can become an entrenched habit, a way of life that overwhelms our cognitive reasoning and entraps us in behaviors that have a deleterious impact on us and others. Even when we know these behaviors are harmful, we struggle to break away from them. That's slavery!

These addictive behaviors come in a wide variety of forms. In some cases, such as alcoholism or drug addiction, the bondage may have a strong physiological component, requiring professional help to overcome. The more common variety, however, is simply bad habits that have become deeply embedded in our character: anger management issues, blame-shifting, holding grudges, laziness, favoritism, cursing and swearing, "white lies" that grow ominously darker, chronic negativity, gossip, ingratitude—the list goes on and on. Early in life, ignorance, stubbornness, and peer influences lead us to get sloppy in all these areas, and through years of constant practice we become chained to a way of life that robs us of joy. We are in bondage to sin, and like every slave, we are miserable in our servitude. And we know it!

How can we escape this wretched life? Earlier in the same context, Jesus said, "You shall know the truth, and the truth shall make you free" (Jn. 8:32). The grip of habitual sin on our lives can be broken only by an intensive education in the truth—the truth about God's purpose for our lives, the truth about the faulty mindset that derails our fulfillment of that purpose, and the truth about the transformation that is possible by surrendering our hearts and lives to His control. This transformation is not instantaneous nor total. But once we embrace that truth and start to see the chains fall away, we will experience the joy and peace of mind that only a free person can know.

Why Suffering?

We have such a shallow, simplistic perspective on the role of suffering in the world. We fail to see suffering, not as a curse, but as an opportunity.

Now as Jesus passed by, He saw a man who was blind from birth. And His disciples asked Him, saying, "Rabbi, who sinned, this man or his parents, that he was born blind?" Jesus answered, "Neither this man nor his parents sinned, but that the works of God should be revealed in him" (Jn. 9:1-3).

ରେକ୍ଷ

The question of *theodicy*—how to reconcile the fact of suffering with the existence of a loving and all-powerful God—has occupied the minds of philosophers and theologians for much of human history. There is so much that could be said on this subject, but this incident in the ministry of Jesus addresses at least one piece of the puzzle.

The disciples were locked into a karma-based view of suffering: Good things happen to good people, and bad things happen to bad people. By that reasoning, this man's blindness must have been the consequence of sins committed by either him or his parents. Many today embrace that same view of life—and are devastated when the formula doesn't play out the way they thought it should. Good people suffer grievously, while bad people skate by without a care in the world. What kind of God would allow such inequity to flourish?

Jesus dismissed this simplistic view of suffering, pointing to a more important component in the equation. By fixating on the "blame" question, the apostles failed to see a greater opportunity in this man's circumstances. It never occurred to them that there might be a deeper metaphysical explanation for his disability. Jesus challenged them to consider that his condition offered an occasion for a greater good: "that the works of God should be revealed in him." He then healed the blind man, thus displaying the love of God in a manner that would not have been possible had there been no suffering to address.

We face the same dilemma today. Given that suffering exists, how should those who believe in God respond to it? By obsessing over *why* God allows disease and illness and natural disasters to occur, we constrict our view of His role in human affairs to a narrow range of possibilities. The preferred response should be, how can we use these occasions as opportunities to glorify God?

God has not put us in this world to be arm-chair philosophers critiquing His business model. He put us here to be agents of His love in response to these calamities. He wants His people to treat the sick, comfort the discouraged, support the weak, lift up the downfallen, counsel the unruly, feed the hungry, care for the orphan, the widow, and the dispossessed. We are God's instruments for addressing these problems. To the extent we are engaged in those activities, "the works of God" are being revealed in the very tragedies the rest of humanity bemoans.

In times of trial, let us all be busy in the work God has given us to do. The world will notice, and God will be glorified.

On Seeing Truth

When we encounter truth, by whatever means, our response to that truth reveals the state of our heart, regardless of our outward circumstances.

And Jesus said, "For judgment I have come into this world, that those who do not see may see, and that those who see may be made blind." Then some of the Pharisees who were with Him heard these words, and said to Him, "Are we blind also?" Jesus said to them, "If you were blind, you would have no sin; but now you say, 'We see.' Therefore your sin remains" (Jn. 9:39-41).

۹৩৩৩

This exchange between Jesus and the Pharisees follows the story of the blind beggar whom Jesus healed at the pool of Siloam. That miracle prompted a formal inquiry by the Pharisees, who were driven by their desire to discredit Jesus as a fraud. To succeed, they had to debunk this miracle as a hoax. So the Pharisees grilled the (formerly) blind beggar mercilessly, and even called in his parents in an effort to obtain incriminating testimony. Throughout the questioning, the beggar more than held his own against his interrogators. In the end, his stubborn defense of the miracle he experienced earned him expulsion from the synagogue.

A significant theme in this story is the gradual development of the beggar's opinion of Jesus. At the beginning of his interrogation, he called Jesus merely "a man" (v. 11); a wonderful man to be sure, but beyond that he could not say. As the Pharisees pressured him to recant his testimony, he firmly clung to his story, even to the point of calling Jesus "a prophet" (v. 17). After being cast out, he encountered Jesus again, who fully revealed His identity. The beggar then became a full-fledged believer ("Lord, I believe," v. 35, 38).

The beggar received two gifts that day: His physical sight was restored, and he came to see Jesus as the Messiah. The Pharisees, on the other hand, retreated deeper behind a curtain of denial. They could believe in miracles performed a thousand years earlier (v. 29), but could not accept one performed right under their noses. Their disbelief exposed hearts black with prejudice.

It's that contrast between the belief of the beggar and the disbelief of the Pharisees—both involving the same body of evidence—that prompted Jesus' remark about judgment. Jesus came into this world to sort humanity into two camps: those who recognize their deficiencies and surrender to the authority of the One they see as their Master; and those who, defiant in their pride, stiffen their necks against the demands of the gospel and reject Jesus as unworthy of their trust. This is not a judgment that God imposes upon them; it is one they choose for themselves.

Moreover, this sorting-out process often follows a familiar pattern. It is usually the weak, the outcast, the unlearned, who possess the innocence of heart to see the truth and respond. And it is often the knowledgeable, the prosperous, the sophisticated, who are hopelessly blind to their need for a Savior.

The challenge that faces each one of us in life is keeping our minds open to new ideas that disrupt our status quo. It's not easy to objectively consider evidence that might force us to revise our thinking. But honesty demands nothing less.

"There are none so blind as those who will not see"— and none who see with such clarity as those who change their minds when truth demands it.

Demonizing the Opposition

When we disagree with others, we are tempted to exaggerate the differences and impugn each others' motives. We hurt ourselves in doing so.

And many of them said, "He has a demon and is mad. Why do you listen to Him?" Others said, "These are not the words of one who has a demon. Can a demon open the eyes of the blind?" (Jn. 10:20-21).

જ✧જ

This exchange among the Jews who heard the teaching of Jesus illustrates a common mistake that people often make when pigeon-holing those with whom they disagree. Notice that some refused even to listen to Jesus because they had concluded "he has a demon and is mad." By labeling Jesus as the very epitome of the devil himself, any possibility of bridging the gap between themselves and Him was lost.

Today, we call this strategy "demonizing the opposition." Political discourse is loaded with it, particularly around election times. Politicians accuse each other of the most sinister motives in an effort to discredit their opponents in front of the electorate ("Why do you listen to him?!"). Married partners employ the same device when explaining their problems to a counselor. Whatever qualities may have attracted them to each other in the beginning are now gone, replaced by the most despicable attitudes and behaviors—at least judging by the language they use to describe each other. Each party is convinced they are now married to a demon. Until the partners can move beyond such alarmist rhetoric, reconciliation will be impossible.

The truth, of course, is that the opposition is almost never as bad as we make them out to be. By painting our opponent in the worst possible light, and ignoring any positive qualities that might exist, we create a caricature of the real person. We may convince ourselves that we're dealing with a devil, but the more likely reality is that we are dealing with another human being, a creature possessing many of the same traits, ambitions, longings, and flaws as ourselves. As long as we fixate on the flaws, even to the point of exaggerating them, we blind ourselves to whatever good qualities or ideas our opponent may possess.

And by refusing to expose ourselves to what is good in others, we rob ourselves of the opportunity to grow from that good. What Jesus taught may have sounded strange to His critics, but by labeling Him as a demon, they never gave themselves a chance to see the wisdom of what He was teaching. We make the same mistake when we demonize those with whom we disagree. They are not nearly as evil as we portray them—and might even have something worthwhile to say, if we would just take the time to listen and understand.

Notice that in our text, those who demonized Jesus were countered by others who sought to evaluate Jesus more objectively: "These are not the words of one who has a demon. Can a demon open the eyes of the blind?" These folks may not have been entirely convinced yet, but at least they allowed the possibility that this was something they needed to seriously consider. God can work with people like that.

In the end, demonizing the opposition is usually just a way of avoiding the hard task of confronting the need for change in our own lives. The real demon is not our opponent, but our own shriveled heart.

For God's Glory

Though we cannot see it, our darkest days are
often a gateway to a glorious future. Our task is to
remain hopeful and trust God to work it all out.

---

*Now a certain man was sick, Lazarus of Bethany, the
town of Mary and her sister Martha. . . . When Jesus heard
that, He said, "This sickness is not unto death, but for the
glory of God, that the Son of God may be glorified through
it" (Jn. 11:1, 4).*

৵৹৵

By the time Jesus got to Bethany, Lazarus had been in
the tomb for four days (v. 17); meaning, he was probably already dead by the time Jesus learned of his illness. Why then
did Jesus announce that his sickness "is not unto death"? Did
His gift of prophecy fail Him?

No, Jesus knew that Lazarus had died. In fact, upon receiving the news, He waited two more days before starting
out for Bethany (v. 6). It's as though Jesus wanted everyone
to know that Lazarus was good and gone. His body had already begun to decay by the time Jesus arrived (v. 39).

So when Jesus raised Lazarus from the dead, the impact
on those who witnessed it was enormous. In fact, the resusci-
tation of Lazarus' rotting corpse was likely the final straw
that sealed Jesus' fate. "From that day on, they plotted to put
Him to death" (v. 53).

Yes, Lazarus died. But Jesus knew that his friend's death
was only temporary. The raising of Lazarus would glorify
both God and Jesus. Furthermore, by resurrecting Lazarus,

Jesus was setting up His own death and resurrection—and God would be glorified even more.

So the sickness and death of this ordinary Jew from Bethany set in motion a cascading series of events that culminated in God's crushing defeat of Satan and sin. Lazarus and his sisters could see nothing good coming from his illness—but the Lord did, and accomplished something far beyond their wildest dreams.

God's method of achieving His purposes has often taken this kind of improbable path:

- Joseph could not envision any purpose to his slavery in Egypt—until the day he saw his long-lost family standing before him pleading for help.
- As Moses tended sheep in the wilderness of Midian, he had no idea how God was preparing him for the greatest rescue mission in history.
- The apostles had their faith shattered when they saw their Lord crucified like a common criminal, not knowing the astonishing triumph that lay just beyond the cross.

Remember this story the next time you feel like God has abandoned you and the end is near. God can use your affliction to accomplish a greater purpose hidden from your view. Your suffering very well may be "for the glory of God, that the Son of God may be glorified through it."

Your job in the moment is to be patient, perform your duty to the best of your ability, and trust God to do what is best.

The Skeptic's Mistake

Atheists are not the only ones who have a
problem grasping the nature and power of God.
Even believers struggle to understand Him.

---

*Now a certain man was sick, Lazarus of Bethany, the
town of Mary and her sister Martha. . . . Therefore the sisters
sent to Him, saying, "Lord, behold, he whom You love is
sick." When Jesus heard that, He said, "This sickness is not
unto death, but for the glory of God, that the Son of God may
be glorified through it" (Jn. 11:1, 3, 4).*

୧∞୬

The resurrection of Lazarus later in this chapter indeed
glorified Jesus. In fact, it was such an astounding miracle that
it sealed His fate. From this point forward, Jesus' enemies
were determined to kill Him (v. 47-53).

But there is one aspect of this story that deserves closer
attention. Jesus responded to the sisters' request by delaying
for two days (v. 6). When He came to Bethany, Lazarus had
already been dead for four days. So when Jesus arrived, both
Martha and Mary met Him—separately—with the same
greeting: "Lord, if You had been here, my brother would not
have died" (v. 21, 32). Later, some of the mourners who had
gathered to support the sisters had a similar reaction: "Could
not this Man, who opened the eyes of the blind, also have
kept this man from dying?" (v. 37).

There is a common thread that runs through all three of
these responses. Each displays a sense of resignation or failure. Jesus could have healed Lazarus if had He arrived in
time; but He was too late, so the opportunity for performing

a miracle had passed. Lazarus was dead, and his body had already begun to decay (v. 39). There would be no miracle. Even Jesus could not overcome this loss.

It occurs to me that these comments bear an uncanny resemblance to the argument of the atheist who rejects the existence of God: "If God really existed, He would not allow all the evil and suffering that afflicts the world." The atheist has his own rigid idea of how God ought to operate ("If this, then that"). Since God does not meet that pre-determined condition, then God obviously does not exist.

The reasoning of the sisters and the Jewish mourners followed much the same line: "If You had been here, this would not have happened." They had a pre-determined idea of the scope of Jesus' power, and since the circumstances did not fit their idea, their minds were completely closed to the possibility of any positive outcome.

The sisters denied the possibility of Lazarus' return, and the atheist denies the existence of God, for the same reason: a faulty mental model of how God works.

Jesus confounded the friends of Lazarus by raising him from the dead in dramatic fashion (v. 38-44). That had been His intention all along, of course, "that the Son of God may be glorified" (v. 4). In like manner, the atheist will some day witness the power of God to make all things new again. On that day, the atheist will realize the smallness of his thinking.

This story teaches us that we need not be atheists to be skeptics. Martha and Mary were loyal friends of Jesus, yet they could not grasp the possibilities available to them through Him. Sometimes we make the same mistake, trying to confine God to a small box, failing to realize the extent of His power.

When it comes to God, we must learn to think big. He is capable of so much more than we realize.

Fearless Thomas

Thomas has been tagged as the "doubter." But there is another side to his character that provides a more balanced and exemplary perspective.

Then Thomas, who is called the Twin, said to his fellow disciples, "Let us also go, that we may die with Him" (Jn. 11:16).

౮౷౪

History remembers Thomas as the apostle who refused to believe that Jesus had risen from the dead until he could see the nail prints in His hands (Jn. 20:25). "Doubting Thomas" has entered our lexicon as a synonym for the pessimist, someone who is prone not to see the good that is in the world.

But there is another side to Thomas that does not get the attention it deserves. On Jesus' previous visit to Jerusalem, His enemies had tried to stone Him (Jn. 10:31). Now He wanted to return to Bethany to visit the family of Lazarus, a friend who was dying from an illness. Bethany was a suburb of Jerusalem, so such a trip would likely risk another brush with death. When Thomas heard Jesus' plan, he feared the worst: "Let us also go, that we may die with Him." True to form, Thomas' pessimism saw only the worst possible outcome.

But Thomas' resignation conceals an admirable attribute for which he rarely gets credit. It's true that Thomas expected the worst in this trip; but he did not flinch in facing it. If Jesus was determined to go to Jerusalem and almost sure death, Thomas would go with Him and share His fate. There was a fearlessness in Thomas, a determination to face evil with resolute courage.

When we are faced with dangers in our life, it is natural to fear the worst. We may have reason to expect the future to be a grim one, with no hope of success. But the key question is, what shall we do with that apprehension? Do we give up and quit? Do we throw away our faith and stop trying? Or do we press on with stubborn determination, resolute in our conviction?

Whatever his faults, Thomas was not a quitter. He remained true to his commitment, and in doing so, found the answer to his doubts. When finally confronted by the resurrected Christ that Sunday evening, his doubts were swept away and a renewed conviction took hold: "My Lord and My God!" (Jn. 20:28). Tradition says that Thomas, like his fellow apostles, stayed true to his faith, and later died as a martyr in India.

"Let us also go, that we my die with Him." Does that describe the intensity of *your* faith in the Lord?

Protecting Our Place

When we view everything and everyone as tools
to preserve our own selfish interests, we set
ourselves up for a spectacular fall.

*Then the chief priests and the Pharisees gathered a
council and said, "What shall we do? For this Man works
many signs. If we let Him alone like this, everyone will believe in Him, and the Romans will come and take away both
our place and nation" (Jn. 11:47-48).*

୧୭

The priests (who dominated the party of the Sadducees)
were political opportunists who benefited financially from
their relationship with the Romans. The Pharisees, who fan-
cied themselves defenders of the Law of Moses, were the
populist party who had the backing of the common people.
Under normal circumstances, these two factions were bitter
rivals who rarely cooperated on anything. The Sanhedrin
Council was a delicately balanced political arrangement that
gave both groups a role in the governance of their nation.

But these were not normal circumstances, and the growing popularity of the Galilean carpenter threatened the power
they shared. This Jesus movement displayed many of the earmarks of a popular uprising, which could trigger a Roman
crackdown. So in their deliberations on how to deal with Jesus, these leaders made a candid admission of their real fear:
"The Romans will come and take away both our place and
nation."

Some commentators and translations take the word
"place" here to be a reference to "the holy place," that is, the

temple. But the more likely meaning is "a position of prominence or authority." Whether Sadducee or Pharisee, everyone in this august body saw Jesus as a threat to their gravy train. They were not concerned about whether Jesus was teaching the truth, or what the will of God was in this matter. Jesus had to be eliminated because their lofty "place" in the local pecking order was threatened. Consequently, they conspired to eliminate Him, using the Romans as convenient pawns.

Of course, by putting Jesus away, they set in motion a chain of events that brought about the very thing they feared. In one of history's great ironies, the Romans came and took away their place and nation. Their envy became their undoing. Meanwhile, the lowly carpenter whom they hated lost His life, but gained an exalted place at the right hand of God.

Before we criticize these leaders for their naked self-interest, we ought to examine our own motivations. How many of our decisions are driven by a perceived threat to our "place" of privilege or authority or advantage? Whether in our family, our workplace, or the church, how often do we assess the behaviors of others strictly in terms of how it impacts our own selfish interests? And how often do our evil machinations blow up in our face, ruining our own reputation in the process?

Our purpose in life is not to "protect our place." It's to serve others in a spirit of love and good will, even if it costs us. How long will it take us to learn that lesson?

Life As a Seed

To those who struggle to understand their purpose in life, Jesus offers a simple but beautiful little metaphor to illustrate the answer.

"The hour has come that the Son of Man should be glorified. Most assuredly, I say to you, unless a grain of wheat falls into the ground and dies, it remains alone; but if it does, it produces much grain. He who loves his life will lose it, and he who hates his life in this world will keep it for eternal life. If anyone serves Me, let him follow Me . . ." (Jn. 12:23-26).

৩৵৵

Jesus spoke these words a short time before He died. His own life was about to reach a climax of glorification, but in a manner quite unlike what anyone would have expected. In His example, we find the secret for living a happy, meaningful life.

Jesus illustrates this principle using the metaphor of a seed. A seed is a small, insignificant bit of organic matter. By itself, it is good for little, except perhaps to eat. Even then, it's contribution is negligible. Set this little seed in a sealed container and it will last for years, intact and whole—but alone and useless.

Yet what happens when that seed is planted in the ground? From a purely selfish standpoint, the seed ceases to exist as a separate entity. It will never be seen again. Of course, no one sheds a tear over the fate of the little seed, because *that's what it's supposed to do*. It ceases to exist in its original form, but it grows into a beautiful plant that produces many other seeds just like itself. The real glory of the seed is seen, not by preserving it, but by exposing it to soil, water and sunlight. Only by "dying" can the seed achieve its full potential.

Like the little seed, each one of us has the potential to glorify God in a way far beyond what we can imagine. But we will never achieve that potential by carefully shielding ourselves from the world. We must surrender our lives to the service of others, exposing ourselves to the harsh elements of life. It's hard, dirty, sometimes painful work. And we cannot perform that work without sacrificing our own comfort and ease.

But like the seed, that is what we were designed to do. That's why God made us! Only in spending ourselves to serve and help others will we find real satisfaction and joy in life. In the end, when the final account is given of our lives, we will be glorified, both by those who knew us in this life, and by the God who will reward us in the next.

So the choice for each one of us is simple—"love" your life by pampering it for your own selfish purposes, or "hate" it by spending it in the service of others. One approach will leave you comfortable, but alone and unappreciated; the other will cost you everything, but leave you loved and happy.

Your life is a seed. Plant it, and see what beauty it can produce.

Knowing and Doing

It is not enough to know God's truth. If we are not
actively implementing it in our daily lives, we are
mocking God and deceiving ourselves.

---

*"If you know these things, blessed are you if you do
them" (Jn. 13:17).*

*Therefore, to him who knows to do good and does not do
it, to him it is sin (Jas. 4:17).*

৩৽৵৶

The Greek historian Plutarch tells the story of an old man
who arrived late at an Olympic event. The Greeks who were
already seated in the amphitheater laughed and mocked the
poor man's stumbling efforts to find a seat. But when he
reached the section where the Spartans were seated, all the
Spartans arose and politely offered the old gentleman their
seats. The other Greeks were silenced by this display of courtesy, then began applauding in admiration. The old man made
this observation: "All Greeks know what is right, but only the
Spartans do it."

Knowledge of the truth will set us free (Jn. 8:32)—but
not if we keep it locked away in our heads. We may *know* the
truth, and *appreciate* its presence in the lives of others, and
even *defend* it vigorously against critics. But if that knowledge is never converted into action in our own lives, what
does it profit us?

Jesus likened those who hear His words but do not do
them to someone building a house on a foundation of sand
(Matt. 7:26-27). Our head knowledge may provide us a false
sense of comfort and security for awhile. But when the

storms of life hit, the lack of practical experience in living that knowledge will expose the weakness of our foundation. We cannot benefit from counsel that we do not live.

A failure to practice what we know to be right is the gravest of offenses, because it amounts to a deliberate rejection of the truth. "That servant who knew his master's will, and did not prepare himself or do according to his will, shall be beaten with many stripes" (Lk. 12:47). If we willfully neglect living out the truth that we know God wants us to live, we are effectively condemning ourselves. It makes no difference what excuses we may offer for our carelessness; we chose not to obey, and we must suffer the consequences.

Like the ancient Spartans, doing the right thing often requires being different from the crowd. But the rewards for such courage—divine favor, personal satisfaction, the admiration of others—make the sacrifice worthwhile. We just need to muster the courage to do it.

The gap between knowing what is right and doing it is as wide as the gap between heaven and hell. Which path are you on?

I Don't Understand

Like the first disciples of Jesus, our walk with Him is complicated by enigmas that we don't understand. That's okay—if we don't quit.

Then He came to Simon Peter. And Peter said to Him, "Lord, are You washing my feet?" Jesus answered and said to him, "What I am doing you do not understand now, but you will know after this." Peter said to Him, "You shall never wash my feet!" (Jn. 13:6-8).

ಊಆ

The humility of Jesus—and the density of His apostles—is nowhere more starkly displayed than in the story of Him washing their feet at the Last Supper. We know that at some point that evening the apostles argued as to which among them was the greatest (Lk. 22:24). Perhaps this foot washing episode was the Master's way of teaching them a lesson that no words could convey: Greatness in the kingdom is the result of serving others, not muscling for power and advantage.

But it was not an easy lesson for them to learn. The reaction of Simon Peter—"You shall never wash my feet!"—is especially instructive. Peter was incredulous at the thought of Jesus performing such a lowly task, and Jesus had to shame him into accepting the honor (v. 8-9). Peter had the same hierarchical view of service that most of us have: Great people perform great feats, while menial tasks are performed by those of low status. It seems so obvious from a worldly perspective. But the kingdom of Christ is not of this world, and the usual rules don't apply here. Peter had yet to learn that lesson.

Jesus knew that His apostles were still not getting it: "What I am doing you do not understand now." But He assured them that someday the veil would be lifted: "You will know after this." Eventually the light would turn on in their heads and it would all make sense. Indeed, following His resurrection the final puzzle pieces fell into place and they saw the mission of Jesus with sharper vision. Their lives and their ministry were transformed by that deeper awareness. Their patience paid off.

This exchange between Jesus and His apostles regarding this one concept offers a good lesson about the gradual nature of growth in all of life. There is so much in our spiritual journey as disciples of Christ that we do not understand, especially at the beginning. Why does God allow suffering in my life? Why should I bother going to church when it is full of so many hypocrites? Why doesn't God remove temptation from my path? How can I meet my obligations to my family without allowing material things to become my idols? We struggle with questions like these every day, all rooted in a struggle to understand why God's creation functions the way it does. Sometimes life just doesn't make any sense, and it's hard to stay focused on the goal.

What we *cannot* do is take the Simon Peter approach and rashly declare what we will or will not accept, as though we know everything already. It is not our place to make demands of the Lord. Our job is to humbly submit to whatever God sends our way, to keep on studying, praying, reflecting, practicing, and seeking the wisdom from above. Some of the answers will be revealed to us in this life; some will not be found until we enter glory. Either way, our task is to stay faithful to the Lord's guidance.

"You do not understand now" is such a discouraging reality. But we can take comfort in the Lord's promise, "You will know after this."

Never give up!

A New Commandment

The command to love one another dates back at least to the time of Moses. But Jesus casts this duty in a new light that can transform our lives.

"A new commandment I give to you, that you love one another; as I have loved you, that you also love one another. By this all will know that you are My disciples, if you have love for one another" (Jn. 13:34-35).

❧

Moses taught Israel at Mount Sinai to "love your neighbor as yourself" (Lev. 19:18). In a world rife with selfishness and hate, the command to love others has potential to fix what's broken in human relations. Jesus labeled it the second greatest commandment in the Law (Matt. 22:37-40).

Yet here at the Last Supper, Jesus calls the instruction to love one another "a new commandment." What was so new about it? Hadn't Moses already covered that ground?

The Leviticus approach to loving others "as yourself" is constrained by one parameter: *how we view ourselves.* For example, if I have a low self-image, seeing myself as a worthless human being deserving of nothing good, I will struggle to view others as objects of compassion. At the other extreme, if I am a narcissist who views myself as the center of the universe and everyone around me as my personal fan club, loving others will be impossible. In both scenarios, "loving others" will always be a challenge. Love that is based only on self-reflection will always be somewhat distorted.

Jesus' teaching on love is different because it is driven by a different motivation. He wants us to love one another, not as we love ourselves, but "as I have loved you." With this addendum, Jesus raises the commandment to love others to a new level. We are to love others, not out of a sense of cold duty, using ourselves as the standard, but out of gratitude for the love that Jesus extended to us in His sacrificial death.

As Jesus spoke these words, He stood in the shadow of the cross, painfully aware of the fate that awaited Him. His disciples, however, had no idea what was about to happen. In His farewell remarks to His disciples, His heart yearned to explain to them something they could not yet comprehend: The sacrifice He was about to suffer would upend everything they thought they knew about serving God and being a "good" person. This new commandment was at the heart of this revolutionary program.

The apostles had no way of knowing it yet, but they were about to witness the most astonishing demonstration of love the world had ever seen. They would come to see the suffering of Christ, not as a *failure* of God's plan, but as the *realization* of that plan. Despite all our failures, weaknesses, and stubborn rebellion, God still loves us, and in Jesus Christ that love was put on display in the most dramatic fashion possible. "God demonstrates His own love toward us, in that while we were still sinners, Christ died for us" (Rom. 5:8). That bedrock truth transformed the lives of the apostles. It even touched the heart of early Christianity's most feared enemy, Saul of Tarsus: "The life which I now live in the flesh I live by faith in the Son of God, *who loved me* and gave Himself for me" (Gal. 2:20). Once we grasp the significance of what Jesus did for us on the cross, it overhauls our concept of love into a power that the world can only gaze upon with awe.

And therein lies the significance of this new commandment. When our love for others reflects the love that Jesus has shown us, the world will see in His disciples a kind of love they've never seen before. That's what makes it so unorthodox—and so powerful.

Why the World Hates Us

As we transition to a post-Christian society, we will more and more experience the world's hatred of our convictions. Are we ready for this?

"If the world hates you, you know that it hated Me before it hated you. If you were of the world, the world would love its own. Yet because you are not of the world, but I chose you out of the world, therefore the world hates you" (Jn. 15:18-19).

The world does not know us, because it did not know Him. . . . Do not marvel, my brethren, if the world hates you (1 Jn. 3:1, 13).

༼ঔ৶ঔ༽

From the beginning of time, the world has had little use for followers of God. From Abel's murder at the hand of his brother, to the martyrdoms of Paul and Peter, and even today in some corners of the world, to be a believer is a death sentence. The world despises with a burning hatred those whose hearts and lives are devoted to God.

This irrational hostility reached its zenith, of course, in the career of Jesus. In His own words, His mission in the world was to "bear witness to the truth" (Jn. 18:37), and it was that commitment to truth that got Him killed. His teaching exposed the selfishness and haughtiness that dominated the society of His day. He modeled what He preached, unmasking the hypocrisy of His critics. That's why they had to eliminate Him.

If we commit to following Jesus, it should come as no surprise that we will share His fate in some measure. Jesus has called us "out of the world," which means we are no longer "of the world." Our performance is not flawless like His, of course; but it's sufficiently different to evoke the same response. "Do not marvel if the world hates you."

In our lifetimes, we have lived through a narrow window of history that has afforded us a remarkable degree of religious freedom. We have equated "the world hates us" to having a door slammed in our face when passing out gospel tracts. Believers in other ages and in other countries today laugh at our weakness.

We are on the verge of finding out what it means to be hated by the world. In our own society now there is a growing visceral contempt for everything that Christ and Christianity stand for. We no longer enjoy the privilege of a live-and-let-live approach to religion. If we hold to the Biblical teaching on gender and sexuality, for example, we are not just ridiculed for our belief; we are vilified as sociopaths whose influence must be crushed. The hatred directed at us is public and intense—including, ironically, labeling us as "haters," the ultimate absurdity.

When you signed up to be a disciple of Jesus, you bade the world goodbye. Whatever comes next—*whatever* comes next—know that it's part of the package. Be strong, and look to the reward beyond.

From Sorrow to Joy

The trauma of the apostles during the trial and crucifixion of Jesus serves as a microcosm of our own struggles with disappointment and pain.

"Most assuredly, I say to you that you will weep and lament, but the world will rejoice; and you will be sorrowful, but your sorrow will be turned into joy" (Jn. 16:20).

༺༅༻

As Jesus stood with His apostles in the shadow of the cross, He knew that His earthly sojourn with them was drawing to a close. The next few hours would be very difficult for these men, and they were unprepared for what was about to hit them. Despite all His teaching and forewarning, the end would fall on them like a hammer. They stood on the precipice of an inferno that would shatter their faith. Worse, the unbelieving world around them would celebrate their defeat with mockery and contempt. "Weep and lament" was a mild understatement of what the apostles were about to experience.

Of course, Jesus also knew what lay beyond this catastrophe. The apostles' sorrow would eventually turn to joy. A brighter day lay beyond the impending gloom.

Two thousand years later, all this makes perfect sense to us. We know exactly what the apostles would experience, and how brief that trauma would last. Resurrection! Victory! Glorious ascent into heaven! Yes, it all had a happy ending, and the apostles really had nothing to worry about.

Except *they* didn't know that. What they witnessed at the trial and crucifixion of Jesus was a complete collapse of everything they had come to believe about their Master. His enemies crushed Him, and He was powerless to resist. All His teachings, the miracles, the clever confrontations with His enemies—it had all been a sham, and now they looked like fools. They scattered like rabbits—exactly the effect their enemies had intended. Let's not take their state of mind lightly. These men endured a sorrow every bit as deep as anything we may experience in our own travails.

But when they finally saw their Master resurrected, their sorrow turned to joy. They finally realized that, as painful as it was, the crucifixion was essential to God's ultimate plan. There could be no victory *over* death *without* death. This insight gave them a new confidence that the world could not touch, and they spent the rest of their lives telling everyone about it—with unbounded joy.

So when we face disasters in our own life, we need to remember the ordeal of the apostles during those hours between the death and resurrection of Jesus. Satan has any number of ways to convince us that the game is over, the outcome is rigged, everything is broken and lost, there's no hope in carrying on—just like the apostles.

But just like the apostles, we, too, have a glorious future awaiting us. The sorrows of the moment are transitory, and will soon be swept away by a beauty that will overwhelm our hearts.

Today you may sorrow, but look to the restoration that is coming. You have every reason to rejoice.

Alone

The real test of our trust in God is when we must stand alone against the forces of evil, with no earthly friend to encourage us. Can we do it?

"Indeed the hour is coming, yes has now come, that you will be scattered, each to his own, and will leave Me alone. And yet I am not alone, because the Father Is with Me" (Jn. 16:32).

❧

Ideally, serving God should be a communal experience. In the Old Testament, God's plan was fulfilled through a family that grew into a nation. The shared culture of these people not only preserved their identity in an alien world, it provided a sense of belonging that gave every individual a foundation for life. In the New Testament, a more universal body of believers finds expression in local churches, little communities in which individuals, whatever their social status or background, find the security of a home and family.

But occasionally circumstances will conspire to remove a servant of God from the embrace of companions. He is plunged into the storms of life alone, without kith or kin, and must endure with whatever resources he possesses within himself—no one to lend encouragement, no one to offer comfort, no one to lean on. It's in times like these that one's faith is stretched to the limit.

In the last hours of His life, Jesus knew that isolation. His enemies had gained the upper hand and were closing in. His closest friends had panicked and fled. He went through His final ordeal utterly alone, cursed by a world that had no clue why He was even here, nor appreciated the significance of what He was doing. As if to intensify His gloom, even the midday skies over His head turned black.

Jesus knew this day would come, and was ready for it. He assured His disciples that whatever disaster befell Him, "I am not alone, because the Father is with Me." He clung to that conviction through the beatings, the mockery, and the stakes pounded through His hands and feet. Even when it became clear that all was lost ("My God, My God, why have You forsaken Me?," Matt. 27:46), He refused to give up. The task had to be finished.

For me, it's easy to glide through the story of Jesus' crucifixion, knowing how the story played out. But what I can't see is the path my own story will take. In the midst of my own distress, the temptation to give up is strong. Nobody cares. Nobody listens. Nobody draws near to help. I am facing this struggle alone, and the pain is unbearable.

Somewhere deep inside, I must cling to one essential truth: "I am not alone, because the Father is with me." Jesus is with Me too, and armed with their presence I will see this through.

In our own nation, we are rapidly approaching a point where those who have convictions regarding truth and righteousness will pay a steep price for standing up for those convictions: social ostracism, loss of employment, financial penalties, maybe even criminal sanctions. The easy thing to do will be to keep quiet. Don't rock the boat. Go along to get along. Cower in fear. By doing so, we will preserve our standard of living—but at what cost to our integrity?

Like Jesus, the hour is coming when each one of us must make a decision: Will I meekly yield to the forces of darkness that are sweeping everything in their path? Or will I stand up —alone if necessary—for the truth of the God whom I serve?

Be of Good Cheer

It's hard to be cheerful in a dark and cruel world.
But thanks to Jesus, we have every reason to face
life with calm confidence and optimism.

---

*"These things I have spoken to you, that in Me you may
have peace. In the world you will have tribulation; but be of
good cheer, I have overcome the world" (Jn. 16:33).*

৶৹৶

Jesus was only hours away from experiencing a brutal
beating and execution. The disciples to whom He was speaking were about to have their entire world ripped out from
under their feet. Yet here He was, in the very shadow of the
cross, talking about "peace" and "good cheer." And given the
crisis that was about to come down upon Him, how could He
boast, "I have overcome the world"? Under the circumstances, this kind of talk bordered on delusion.

Of course, two thousand years later we don't look at His
words that way at all. It makes perfect sense: Yes, He would
die painfully, but shortly thereafter He would be resurrected
and ascend into heaven to sit at the right hand of God. He
could speak as a victor because He had run the race well and
was now only a few steps from the finish line. One more hur-
dle to clear, then He was home free.

In Jesus' victory, we have a glimpse of our own. He lived
the perfect life we could not live. His death paid the ransom
price for all the sins that have held us in bondage to Satan.
And in His glorious resurrection we see the hope of our own
bodily redemption some day. This world and its sorrows can
be painful, that's true. But, oh, what a magnificent future

awaits us just across the river! A few more days, and we will share eternity with Him in a place of such exquisite beauty that we can't stop thinking about it.

In your darkest hour, when it seems that life can't get any more cruel and bleak, remember what Jesus has done for you. He overcame the world, clearing a path to heaven so that you can follow Him there. He has won the victory in your behalf, and soon He will receive you to Himself in that fair realm. What can the world do to rob you of that hope?

In the meantime, be of good cheer. Let your outward countenance radiate the joy that inspires your inner life. Be at peace with yourself and the world, knowing that you are at peace with God through Christ. The storms that swirl around you may be intense, but you have found a harbor that will protect your soul until that storm passes.

This will all be over soon enough.

The Clash of Kingdoms

The confrontation between Pilate and Jesus lasted only a few minutes, but the outcome of their exchange shook the world to its foundation.

Pilate entered the Praetorium again, called Jesus, and said to Him, "Are You the King of the Jews?" (Jn. 18:33).

Then Pilate said to Him, "Are You not speaking to me? Do You not know that I have power to crucify You, and power to release You?" (Jn. 19:10).

৯৹৫৩

Pilate's interrogation of Jesus spans several verses in John's gospel from chapter 18 into chapter 19. The two questions listed here—the first and last questions Pilate asked in this exchange—highlight the cosmic significance of the battle that was fought that day.

Consider the antagonists: Pilate was Caesar's emissary in Judea, representing Rome, the most powerful and advanced empire the world had known to that time. He reminded Jesus that he had absolute power over His fate, to release Him or to crucify Him.

Pilate's opponent was Jesus, the Son of God, "the king of the Jews," an emissary of God sent from heaven, disguised as an ordinary peasant.

This was Rome versus God, the final climax of a long struggle that had been building throughout the ages. Both David (Psalm 2) and Daniel (Daniel 2) had predicted this day. Now it had arrived. Who would win?

Superficially, this contest was a terrible mismatch. Pilate had the legal authority and the political advantage to condemn Jesus to death, with many soldiers at his disposal to carry out his orders. No one could resist him.

Jesus, on the other hand, was a blue-collar worker, an itinerant preacher whose few friends scattered like roaches when their master was taken into custody. He had no army, no allies, no secret weapon, nothing with which He could prevent the inevitable Roman victory. When pressed to reveal where He was from, Jesus "gave him no answer" (Jn. 19:9), a silence that baffled Pilate (Mk. 15:5). He was accustomed to watching doomed men beg for their lives; eliminating this loser was too easy.

It was so easy, in fact, that Pilate saw no threat in Jesus. But yielding to pressure from the mob, he gave the order to have Jesus crucified anyway, then washed his hands of the affair. The "king of the Jews" was executed, and life went on as usual. Rome won a quick and decisive victory that day.

Of course, Rome's victory was short-lived. Three days later, Jesus rose from the grave. Within months, Jerusalem was electrified by the testimony of those who had seen Him after His resurrection, and thousands took up His cause. Within a few years, this Jesus movement spread to surrounding cities and provinces, attracting both Jews and Gentiles. Within a few decades, one of those who had witnessed the resurrected Jesus stood before Caesar himself in Rome, testifying of Jesus' resurrection and His teachings.

Today, Rome and its rulers are long gone. Other empires have followed, each imposing its will on its neighbors for a short while, then crumbling into the dust bin of history. But despite every effort by tyrants and traitors to destroy it, the kingdom of God remains. Ultimately, Jesus won the war, not through political or military power, but through the power of truth (Jn. 18:37).

Question: Which side are you on?

It Is Finished!

The measure of our life is not determined by the number of years we live, but what we do with the years we have been given.

So when Jesus had received the sour wine, He said, "It is finished!" And bowing His head, He gave up His spirit (Jn. 19:30).

❦

Thus ended the earthly career of Jesus of Nazareth. He was only thirty-three years old when He died, following a ministry that lasted barely three and a half years.

Considering what Jesus accomplished during those few years, think what He could have accomplished had He lived a long, full life.

- He could have traveled far beyond Judea and Galilee, taking His unique brand of preaching to the Gentiles.
- He could have debated—and defeated—the leaders of every major religious system in His day, thoroughly exposing their weaknesses.
- He could have personally trained many more than twelve apostles, leaving behind a much larger cadre of well-prepared disciples to carry on His work.

Of course, He never got a chance to do all those things. He died young, snatched away in the prime of His life. What a terrible loss!

Or was it? When we consider the life and death of Jesus, we never think in terms of "what might have been," because we know that Jesus accomplished everything He came to do. His life was not "wasted"—it was completed, fulfilled, successful. His last words were not, "I'm finished!", but "It is finished!" The Message translation renders the single Greek word used here as, "It's done . . . complete!" Jesus was not lamenting a life cut short, but celebrating a mission accomplished. He had fulfilled the task His Father had sent Him to perform.

I reflect on this every time I hear of a young person who dies. Whether killed in an accident, taken by an illness, or a casualty of war, it is painful to hear of one who dies so young. The usual response is to bewail the loss of "what might have been," had the young person lived a long life.

But is that the right question to ask? Perhaps we should be asking, what did this young person accomplish during his or her young life? How many other lives were touched by his or her example? When we recall all the good things that a young person has done in their short life, do we ever consider that maybe that was their purpose all along?

In the end, does it really matter how long we live? The true measure of a life is not the *number* of our years, but the *quality* of what we do during those years, however few or many.

The real tragedy is not when a young person is cut down in their tender years; it is when an old person dies after many years of life, having accomplished nothing of any significance. No friends, no family, no legacy, and no hope. An entire lifetime wasted. And so much work left unfinished.

Instead of marking days off a calendar, we should be tracking the things that matter: the friends we've made, the good deeds we've performed, the encouragement and counsel we've shared with others, the integrity of a pure heart. So when the time comes that we, like Jesus, must give up our spirit, we can say with satisfaction, "It is finished!"

Even if we're only thirty-three years old.

The Ark and the Empty Tomb

John's account of the resurrection includes an odd
detail that is easy to overlook. But it reveals a
significant connection to an Old Testament relic.

*But Mary stood outside by the tomb weeping, and as she
wept she stooped down and looked into the tomb. And she
saw two angels in white sitting, one at the head and the other
at the feet, where the body of Jesus had lain (Jn. 20:11-12).*

*"You shall make two cherubim of gold; of hammered
work you shall make them at the two ends of the mercy seat.
Make one cherub at one end, and the other cherub at the
other end . . ." (Ex. 25:18-19).*

୧୦୶୬

Commentaries on the gospel of John often mention the
striking similarity between what Mary Magdalene saw in the
tomb and the physical description of the ark of the covenant.
The text does not offer an explanation that would connect
these stories, but the wording is too similar to be mere coin-
cidence.

The ark of the covenant was the single most important
relic to the ancient Israelites. This ark, which contained the
stone tablets given to Moses at Mt. Sinai, rested in the innermost chamber of the tabernacle, the "Holy of Holies."

The lid that covered this ark—a slab of pure gold—was
called "the mercy seat." On each end of the mercy seat was a
cherub, or angel, facing its counterpart on the other end. (If
you watched the Spielberg movie, *Raiders of the Lost Ark*,
you've seen a decent representation of what the ark and these
cherubim probably looked like.)

God described the mercy seat as the place where He "will meet with you, and . . . speak with you" (Ex. 25:22). It was accessible only to the High Priest, and he could come into its presence only once a year, on the Day of Atonement. On that day, the High Priest would make atonement for the sins of all the people by sprinkling the blood of a sacrifice on the mercy seat, in the presence of God.

The ark disappeared from history no later than the destruction of Solomon's temple in the sixth-century BC, and was never replaced. According to Josephus, the Holy of Holies in Herod's temple during the time of Christ was completely empty. The Jews continued to worship God at the temple, but the physical relic that connected them to God was gone.

That brings us to John's account of the resurrection. John records that Mary saw two angels in the empty tomb. But why does he add the little detail that the angels sat on each end of the ledge where Jesus had been laid?

The parallel to the cherubim over the mercy seat is unmistakable. The empty Holy of Holies in the temple had now been replaced by an empty tomb. The former offered no permanent solution to sin; the latter abolished the final barrier between God and man. In both cases, angels guarded a sacred place, but the empty tomb in one stroke provided access to God for all humanity.

One final thought: In the tabernacle, it was the High Priest alone who had the right to come before the mercy seat and see the cherubim. In the empty tomb, it was a woman with a tainted past and a deep love for her Savior, who came into the presence of the Divine. The angels in the empty tomb of Jesus are inviting all of us, whatever our social status, whatever our past mistakes and failures, to come into the presence of God. The resurrected Jesus has opened the way!

"You Follow Me"

We are too easily influenced by what others think, say, or do. Our challenge is to live our lives by only one standard: What Jesus tells us to do.

Peter, seeing him, said to Jesus, "But Lord, what about this man?" Jesus said to him, "If I will that he remain till I come, what is that to you? You follow Me" (Jn. 21:21-22).

৩৽৻৶

After His resurrection, Jesus had a private meeting with Simon Peter to restore the relationship that had been lost with Peter's denial during the trial. This was a painful reunion for Peter, but essential to his restoration.

Jesus' message included a cryptic description of the manner of Peter's death (v. 17-18). Rather than become fixated on the manner of his death, however, Jesus encouraged Peter to concentrate on the work before him. Peter's mission was simple: "Follow Me."

Peter's reaction was so typical of the man. Still lost in thought about Jesus' prophecy of his death, he motioned to his fellow apostle, John, standing nearby: "But what about this man?" Peter was curious about the fate of his fellow apostle; the injunction to "follow Me" got lost in this mental rabbit trail.

The task that Jesus laid upon Peter was not hard to understand. "Follow Me" involves only two people: Jesus and the disciple who would become like Him. But Peter's duty to "follow Me" got derailed by curiosity over what would happen to John. Of course, John's manner of death would have no bearing on Peter's life, so Jesus had to gently chide him: "What is that to you? *You follow me.*"

This was not the only time Peter made this kind of mistake. His earlier denial of Jesus in the courtyard while Jesus was on trial was triggered by his fear of what others would think of him. Years later at a Gentile church in Antioch—even after defending the right of the Gentiles to have access to the grace of God without circumcision or the Law of Moses—he refused to eat with them, "fearing those who were of the circumcision" (Gal. 2:12). Instead of following Jesus, he yielded to the prejudices of those around him.

Peter's inclination to get distracted by the expectations and circumstances of others mirrors our own. Jesus bids us follow Him, too. But it's easy to become so preoccupied with what others are thinking or doing that we lose sight of that primary objective. We fear that the world will brand us as religious kooks, so we disguise our convictions and compromise our morals. Or we meekly allow the shifting winds of brotherhood politics to set the agenda for us in making decisions regarding doctrine or polity. In either case, the root problem is the same: We are no longer following Jesus, but the influence of others who are just as lost as we are.

Jesus' rebuke to Peter is the same one we need to hear today: "What is that to you? *You follow me.*" Both as individuals and as a local congregation, we need to look past what others are thinking or doing and concentrate our attention on what Jesus wants us to do. That path requires a lot more study and thought, but it is the only path that pleases our Master.

Scripture Index

Items highlighted in **bold text** are primary passages upon which the related articles are based. Items that are not bolded receive some level of additional treatment in articles. Incidental scripture references are not included here.

Subject Index